English-Urdu
Urdu-English

Word to Word®
Bilingual Dictionary

Compiled by:
C. Sesma, M.A.

Translated by:
Aatika khattak

Bilingual Dictionaries, Inc.

Urdu Word to Word® Bilingual Dictionary
2nd Edition © Copyright 2011

Published in the United States by:

Bilingual Dictionaries, Inc.
PO Box 1154
Murrieta, CA 92562
T: (951) 461-6893 • F: (951) 461-3092
www.BilingualDictionaries.com

ISBN13: 978-0-933146-39-6
ISBN: 0-933146-39-6
Printed in India

Preface

Bilingual Dictionaries, Inc. is committed to providing schools, libraries and educators with a great selection of bilingual materials for students. Along with bilingual dictionaries we also provide ESL materials, children's bilingual stories and children's bilingual picture dictionaries.

Sesma's Urdu Word to Word® Bilingual Dictionary was created specifically with students in mind to be used for reference and testing. This dictionary contains approximately 18,500 entries targeting common words used in the English language.

List of Irregular Verbs

present - past - past participle

arise - arose - arisen
awake - awoke - awoken, awaked
be - was - been
bear - bore - borne
beat - beat - beaten
become - became - become
begin - began - begun
behold - beheld - beheld
bend - bent - bent
beseech - besought - besought
bet - bet - betted
bid - bade (bid) - bidden (bid)
bind - bound - bound
bite - bit - bitten
bleed - bled - bled
blow - blew - blown
break - broke - broken
breed - bred - bred
bring - brought - brought
build - built - built
burn - burnt - burnt *
burst - burst - burst
buy - bought - bought
cast - cast - cast
catch - caught - caught
choose - chose - chosen
cling - clung - clung
come - came - come
cost - cost - cost
creep - crept - crept
cut - cut - cut
deal - dealt - dealt

dig - dug - dug
do - did - done
draw - drew - drawn
dream - dreamt - dreamed
drink - drank - drunk
drive - drove - driven
dwell - dwelt - dwelt
eat - ate - eaten
fall - fell - fallen
feed - fed - fed
feel - felt - felt
fight - fought - fought
find - found - found
flee - fled - fled
fling - flung - flung
fly - flew - flown
forebear - forbore - forborne
forbid - forbade - forbidden
forecast - forecast - forecast
forget - forgot - forgotten
forgive - forgave - forgiven
forego - forewent - foregone
foresee - foresaw - foreseen
foretell - foretold - foretold
forget - forgot - forgotten
forsake - forsook - forsaken
freeze - froze - frozen
get - got - gotten
give - gave - given
go - went - gone
grind - ground - ground
grow - grew - grown
hang - hung * - hung *
have - had - had

hear - hear - heard	**ring -** rang - rung
hide - hid - hidden	**rise -** rose - risen
hit - hit - hit	**run -** ran - run
hold - held - held	**saw -** sawed - sawn
hurt - hurt - hurt	**say -** said - said
hit - hit - hit	**see -** saw - seen
hold - held - held	**seek -** sought - sought
keep - kept - kept	**sell -** sold - sold
kneel - knelt * - knelt *	**send -** sent - sent
know - knew - known	**set -** set - set
lay - laid - laid	**sew -** sewed - sewn
lead - led - led	**shake -** shook - shaken
lean - leant * - leant *	**shear -** sheared - shorn
leap - lept * - lept *	**shed -** shed - shed
learn - learnt * - learnt *	**shine -** shone - shone
leave - left - left	**shoot -** shot - shot
lend - lent - lent	**show -** showed - shown
let - let - let	**shrink -** shrank - shrunk
lie - lay - lain	**shut -** shut - shut
light - lit * - lit *	**sing -** sang - sung
lose - lost - lost	**sink -** sank - sunk
make - made - made	**sit -** sat - sat
mean - meant - meant	**slay -** slew - slain
meet - met - met	**sleep -** sleep - slept
mistake - mistook - mistaken	**slide -** slid - slid
must - had to - had to	**sling -** slung - slung
pay - paid - paid	**smell -** smelt * - smelt *
plead - pleaded - pled	**sow -** sowed - sown *
prove - proved - proven	**speak -** spoke - spoken
put - put - put	**speed -** sped * - sped *
quit - quit * - quit *	**spell -** spelt * - spelt *
read - read - read	**spend -** spent - spent
rid - rid - rid	**spill -** spilt * - spilt *
ride - rode - ridden	**spin -** spun - spun

spit - spat - spat
split - split - split
spread - spread - spread
spring - sprang - sprung
stand - stood - stood
steal - stole - stolen
stick - stuck - stuck
sting - stung - stung
stink - stank - stunk
stride - strode - stridden
strike - struck - struck (stricken)
strive - strove - striven
swear - swore - sworn
sweep - swept - swept
swell - swelled - swollen *
swim - swam - swum
take - took - taken
teach - taught - taught
tear - tore - torn

tell - told - told
think - thought - thought
throw - threw - thrown
thrust - thrust - thrust
tread - trod - trodden
wake - woke - woken
wear - wore - worn
weave - wove * - woven *
wed - wed * - wed *
weep - wept - wept
win - won - won
wind - wound - wound
wring - wrung - wrung
write - wrote - written

**Those tenses with an * also
 have regular forms.**

English-Urdu

Bilingual Dictionaries, Inc.

Abbreviations

a - article
n - noun
e - exclamation
pro - pronoun
adj - adjective
adv - adverb
v - verb
iv - irregular verb
pre - preposition
c - conjunction

A

a *a* ایک

abandon *v* چھوڑ رینا

abandonment *n* کنارہ کشی

abbey *n* خانقاہ

abbot *n* صدر راہب

abbreviate *v* اختصار کرنا

abbreviation *n* اختصار

abdicate *v* دست بردار ہونا

abdication *n* دست برداری

abdomen *n* شکم

abduct *v* اغوا کرنا

abduction *n* اغوا

aberration *n* انحراف

abhor *v* نفرت کرنا

abide by *v* پابند رہنا

ability *n* قابلیت

ablaze *adj* فروزاں

able *adj* قابل

abnormal *adj* خلاف معمول

abnormality *n* غیر معمولی پن

aboard *adv* جہاز پر

abolish *v* توڑ دینا

abort *v* حمل گرانا

abortion *n* اسقاطِ حمل

abound *v* وافر ہونا

about *pre* بابت

about *adv* ارد گرد

above *pre* اوپر

abreast *adv* ہم قدم

abridge *v* گھٹانا

abroad *adv* دور دراز

abrogate *v* منسوخ کرنا

abruptly *adv* ایکا ایکی

absence *n* غیر حاضری

absent *adj* غیر حاضر

absolute *adj* غیر مشروط

absolution *n* خلاصی

absolve *v* چھوڑنا

absorb *v* جذب کرنا

absorbent *adj* جاذب

abstain *v* باز رہنا

abstinence *n* اجتناب

abstract *adj* قیاسی

absurd *adj* نامعقول

abundance *n* بہتات

abundant *adj* بہت سا

abuse *v* گالی دینا

abuse *n* گالی گلوچ

abusive *adj* بد زبان

abysmal *adj* بے انتہا گہرا

abyss *n* غار

academic *adj* اشراقی

academy *n* جامعہ

accelerate *v* رفتار بڑھانا

accent *n* لہجہ

accept *v* قبول کرنا

acceptable *adj* قابل قبول

acceptance *n* رضا مندی

access *n* رسائی

accident *n* حادثہ

accidental *adj* اتفاقی

acclaim v تحسین

acclimatize v آب و ہوا راس آنا

accommodate v انتظام کرنا

accompany v ہمراہ ہونا

accomplice n رفیق جرم

accomplish v انجام دینا

accord n میل ملاپ

according to pre حسب الحکم

accordion n بلحاظ

account n حساب کتاب

account n تفصیل

account for جواب دہی کرنا

accountable adj ضامن

accumulate v جمع کرنا

accuracy n درستی

accurate adj درست

accusation n الزام

accuse v الزام لگانا

accustom v عادت ڈالنا

ace n اکا

ache n درد

achieve v حاصل کرنا

achievement n کار نمایاں

acid n تیزاب

acidity n تیزابیت

acknowledge v تسلیم کرنا

acorn n بلوط

acoustic adj سماعتی

acquaintance n شناسائی

acquire v حاصل کرنا

acquisition n حصول

acquit v ربا کرنا

acquittal n رہائی

acrobat n قلاباز

across pre آڑا

act v عمل

action n فعل

activate v متحرک کرنا

activation n متحرک کاری

active adj سرگرم

activity n سرگرمی

actor n اداکار

actress n اداکارہ

actual adj حقیقی

actually adv در حقیقت

acute adj نوکدار

adamant adj ناقابل شکست

adapt v مطابق کرنا

adaptable adj مطابقت پذیر

adaptation n مطابقت

adapter n بدلنے والا

add v جمع کرنا

addicted adj عادی

addiction n عادت

addictive adj نشہ آور

addition n اضافہ

additional adj اضافہ شدہ

address n خطبہ

address v خطاب کرنا

addressee n مکتوب الیہ

adequate adj مناسب

adhere v جما رہنا

adhesive adj چپکانے والے

adjacent adj ملحق

اضافی **adjective** n	پیشگی **advance** n
جوڑنا **adjoin** v	فائدہ **advantage** n
ملحقہ **adjoining** adj	آمد یا وَرُود **Advent** n
ملتوی کرنا **adjourn** v	مُہم **adventure** n
لگانا ۔ مطابق بنانا **adjust** v	متعلق فعل **adverb** n
قابلِ ترتیب **adjustable** adj	حَریف **adversary** n
ہم آہنگی ۔ تطابق **adjustment** n	بر عکس **adverse** adj
اِنتظام کرنا **administer** v	بَد بَختی **adversity** n
قابلِ تَعریف **admirable** adj	اشتہار دینا **advertise** v
امیرُ البَحَر **admiral** n	اِشتِہار بازی **advertising** n
تعریف **admiration** n	مشورہ **advice** n
سراہنا **admire** v	مشورہ دینا **advise** v
مَدّاح **admirer** n	مشیر **adviser** n
قابلِ قُبُول **admissible** adj	وکالت کرنا **advocate** v
داخلہ **admission** n	ہوائی جہاز **aeroplane** n
قبول کرنا **admit** v	جمالیاتی **aesthetic** adj
داخلہ **admittance** n	فاصِلے پَر **afar** adv
ہدایت کرنا **admonish** v	خُوش اِخلاق **affable** adj
نصیحت **admonition** n	معاملہ **affair** n
نوجوانی **adolescence** n	اثر انداز ہونا **affect** v
بالغ **adolescent** n	محبت **affection** n
گود لینا **adopt** v	مشتاق **affectionate** adj
اِنتِخاب **adoption** n	الحاق کرنا **affiliate** v
اختیاری **adoptive** adj	الحاق **affiliation** n
اِنتہائی دِلکَش **adorable** adj	رَبط یا اِتحاد **affinity** n
عقیدَت **adoration** n	حَق جَتانا **affirm** v
سَجانا **adorn** v	اِجاب **affirmative** adj
چاپلُوسی **adulation** n	نَتھّی کَرنا **affix** v
بالغ **adult** n	ذَلیل کَرنا **afflict** v
مِلاوٹ کرنا **adulterate** v	ایذا **affliction** n
زَنا کاری **adultery** n	دولت **affluence** n
بڑھنا **advance** v	رَواں **affluent** adj

afford v استطاعت رکھنا	aid n امداد
affront v گُستاخی کَرنا	aid v مَدَد کَرنا
affront n حقارت	aide n نائب
afloat adv پانی پر	ailing adj علیل
afraid adj خوف زدہ	ailment n علالت
afresh adv از سر نو	aim v ہَدَف لینا
after pre پیچھے	aimless adj بے مَقصَد
afternoon n دوپہر	air n ہَوا
afterwards adv بَعد میں	air v ہَوا دینا
again adv دوبارہ	aircraft n طَیّارہ
against pre بَرخِلاف	airfare n جہاز کا کرایہ
age n عمر	airfield n ہَوائی اڈّا
agency n نمائندگی	airline n ہَوائی کَمپنی
agenda n پیش نامَہ	airmail n ہَوائی ڈاک
agent n کارندہ	airplane n ہَوائی جَہاز
agglomerate v انبار لَگانا	airstrip n رَن وے
aggravate v بگاڑنا	airtight adj ہَوا بَند
aggravation n سنگینی	aisle n برآمدہ
aggregate v جَمَع کَرنا	ajar adj نیم وا ۔ آدھ کھُلا
aggression n جارحیت	akin adj سگا ۔ رشتہ دار
aggressive adj جارحانہ	alarm n خطرے کی اطلاع
aggressor n جارحیت پسند	alarming adj خلل ڈالنے والا
aghast adj سَرا سیمَہ	alcoholic adj عادی شَرابی
agile adj پھُرتیلا	alcoholism n شَراب خوری
agnostic n لا اَدری	alert n چوکس
agonizing adj اذِیت خیز	alert v چوکَس
agree v اقرار کرنا	alight adv نیچے اُتَرنا
agreeable adj قابلِ مُطابقَت	align v ایک خَط میں لانا
agreement n اقرار نامہ	alike adj یکساں ۔ ایک سا
agricultural adj زرعی	alive adj زِندَہ ۔ جیتا جاگتا
agriculture n کاشتکاری	all adj تمام ۔ سب
ahead pre آگے	allege v الزام دینا

allegedly *adv* مبینہ طور پر	altar *n* قُربان گاہ
allegiance *n* وَفا داری ۔ اطاعت	alter *v* تبدیل کرنا
allergy *n* الَرجی ۔ خارش	alteration *n* ردوبدل تبدیلی
alleviate *v* کم کرنا ۔ گھٹانا	altercation *n* مباحثہ
alley *n* گلی	alternate *v* ادَل بَدَل کَرنا
alliance *n* معاہدہ ۔ میثاق	alternative *adj* متبادل
allied *adj* حلیف	although *c* اگرچہ
alligator *n* مگر مچھ	altitude *n* اونچائی
allocate *v* مُقَرَّر کَرنا	altogether *adj* کلی طَور پَر
allot *v* تَقسیم کَرنا	aluminum *n* ایلومنم
allotment *n* خوراک	always *adv* ہمیشہ
allow *v* اجازت دینا	amass *v* ڈھیر لَگانا
allowance *n* وظیفہ	amateur *adj* غَیر پیشہ وَر
alloy *n* دھاتی مرکب	amaze *v* متحیر کرنا/ہونا
allure *n* دِلرُبائی	amazement *n* اچنبھا ۔ حیرانی
alluring *adj* دل کش	amazing *adj* حیرت انگیز
ally *n* ساتھی	ambassador *n* سَفیر ۔ ایلچی
ally *v* شامل ہونا	ambiguous *adj* مبہم ۔ ذو معنی
almanac *n* تَقویم ۔ جَنتری	ambition *n* آرزو ۔ تمنا
almighty *adj* قادرِ مطلق	ambitious *adj* حوصلہ مند
almond *n* بادام	ambivalent *adj* مبہم
almost *adv* تقریباً	amenable *adj* اصیل
alms *n* خیرات	amend *v* ترمیم کرنا
alone *adj* اکیلا ۔ تنہا	amendment *n* ترمیم
along *pre* ساتھ ساتھ	amenities *n* مَدنی سَہُولتیں
alongside *pre* بَرابَر بَرابَر	American *adj* امریکی
aloof *adj* جُدا	amiable *adj* شفیق
aloud *adv* بہ آوازِ بُلَند	amicable *adj* دوستانہ ۔ پرامن
alphabet *n* حروفِ تہجی	amid *pre* بیچ میں
already *adv* پہلے ہی سے	ammunition *n* گولہ بارود
alright *adv* ٹھیک ہے	amnesty *n* تحفظ
also *adv* بھی ۔ مزید	among *pre* دَرمیان

amoral *adj* غَیر اِخلاقی	animal *n* ۔ جانور
amorphous *adj* بے شَکلا	animate *v* جان ڈالنا
amount *n* رقم	animosity *n* بُغَض ۔ کِینَہ
amount to *v* مساوی ہے	ankle *n* ٹخنہ
ample *adj* فراخ	annex *n* شامل کرنا ۔ ملانا
amplify *v* بڑھانا	annexation *n* شمول ۔ ضبطی
amputate *v* قَطَع کَر دینا	annihilate *v* نابُود کَر دینا
amputation *n* بُریدگی	annihilation *n* نیستی ۔ فنا
amuse *v* دل بہلانا	anniversary *n* بَرسی
amusement *n* تفریح	annotate *v* لکھ لینا
amusing *adj* تَفریحی	annotation *n* شرح نویسی
an *a* ایک	announce *v* اعلان کَرنا
analogy *n* تَمثیلی اِستَدلال	announcement *n* اعلان
analysis *n* تجزیہ	announcer *n* اعلانچی
analyze *v* تَجزیَہ کَرنا	annoy *v* زحمت دینا
anarchy *n* بے حَکومتی	annoying *adj* تَکلیف دہ
anatomy *n* تشریح الاعضا	annual *adj* سالانہ
ancestor *n* آباو اجداد	annul *v* منسوخ کرنا
ancestry *n* حَسب و نَسَب	anoint *v* چُپَڑنا
anchor *n* لَنگر	anonymity *n* بے نامی
ancient *adj* قدیم ۔ موروثی	anonymous *adj* گمنام
and *c* اور	another *adj* دوسرا
anecdote *n* قِصَّہ ۔ حَکایَت	answer *v* جواب
anemia *n* انیمیا	answer *n* جواب دینا
anemic *adj* انیمیا کا مریض	ant *n* چیونٹی
anew *adv* ازسر	antagonize *v* دشمن بنانا
angel *n* فرشتہ	antecedent *n* ماقبل
anger *v* غصہ آنا	antecedents *n* حالات ۔ مقابل
anger *n* غیظ ۔ طیش	antelope *n* غزال
angle *n* زاویہ	anthem *n* قَومی تَرانَہ
angry *adj* ناراض	antibiotic *n* ضَدِ نامِیَہ
anguish *n* کوفت	anticipate *v* پہلے سے اندازہ

anticipation *n* پیش بندی	appeal *v* التجا کرنا
antidote *n* تریاق	appealing *adj* دلکش
antipathy *n* عداوت	appear *v* نگاہ میں آنا
antiquated *adj* پُرانا	appearance *n* موجُودگی
anvil *n* سِندان	appease *v* دِلاسا دینا
anxiety *n* اِضطَراب	appeasement *n* دِلاسا
anxious *adj* مُتَفَکّر	appendicitis *n* سوزَشِ زائدَہ
any *adj* کوئی ۔ کِسی	appendix *n* ضَمیمَہ
anybody *pro* کوئی بھی	appetite *n* ذوق ۔ میلان
anyhow *pro* بَہَر صُورَت	appetizer *n* اِشتِہا آوَر
anyone *pro* کوئی اکیلا	applaud *v* تالی بَجانا
anything *pro* کُچھ بھی	applause *n* آفرین
apart *adv* جدا ۔ الگ	apple *n* سیب
apartment *n* مشترکہ جائیداد	appliance *n* ذریعہ؛آلہ
apathy *n* بے حِسی	applicable *adj* قابلِ اطلاق
ape *n* بن مانس	applicant *n* دَرخُواست گُزار
apex *n* چوٹی	application *n* عرضی
aphrodisiac *adj* شہوَت انگیز	apply *v* مَلنا؛ لگانا
apiece *adv* فی کَس	apply for *v* درخواست دینا
apocalypse *n* کَشَف ۔ الہام	appoint *v* تَقرّر کَرنا
apologize *v* معذرت کرنا	appointment *n* تقرری
apology *n* معذرت	appraisal *n* تخمینہ
apostle *n* مثل مقدمہ	appraise *v* جانچنا
apostolic *adj* پاپائی	appreciate *v* قدردانی کرنا
apostrophe *n* حَذفی علامَت	appreciation *n* تحسین
appall *v* خَوف زَدَہ کَرنا	apprehend *v* گِرَفتار کَرنا
appalling *adj* ہولناک	apprehensive *adj* سَرا سیمَہ
apparel *n* لِباس	apprentice *n* مُبتَدی ۔ شاگِرد
apparent *adj* ظاہری	approach *v* قریب ہونا ۔ پاس آنا
apparently *adv* بَظاہِر	approach *n* رَسائی
apparition *n* ظُہُور	approachable *adj* قابلِ رسائی
appeal *n* مرافعہ کرنا	approbation *n* قَبُولِیَت

appropriate adj مناسب

approval n مَنظوری

approve v مَنظور کَرنا

approximate adj تَقریباً

apricot n خُوبانی

apron n ایپرن ۔ تہ بند

aptitude n رُجحان

aquatic adj آبی

aqueduct n آبراہ ۔ نالی

Arabic adj عَربی

arable adj زَراعتی

arbiter n ثالث

arbitrary adj خود مختارانہ

arbitrate v ثالث بَننا

arbitration n ثالثی

arc n آرک ۔ قَوس

arch n محراب

archaeology n عِلم آثار قدیمہ

archaic adj قَدیم

archbishop n صَدَر أسقُف

architect n ماہر تَعمیرات

architecture n فنِ تعمیر

ardent adj جَلنے کا إحساس

ardor n رَغبَت ۔ حَرارَت

arduous adj کَٹھَن ۔ دُشوار

area n رَقبہ

arena n اکھاڑا؛ میدان

argue v دلیل دینا

arid adj بَنجَر

arise iv طُلُوع ہونا

aristocracy n اشرافِیہ

aristocrat n اشراف

arithmetic n عِلم حِساب

arm n بازُو

arm v بانہ

armaments n اسلَحَہ

armchair n بازو دار کُرسی

armed adj مَسلح

armistice n عارضی صُلَح

armor n آلاتِ جَنگ

armpit n بغل

army n فَوج

aromatic adj خُوشبُو دار

around pre چاروں طرف

arouse v بیدار ہونا؛ أکسانا

array n صَف بَندی

arrest v گِرَفتار کَرنا

arrest n گِرَفتاری

arrival n آمد

arrive v پَہنچنا ۔ آنا

arrogance n نخوت

arrogant adj گھَمَنڈی

arrow n تِیر

arsenal n بارود خانَہ

arsenic n سَنکھِیا

arson n آتَش زَنی

arsonist n آتَش زَن

art n فن

artery n نَسّ

arthritis n جوڑ کی سوزش

artichoke n فَرشوف

article n آیٹَم؛ چیز

articulate v صاف تلفظ کَرنا

articulation n گویائی

artificial *adj* جعلی	assemble *v* اِکٹھَا کرنا
artillery *n* توپخانَہ	assembly *n* اجتماع
artisan *n* کاریگر	assent *v* ماننا ۔ ہاں کہنا
artist *n* مُصَوَر ۔ آرٹِسٹ	assert *v* حَق جَتانا
artistic *adj* جَمالیاتی	assertion *n* دعویٰ ۔ اصرار
artwork *n* فنی کام	assess *v* تشخیص کرنا
as *c* چونکہ	assessment *n* تشخیص کا عمَل
as *adv* جیسا	asset *n* اثاثہ
ascend *v* اوپر چڑھنا	assets *n* اثاثے
ascendancy *n* حَسب و نَسَب	assign *v* مقرر کردہ
ascertain *v* یَقینی بَنانا	assignment *n* تفویض
ascetic *adj* زاہدانَہ	assimilation *n* اِستحالَہ
ash *n* راکھ	assist *v* مدد دینا
ashamed *adj* شرمندہ	assistance *n* مدد کرنا
ashtray *n* راکھ دان	associate *v* شَریک کَرنا
aside *adv* ایک طرف	association *n* شِرکَت
aside from *adv* علاوہ	assorted *adj* مختلف
ask *v* پوچھنا	assortment *n* قِسم بَندی
asleep *adj* سویا ہُوا	assume *v* اخَذ کَرنا
asparagus *n* مارچوب	assumption *n* مفروضہ
aspect *n* پہلو	assurance *n* بھروسا
asphalt *n* مَعدنی تارکول	assure *v* یقین دِلانا
asphyxiate *v* دَم گھونٹنا	asterisk *n* ستارہ
aspiration *n* خواہش	asteroid *n* سیّارچہ
aspire *v* چاہنا	asthma *n* دمہ
assail *v* بَلَم بولنا	asthmatic *adj* دمہ زدہ
assailant *n* حَملَہ آور	astonish *v* ششدر کرنا
assassin *n* قاتل	astonishing *adj* حیرت انگیز
assassinate *v* مار دینا	astound *v* بَکا بَکا کَر دینا
assassination *n* قتل	astounding *adj* حیرَت انگیز
assault *n* حملہ	astray *v* گُمراہ
assault *v* حملہ کرنا	astrologer *n* نَجومی

astrology *n* عِلم نَجُوم	attend *v* حاضر ہونا
astronaut *n* خلانورد	attendance *n* حاضری
astronomer *n* مابر فَلکِیات	attendant *n* خِدمَت گار
astronomic *adj* فَلکِیاتی	attention *n* تَوَجُہ
astronomy *n* فَلَک شَناسی	attentive *adj* چوکَس
astute *adj* زِیرَک	attenuate *v* کم کرنا
asunder *adv* الَگ ۔ جُدا	attenuating *adj* کمزور بنانا
asylum *n* دارُالامان	attest *v* تصدیق کرنا
at *pre* پر ۔ کے ۔ سے	attic *n* بالا خانہ
atheism *n* الحاد	attitude *n* رَوَیَّہ
atheist *n* مُلحِد	attorney *n* مختار
athletic *adj* چُست ۔ تَوانا	attraction *n* دِلکَشی
atmosphere *n* کرہ ہوا ۔ فضا	attractive *adj* دل کَش
atmospheric *adj* فِضائی	attribute *v* سبب قرار دینا
atom *n* ذَرَہ ۔ جَوہر	auction *n* نیلامی
atomic *adj* جوہری ۔ ذَراتی	auction *v* نیلام کرنا
atone *v* تلافی کرنا	audacious *adj* نڈر
atonement *n* تلافی	audacity *n* جسارت
atrocious *adj* سفاک یا ظَالِم	audible *adj* قابِل سَماعت
atrocity *n* سنگ دلی	audience *n* سامعین
atrophy *v* لاغَری	audit *v* محاسبہ کرنا
attach *v* نتھی کرنا	auditorium *n* سَماعت گاہ
attached *adj* وابَستَہ	augment *v* بڑھانا
attachment *n* وابَستَگی	August *n* اگست
attack *n* حَملَہ	aunt *n* چچی
attack *v* حَملَہ کرنا	auspicious *adj* مُبارَک
attacker *n* حملہ آور	austere *adj* دَرُشت
attain *v* حاصل کرنا	austerity *n* دَرُشتی
attainable *adj* قابِل حَصُول	authentic *adj* مصدقہ
attainment *n* حصول	authenticate *v* تَصدیق کرنا
attempt *v* کوشش کرنا	authenticity *n* صَداقَت
attempt *n* سَعی	author *n* مُصَنِّف

A
B

authoritarian *adj* آمرِیَت پَسَند	**awake** *iv* جاگنا
authority *n* اختیار	**awake** *adj* بیدار
authorization *n* اِختیار نامَہ	**award** *v* عطا کَرنا
authorize *v* مَجاز ٹھہرانا	**award** *n* اِنعام
auto *n* خُود	**aware** *adj* آگاہ
autograph *n* دَستَخَط	**awareness** *n* آگاہی
automatic *adj* خُود کار	**away** *adv* پَرے
automobile *n* خُود مُتَحَرِک	**awe** *n* رُعب
autonomous *adj* خود آئینی	**awesome** *adj* رعب دار
autonomy *n* اختیار	**awful** *adj* ناگوار
autopsy *n* مُعائنہ لاش	**awkward** *adj* بے ڈَھب
autumn *n* خزاں	**awning** *n* سائبان
auxiliary *adj* ذیلی	**ax** *n* کُلہاڑی
avail *v* فائدَہ پَہُنچانا	**axiom** *n* اصول مُتعارفَہ
available *adj* دستیاب	**axis** *n* محوَر
avalanche *n* بَرَفشار	
avarice *n* حِرَص	
avaricious *adj* حَریص	
avenge *v* بَدلا لینا	
avenue *n* خَیابان	
average *n* اوسط	**B**
averse *adj* خِلاف	
aversion *n* کراہَت	
avert *v* موڑ دینا	**baby** *n* شیر خوار
aviation *n* ہوا بازی	**bachelor** *n* کنوارہ
aviator *n* ہَوا باز	**back** *n* پشت
avid *adj* مُشتاق	**back** *adv* واپس
avoid *v* گریز کرنا	**back** *v* واپس کرنا/لینا
avoidable *adj* قابِل گَریز	**back down** *v* تَرک کوشِش
avoidance *n* اِجتَناب	**back up** *v* واپس آنا
avowed *adj* واشگاف	**backbone** *n* ریڑھ کی ہڈّی
await *v* اِنتَظار کَرنا	**backdoor** *n* عقبی دَروازہ
	backfire *n* الٹا نتیجہ نکالنا

B

background n پس منظر	**ballot** n رائے پَرچی
backing n پشت پناہی	**ballroom** n رَقص گاہ
backlash n پَس زَنی	**balm** n بام
backlog n پَس انبار	**balmy** adj چِکنا
backpack n پشتی تھیلا	**bamboo** n بانس
backup n متبادل	**ban** n ممانعت
backward adj پس ماندہ	**ban** v مَنع کرنا
backwards adv پِچھلی جانب	**banality** n فُرسُودگی
bacon n سُوَر کا گوشت	**banana** n کیلا
bacteria n بیکٹیریا	**band** n باندھنا؛ گروہ
bad adj خراب	**bandage** n پَٹی
badge n علامَت	**bandage** v مَرہم پَٹی کرنا
badly adv بُری طرح	**bandit** n غارت گر
baffle v چَکرا دینا	**bang** v بَجانا
bag n بَستَہ	**banish** v جلا وطن کرنا
baggage n سازو سامان	**banishment** n جلا وطنی
baggy adj ڈھیلا ڈھالا	**bank** n کِنارَہ
baguette n ڈھَلا ہُوا	**bankrupt** v دیوالیہ ہونا
bail n ضمانت	**bankrupt** adj دیوالیہ
bail out v ضمانت پر چھوڑنا	**bankruptcy** n دیوالیہ پن
bailiff n ناظر	**banner** n جھَنڈا
bait n چارہ	**banquet** n ضَیافَت
bake v دَم پُخت کرنا	**baptism** n مسِحیّت
baker n طَبّاخ	**bar** n سلاخ
bakery n بیکری	**bar** v منع کرنا
balance v بقایا	**barbarian** n وحشی
balance n میزان	**barbaric** adj وحشیانہ
balcony n بالکَنی	**barbarism** n جَہالَت
bald adj گنجا	**barbecue** n باربِکیُو
bale n گانٹھ	**barber** n حَجّام
ball n گیند	**bare** adj ننگا
balloon n غُبارَہ	**barefoot** adj وُںننگے پا

barely adv مشکل سے	**bath** n غُسَل
bargain n مول تول	**bathe** v غُسَل کرنا
bargain v مول تول کرنا	**bathrobe** n جامَہ غُسَل
bargaining n سودا بازی	**bathroom** n غُسَل خانہ
barge n بجرا	**bathtub** n نَہانے کا ٹَب
bark v بھونکنا	**battalion** n فوجی دَستَہ
bark n چھال	**batter** v بدسلوکی کرنا
barley n جَو	**battery** n زودکوب
barn n کھلیان	**battle** n جدوجہد
barrage n بیراج	**battle** v جدوجہد کرنا
barrel n بندوق کی نال	**battleship** n جَنگی جَہاز
barren adj بَنجَر	**bay** n خَلیج
barricade n مورچَہ	**bayonet** n چھرا
barrier n باڑ	**bazaar** n بازار
bartender n کلال	**be** iv ہونا
barter v تبادلہ	**be born** v پیدا ہونا
base n بنیاد	**beach** n ساحِلِ سَمَندَر
baseball n بیس بال	**beacon** n روشَن مینار
baseless adj بے بنیاد	**beak** n چونچ
basement n تم خانہ	**beam** n شہتیر
bashful adj شَرمیلا	**bean** n لوبیا سیم
basic adj بنیادی	**bear** n ریچھ
basics n ئیاتابتدا	**bear** iv برداشت کرنا
basin n لَگَن	**bearable** adj قابِلِ بَرداشت
basis n بُنیاد	**beard** n داڑھی
bask v سینکنا	**bearded** adj باریش
basket n ٹوکری	**bearer** n حامِل
basketball n باسکِٹ بال	**beast** n حیوان
bastard n حرامی	**beat** iv مارنا
bat n بَلا	**beat** n دھڑکَن
bat n بَلا	**beaten** adj پامال
batch n جتھا	**beating** n دھڑکَن

B

beautiful *adj* خوبصورت	**behead** *v* گردَن اُڑانا
beautify *v* سَنوارنا	**behind** *pre* پیچھے
beauty *n* خوبصورتی	**behold** *iv* دیکھنا
beaver *n* اودبلا	**being** *n* وجود
because *c* کیُونکہ	**belated** *adj* بعد از وقت
because of *pre* بَوَجہ	**belch** *v* ڈکار لینا
beckon *v* اشارَہ دینا	**belch** *n* ڈکار
become *iv* ہونا آنا	**belfry** *n* گھنٹہ گھر
bed *n* بِستَر	**Belgian** *adj* بیلجئیم کا
bedding *n* بسترا	**Belgium** *n* بیلجئیم
bedroom *n* خواب گاہ	**belief** *n* عقیدہ
bedspread *n* پَلَنگ پوش	**believable** *adj* قابل یقین
bee *n* شہَد کی مَکھی	**believe** *v* ماننا
beef *n* گائے کا گوشت	**believer** *n* ایماندار
beef up *v* اضافہ	**belittle** *v* گھٹانا
beehive *n* شہَد کا چھَتّا	**bell** *n* گھنٹی
beer *n* شَراب	**bell pepper** *n* شملہ مرچ
beet *n* چقندر	**belligerent** *adj* جنگ جو
beetle *n* بھوترا	**belly** *n* پیٹ
before *adv* سامنے	**belly button** *n* ناف
before *pre* پہلے	**belong** *v* کا ہونا۔
beforehand *adv* پہلے ہی	**belongings** *n* مال و اسباب
befriend *v* رفاقت کرنا	**beloved** *adj* محبُوب
beg *v* بھیک مانگنا	**below** *adv* ادنیٰ
beggar *n* بھکاری	**below** *pre* نیچے
begin *iv* آغاز ہونا	**belt** *n* کَمَر بَند
beginner *n* مُبتَدی	**bench** *n* بینچ
beginning *n* ابتداء	**bend** *iv* ٹیڑھا گَرنا
beguile *v* دھوکا دینا	**bend down** *v* مائل کرنا
behalf (on) *adv* جانِب سے	**beneath** *pre* خِلافِ شان
behave *v* پیش آنا	**benediction** *n* کلماتِ برکات
behavior *n* تاثر	**benefactor** *n* مُحسِن

beneficial *adj* مفید ۔ کار آمد	**bias** *n* طَرَفداری
beneficiary *n* مُستَفید	**bible** *n* انجیل
benefit *n* نفع منفعت	**bicycle** *n* سائیکل
benefit *v* فائده ہونا	**bid** *n* بولی
benevolence *n* فیض رَسانی	**bid** *iv* بولی دینا
benevolent *adj* مدد کرنے والا	**big** *adj* بَڑا
benign *adj* مَعمُولی مَرض	**bigamy** *n* دو زوجیَت
bereaved *adj* اداس	**bigot** *adj* کٹر
bereavement *n* صَدمَہ	**bigotry** *n* کَٹَر پَن
beret *n* فوجی ٹوپی	**bike** *n* سائیکل
berserk *adv* پاگل	**bile** *n* صَفرا
berth *n* جہاز کا کمرا	**bilingual** *adj* دو زُبانی
beseech *iv* التجا کرنا	**bill** *n* مسودہ قانون؛ بل
beset *iv* گھیر لینا	**bimonthly** *adj* دو ماہی
beside *pre* نَزدیک	**bin** *n* صَندُوق
besides *pre* مزید برآں	**bind** *iv* باندھنا
besiege *iv* مُحاصرہ کَرنا	**binding** *adj* قابلِ پابندی
best *adj* بہترین	**binoculars** *n* دو چشمہ
best man *n* شَہ بالا	**biography** *n* سوانح حیات
bestial *adj* حیوانی	**biological** *adj* حَیاتیاتی
bestow *v* عطا کرنا	**biology** *n* عِلم حَیات
bet *iv* شرط لگانا	**bird** *n* پرندہ
bet *n* شَرط	**birth** *n* پیدائش
betray *v* دھوکا دینا	**birthday** *n* یوم پیدائش
betrayal *n* غداری	**biscuit** *n* بِسکِٹ
better *adj* بہتر	**bishop** *n* بڑا لاٹھ پادری
between *pre* بیچ میں	**bison** *n* بائسن
beverage *n* کَشید	**bit** *n* چھوٹا سا ٹکڑا
beware *v* آگاہ ہونا	**bite** *iv* دانت سے کاٹنا
bewilder *v* سَرا سیمَہ کَرنا	**bite** *n* بُڑکا
bewitch *v* سَحَر ذَدہ ہونا	**bitter** *adj* کڑوا
beyond *adv* کے پار	**bitterly** *adv* تَلخی سے

B

bitterness _n_ کڑواہٹ	**blessed** _adj_ مبترک
bizarre _adj_ کڑواہٹ	**blessing** _n_ فضل
black _adj_ سیاہ	**blind** _v_ خیرہ کرنا
blackberry _n_ سَیاہ نُوت	**blind** _adj_ اندھا
blackboard _n_ تختَہ سَیاہ	**blindfold** _n_ پردہ یا پٹی
blackmail _n_ سَیاہ مُعابَدَه	**blindfold** _v_ آنکھیں بند کرنا
blackmail _v_ دھمکی دینا	**blindly** _adv_ اندھا دھند
blackness _n_ سَیابی	**blindness** _n_ اندھا پن
blackout _n_ گھپ اندھیرا	**blink** _v_ آنکھ جھپکنا
blacksmith _n_ لوہار	**bliss** _n_ مسرت
bladder _n_ مثانہ	**blissful** _adj_ پُر مسرت
blade _n_ پٹا	**blister** _n_ چھالا
blame _n_ الزام	**blizzard** _n_ برفابی طوفان
blame _v_ الزام دینا	**bloat** _v_ پھول جانا
blameless _adj_ بے قصور	**bloated** _adj_ پھولا ہوا
bland _adj_ نازک	**block** _n_ بلاک
blank _adj_ کورا	**block** _v_ راستہ روکنا
blanket _n_ کمبَل	**blockade** _v_ محاصرہ کرنا
blasphemy _n_ بے حرمتی	**blockade** _n_ محاصرہ
blast _n_ دھماکا	**blockage** _n_ گھیرائو
blaze _v_ بھڑک پڑنا	**blond** _adj_ گوری اور بھورے
bleach _v_ رنگ کاٹنا	**blood** _n_ خون
bleach _v_ رنگ کاٹ	**bloodthirsty** _adj_ خون کا پیاسا
bleak _adj_ سرد	**bloody** _adj_ خونی
bleed _iv_ خون نکلنا	**bloom** _v_ کھلنا
bleeding _n_ اخراج خون	**blossom** _v_ پھولوں کو کھلنا
blemish _n_ داغ دوش	**blot** _n_ دھبہ
blemish _v_ داغ لگانا	**blot** _v_ دھبہ لگانا
blend _n_ آمتزاج	**blouse** _n_ کُرتی
blend _v_ یکجان کرنا	**blow** _n_ ضرب
blender _n_ ملانے والا	**blow** _iv_ بجھانا؛ پھونک مارنا
bless _v_ دعا کرنا	**blow out** _iv_ بجھنانا

blow up iv بھک سے اڑنا	**bond** n بندھن؛ تعلق
bludgeon v ڈنڈے سے پیٹنا	**bondage** n غلامی
blue adj نیلا	**bone** n ہڈی
blueprint n بنیادی خاکہ	**bone marrow** n ہڈی کا گودا
bluff v گمراہ کرنا	**bonfire** n الائو
blunder n فاش غلطی	**bonus** n بونس
blunt adj کند؛ کھنڈا	**book** n کتاب
bluntness n کھنڈا پن	**bookcase** n کتاب دان
blur v دھندلا کرنا	**bookkeeper** n منشی
blurred adj دھندلا	**bookkeeping** n منیمی
blush v تمتما اٹھنا	**booklet** n کتابچہ
blush n شرم	**bookseller** n کتب فروش
boar n سور	**bookstore** n کتب خانہ
board n تختہ؛ کونسل	**boom** n گونج؛ گرج
board v تختہ لگانا	**boom** v گرجنا
boast v شیخی بھگارنا	**boost** v دھیکیلنا
boat n کشتی	**boost** n افزائش
bodily adj جسمانی	**boot** n جوتا
body n جسم؛ بدن	**booth** n بوتھ
bog n دلدل	**booty** n لوٹ کامال
boil v ابالنا	**booze** n شراب
boil over v جوش آنا	**border** n سرحد؛ کنارا
boiler n بوائلر	**border on** v قریب آنا
bold adj دلیر	**borderline** adj حدِ فاصل
boldness n بے باکی	**bore** v چھیدنا
bolster v تکیہ لگانا	**bored** adj اکتایا ہوا
bolt n کنڈی؛ کنڈا	**boredom** n اکتاہٹ
bolt v کنڈی لگانا	**boring** adj کند ذبن
bomb n بم	**born** adj زائیدہ
bomb v بم برسانا	**borough** n قصبہ
bombing n بمباری	**borrow** v ادھار لینا
bombshell n توپ کا گولا	**bosom** n چھاتی

B

قائد **boss** _n_	مقاطعہ **boycott** _v_
حکم دیتے رہنا **boss around** _v_	دوست لڑکا **boyfriend** _n_
نباتیات **botany** _n_	لڑکپن **boyhood** _n_
ستیاناس کرنا **botch** _v_	بریسیئر **bra** _n_
دونوں **both** _adj_	تیار کرنا **brace for** _v_
زحمت دینا **bother** _v_	کنگن **bracelet** _n_
پریشان کن **bothersome** _adj_	قوسین **bracket** _n_
بوتل **bottle** _n_	ڈینگیں مارنا **brag** _v_
بوتلوں میں بھرنا **bottle** _v_	مینڈھی **braid** _n_
تنگ راستہ **bottleneck** _n_	دماغ **brain** _n_
پیندا **bottom** _n_	بریک **brake** _n_
اتھاہ **bottomless** _adj_	بریک لگانا **brake** _v_
ٹہنی **bough** _n_	شاخ **branch** _n_
گوم مٹول بٹا **boulder** _n_	پھیلانا **branch out** _v_
شاہراہ **boulevard** _n_	برانڈ **brand** _n_
اچھلنا **bounce** _v_	بالکل نیا **brand-new** _adj_
اچھل کود **bounce** _n_	برانڈی **brandy** _n_
پابند **bound** _adj_	بچہ **brat** _n_
سرحد **boundary** _n_	بہادر **brave** _adj_
بے اتھاہ **boundless** _adj_	بہادری سے **bravely** _adv_
سخاوت **bounty** _n_	بہادری **bravery** _n_
بورژوا **bourgeois** _adj_	جھگڑا **brawl** _n_
جھکائو؛ کمان **bow** _n_	ان بن؛ قطع تعلق **breach** _n_
آگے کو جھکنا **bow** _v_	روٹی **bread** _n_
واپس لے لینا **bow out** _v_	چوڑائی **breadth** _n_
بائولز **bowels** _n_	ٹوٹ؛ شکستگی **break** _n_
پیالی **bowl** _n_	ٹوٹنا **break** _iv._
ڈبہ **box** _n_	خراب ہوجانا **break down** _v_
تفریح **box office** _n_	فرار ہونا **break free** _v_
مکے باز **boxer** _n_	لوٹنا **break in** _v_
مکے بازی **boxing** _n_	توڑ کر کھولنا **break open** _v_
لڑکا **boy** _n_	آغاز **break out** _v_

break up v علیحدہ	**briefly** adv مختصراً
breakable adj بھربھرا	**briefs** n جانگھیا
breakdown n تعطل	**brigade** n بریگیڈ
breakfast n ناشتہ	**bright** adj روشن
breakthrough n مداخلت	**brighten** v چمکانا
breast n چھاتی	**brightness** n چمک
breath n سانس	**brilliant** adj چمک والا
breathe v سانس لینا	**brim** n منہ تک بھرے جانا
breathing n عمل تنفس	**bring** iv لانا
breathtaking adj متاثرکن	**bring back** v واپس لانا
breed iv سینا	**bring down** v کم کرنا
breed iv سدھارنا	**bring up** v پرورش کرنا
breed n نسل	**brink** n سِرا
breeze n نسیم	**brisk** adj تیز
brethren n بھائی	**Britain** n برطانیہ
brevity n اختصار	**British** adj برطانوی
brew v کشید کرنا	**brittle** adj بھوٹک
bribe v رشوت دینا	**broad** adj چوڑ
bribe n رشوت	**broadcast** v نشر کرنا
bribery n رشوت ستانی	**broadcast** n نشریہ
brick n اینٹ	**broadcaster** n ناشر
bricklayer n راج	**broaden** v چوڑا کرنا
bridal adj عروسی	**broadly** adv کھلا کھلا
bride n دلہن	**broadminded** adj کشادہ ذہن
bridegroom n دلہا	**brochure** n بروشر
bridesmaid n دلہن کی خادمہ	**broil** v بھوننا
bridge n پل	**broiler** n بھوننے والا
bridle n لگام	**broke** adj مفلس
brief adj مختصر	**broken** adj ٹوٹا ہوا
brief v ہدایت دینا	**bronchitis** n برونکائیٹس
briefcase n بریف کیس	**bronze** n کانسی
briefing n ابتدائی ہدایات	**broom** n جھاڑو

B

broth n شوربہ	**bug** v ستانا
brothel n قحبہ خانہ	**build** iv تعمیر کرنا
brother n بھائی	**builder** n معمار
brotherhood n برادری	**building** n عمارت
brother-in-law n برادرِ نسبتی	**buildup** n اٹھان
brotherly adj برادرانہ	**built-in** adj دربستہ
brow n ابرو	**bulb** n بلب
brown adj بھورا	**bulge** n ابھار
browse v سرسری پڑھنا	**bulk** n حجم؛ جسامت
browser n پڑھنے والا	**bulky** adj بڑا
bruise n خراش	**bull** n بیل
bruise v چھل جانا	**bulldoze** v تباہ کرنا
brunch n برنچ	**bullet** n گولی
brush n برش	**bulletin** n اطلاع نامہ
brush v برش کرنا	**bully** adj جارحانہ
brush up v اجالنا	**bulwark** n فصیل
brusque adj اجڈ	**bum** n آوارہ گرد
brutal adj وحشی	**bump** n بھڑنا؛ دے مارنا
brutality n وحشیانہ پن	**bump into** v مڈبھیڑ
brute adj وحشی	**bumper** n ٹکر روک
bubble n بلبلہ	**bumpy** adj نابموار
bubble gum n ببل گم	**bun** n بن
buck n کالا برن	**bunch** n گچھا
bucket n ڈول	**bundle** n گٹھا
buckle n بکسوا	**bundle** v گٹھا بنانا
buckle up v باندھنا	**bunker** n مورچہ
bud n شگوفہ؛ غنچہ	**buoy** n تَرنا
buddy n دوست	**burden** n بوجھ
budge v سرکنا	**burden** v لادنا
budget n بجٹ	**burdensome** adj بھاری
buffalo n بھینس	**bureau** n دفتر
bug n کیڑا	**bureaucracy** n افسر شاہی

B
C

bureaucrat n افسر

burger n برگر

burglar n نقب زن

burglarize v نقب لگانا

burglary n نقب زنی

burial n تدفین

burly adj ابھرا ہوا

burn iv جلنا

burn n جلن

burp n ڈکار

burrow n بِل

burst iv بھڑکنا

burst into v پھٹ پڑنا

bury v دفن کرنا

bus n بس

bush n جھاڑی

busily adv مصروفیت سے

business n کاروبار

businessman n کاروباری آدمی

bustling adj دوڑدوپ کرنا

busy adj مصروف

but c لیکن

butcher n قصاب

butchery n قصاب خانہ

butler n خانساماں

butt n ہدف؛ نشانہ

butter n مکھن

butterfly n تتلی

button n بٹن

buttonhole n کاج

buy iv خریدنا

buyer n خریدار

buzz n بھنھناہٹ

buzz v بھنبھنانا

buzzer n بَزر

by pre نزدیک

bye e الوداع

bypass n بائی پاس

bypass v نظر انداز کرنا

by-product n ضمنی پیداوار

bystander n ناظر

C

cab n ٹیکسی

cabbage n بند گوبھی

cabin n حجرہ

cabinet n الماری

cabinet n الماری

cable n تار

cafeteria n قہوہ خانہ

caffeine n جوہرِ قہوہ

cage n پنجرہ

cake n چپاتی

calamity n آفت

calculate v شمار کرنا

calculation n شمار

calculator n شمار کندہ

calendar n جنتری

calf n بچھڑا

C

caliber *n*	لیاقت
calibrate *v*	پیمائش کرنا
call *n*	پکار؛ بلاوا
call *v*	پکارنا؛ بلانا
call off *v*	ملتوی کرنا
call on *v*	ملاقات کرنا
call out *v*	طلب کر لینا
calling *n*	پکار
callous *adj*	سخت
calm *adj*	خاموش
calm *n*	سکون
calm down	دھیما ہونا
calorie *n*	حرارہ
calumny *n*	تہمت
camel *n*	اونٹ
camera *n*	آلہ تصویر کشی
camouflage *v*	تلبیس کرنا
camouflage *n*	تلبیس
camp *n*	خیمہ
camp *v*	خیمہ زن ہونا
campaign *v*	مہم چلانا
campaign *n*	مہم
campfire *n*	الانو
can *iv*	سکنا
can *v*	کر سکنا
can *n*	ڈبہ
canal *n*	نہر
canary *n*	زرد بلبل
cancel *v*	منسوخ کرنا
cancellation *n*	تنسیخ
cancer *n*	سرطان
candid *adj*	صاف گو

candidacy *n*	امیدواری
candidate *n*	امیدوار
candle *n*	شمع
candlestick *n*	شمع دان
candor *n*	صاف گوئی
candy *n*	قندی
cane *n*	بید؛ چھڑی
canister *n*	کنستر
canned *adj*	ڈبہ بند
cannibal *n*	آدم خور
cannon *n*	توپ
canoe *n*	ڈونگی
canonize *v*	ولی گراننا
cantaloupe *n*	خربوزہ نما پھل
canteen *n*	کینٹین
canvas *n*	کرمچ
canyon *n*	آب درہ
cap *n*	ٹوپی؛ ڈھکنا
capability *n*	صلاحیت
capable *adj*	اہل
capacity *n*	گنجائش
cape *n*	راس کوہ
capital *n*	سرمایا
capital letter *n*	بڑے حروف
capitalism *n*	سرمایا داری
capitulate *v*	مطیع ہو جانا
capsize *v*	الٹنا
capsule *n*	کیس بندی
captain *n*	کپتان
captivate *v*	گرویدہ کر لینا
captive *n*	قیدی
captivity *n*	قیدی

capture v قابو کرنا	carry v اٹھانا
capture n ملاپ	carry on v جاری رکھنا
car n کار	carry out v تعمیل کرنا
carat n قیرات	cart n ٹھیلا
caravan n کاروان	cart v لاد کر لیجانا
carburetor n کلسائو	cartoon n کارٹون
carcass n لاش	cartridge n کارتوس
card n کارڈ؛ پت	carve v کندہ کرنا؛ کاٹنا
cardboard n گتہ	cascade n آبشار
cardiac adj قلبی	case n معاملہ؛ ڈبہ
cardiac arrest n قلب گرفتی	cash n زر نقد
cardiology n قلبیات	cashier n خزانچی
care n خیال	casino n کسینو
care v خیال رکھنا	casket n تابوت
care about v پرواہ ہونا	casserole n بنڈیا
career n زریعہ معاش	cassock n جبہ
carefree adj بے فکرا	cast iv ڈھالنا؛ پھینکنا
careful adj محتاط	castaway n آوارہ
careless adj بے پرواہ	caste n ذات
carelessness n بے پرواہی	castle n قلعہ
caress n لاڈ پیار	casual adj اتفاقی
caretaker n نگران	casualty n حادثہ
cargo n کھیپ	cat n بلی
carnage n قتل عام	cataclysm n جل اجھل
carnal adj نفسانی	catacomb n تہہ خانہ
carnation n گلناری پھول	catalog n فہرست
carol n بڑے دن کا گیت	cataract n موتیا؛ آبشار
carpenter n ترکھان	catastrophe n آفت
carpentry n ترکھان کا پیشہ	catch iv پکڑنا
carpet n قالین	catch up v اٹھانا
carriage n بھگی	catching adj دلکش
carrot n گاجر	catchword n تکیہ کلام

C

category *n* ذمرہ	censorship *n* احتساب
cater to *v* توجہ دینا	censure *v* مزمت کرنا
caterpillar *n* سنڈی	census *n* مردم شماری
cathedral *n* بڑا گرجا	cent *n* سواں حصہ
catholic *adj* کیتھولک	centenary *n* صدسالہ جشن
Catholicism *n* کیتھولک مذہب	center *n* مرکز
cattle *n* مویشی	center *v* مرتکز ہونا یا کرنا
cauliflower *n* گوبھی	centimeter *n* سینٹی میٹر
cause *n* سبب	central *adj* مرکزی
cause *v* سبب بننا	centralize *v* مرکز گیر بنانا
caution *n* انتباہ	century *n* صدی
cautious *adj* محتاط	ceramic *n* سرامک
cavalry *n* رسالہ	cereal *n* اناج
cave *n* غار	cerebral *adj* دماغی
cave in *v* دھنس جانا	ceremony *n* تقریب
cavern *n* کھوہ	certain *adj* یقینی
cavity *n* کھوکھلی جگہ	certainty *n* یقین
cease *v* رکنا	certificate *n* سند
cease-fire *n* فاءر بندی	certify *v* تصدیق کرنا
ceaselessly *adv* لاپروایی سے	chagrin *n* برہمی
ceiling *n* چھت	chain *n* زنجیر
celebrate *v* منانا	chain *v* باندھنا
celebration *n* تقریب	chainsaw *n* زنجیری آرا
celebrity *n* نامور شخصیت	chair *n* کرسی
celery *n* اجوائن	chair *v* صدارت کرنا
celestial *adj* سماوی	chairman *n* صدر
celibacy *n* ناتخدائی	chalet *n* پہاڑی بنگلہ
celibate *adj* کنوارہ	chalice *n* جام
cellar *n* تہہ خانہ	chalk *n* چاک
cellphone *n* موبائل ٹیلی فون	challenge *v* للکارنا
cement *n* سیمنٹ	challenge *n* مبازرت
cemetery *n* قبرستان	challenging *adj* صلاحیت آزما

C

chamber *n* کمره	**chart** *n* چارٹ؛ جدول
champ *n* چمپین	**charter** *n* منشور؛ اختیار
champion *n* چمپین	**charter** *v* اختیار دینا
champion *v* معرکه مارنا	**chase** *n* تعاقب
chance *n* موقع	**chase** *v* تعاقب کرنا
chance *n* اتفاق	**chase away** *v* بھاگ نکلنا
chancellor *n* امیر	**chasm** *n* کھائی
chandelier *n* پنساریا	**chaste** *adj* پاک دامن
change *v* بدلنا	**chastise** *v* سزا دینا
change *n* تبدیلی	**chastisement** *n* سزا
channel *n* ندی	**chastity** *n* پاکدامنی
chant *n* بھجن	**chat** *v* گفتگو کرنا
chaos *n* ابتری	**chauffeur** *n* شوفر
chaotic *adj* ابتر	**cheap** *adj* سستا
chapel *n* گرجا	**cheat** *v* دھوکا دینا
chaplain *n* پادری	**cheater** *n* دھوکے باز
chapter *n* باب	**check** *n* پڑتال کرنا؛ روکنا
char *v* کوئلہ بنانا	**check** *v* پڑتال کرنا
character *n* کردار	**check up** *n* جسمانی معائنہ
characteristic *adj* خاصیت	**checkbook** *n* چیک بک
charade *n* شراڈ کھیل	**cheek** *n* رخسار
charbroiled *adj* سیخ پر بھوننا	**cheekbone** *n* رخساری ہڈی
charcoal *n* کوئلہ	**cheeky** *adj* ڈھیٹ
charge *v* بھرنا؛ الزام لگانا	**cheer** *v* خوش کرنا
charge *n* قیمت؛ الزام	**cheer up** *v* حوصلہ بڑھانا
charisma *n* کرشمہ	**cheerful** *adj* بشاش بشاش
charismatic *adj* کرشمہ ساز	**cheese** *n* پنیر
charitable *adj* دریادل	**chef** *n* باورچی
charity *n* نیکی	**chemical** *adj* کیمیکل
charm *v* لبھانا	**chemist** *n* کیمسٹ
charm *n* سحر	**chemistry** *n* کیمیا
charming *adj* پرکشش	**cherish** *v* عزیزرکھنا

C

cherry n شاه دانہ	**chore** n چھوٹاموٹا کام
chess n شطرنج	**chorus** n سنگت
chest n چھاتی؛ صندوق	**christen** v بپتسمہ دینا
chew v چبانا	**christening** n رسم بپتسمہ
chick n چوزہ	**christian** adj عیسائی
chicken n مرغی	**Christianity** n عیسائیت
chicken pox n خسرہ	**Christmas** n کرسمس
chide v ڈانٹنا	**chronic** adj دائمی
chief n سربراہ	**chronicle** n سرگزشت
chiefly adv زیادہ تر	**chronology** n زمانی ترتیب
child n بچہ	**chubby** adj گول مٹول
childhood n بچپن	**chuckle** v کھل کر ہنسنا
childish adj بچگانہ	**chunk** n ٹکڑا
childless adj بے اولاد	**church** n گرجا
children n بچے	**chute** n جھرنا
chill n سردی	**cider** n شراب سیب
chill v ٹھنڈا کرنا	**cigar** n سگار
chilly adj ٹھنڈا	**cigarette** n سگریٹ
chimney n چمنی	**cinder** n لوہے کا میل
chin n ٹھوڑی	**cinema** n سنیما
chip n پھانک؛ ٹکڑ	**cinnamon** n دار چینی
chisel n چھینی	**circle** n حلقہ
chocolate n چاکلیٹ	**circle** v چکر کاٹنا؛ گھیرنا
choice n انتخاب	**circuit** n سرکٹ
choir n طائفہ	**circular** adj دائرہ نما
choke v گھوٹنا	**circulate** v گردش کرانا
cholera n ہیضہ	**circulation** n تشہیر
cholesterol n کولسٹرول	**circumcise** v ختنہ کرنا
choose iv منتخب کرنا	**circumcision** n ختنے
chop v کاٹ ڈالنا	**circumstance** n حالات
chop n تکہ بوٹی	**circus** n سرکس
chopper n ہیلی کاپٹر	**cistern** n حوض

close

citizen *n* شہری	cleanse *v* مصفا بنانا
citizenship *n* شہریت	cleanser *n* صفائی کا آلہ
city *n* شہر	clear *adj* صاف؛ واضح
city hall *n* ایوانِ بلدیہ	clear *v* صاف کرنا
civil *adj* مہذب	clearance *n* صفائی
civilization *n* تہذیب	clear-cut *adj* واضح
civilize *v* مہذب بنانا	clearly *adv* واضح طور پر
claim *v* مطالبہ کرنا	clearness *n* صراحت
claim *n* دعویٰ؛ تقاضا	cleft *n* دراڑ
clam *n* شکنجہ	clemency *n* نرم دلی
clamp *n* شکنجہ	clench *v* کسنا
clan *n* کنبہ	clergyman *n* پادری
clandestine *adj* پوشیدہ	clerk *n* کلرک
clap *v* تالی بجانا	clever *adj* چالاک
clarification *n* تصفیہ	client *n* موکل
clarify *v* وضاحت کرنا	cliff *n* کھڑی چٹان
clarinet *n* بانسری	climate *n* آب و ہوا
clarity *n* وضاحت	climax *n* عروج
clash *v* تصادم ہونا	climb *v* چڑھنا
clash *n* تصادم	climbing *n* چرٹیوں پر چڑھنا
class *n* جماعت؛ درجہ	clinch *v* بھینچنا
classic *adj* حسین	cling *iv* چمٹنا
classmate *n* ہم جماعت	clinic *n* مطب
classroom *n* کمرہ جماعت	clip *v* کاٹنا
classy *adj* حسین	clipping *n* کاٹنے کا عمل
clause *n* ذیل جملہ	cloak *n* چغہ
claw *n* پنجہ	clock *n* گھڑیال
claw *v* نوچنا	clog *v* روک لگانا
clay *n* مٹی	cloister *n* خانقاہ
clean *adj* صاف	clone *v* قلمیہ
clean *v* صاف کرنا	close *v* قریب ہونا
cleaner *n* صفائی کرنے والا	close *adj* قریب

C

close to *pre* قریب قریب	coastline *n* ساحلی خط
closed *adj* بند	coat *n* کوٹ
closely *adv* تقریباً	coat *n* تہہ
closet *n* خلوتی کمرہ	coax *v* پھسلانا
closure *n* خاتمہ	cob *n* مکئی کا بھٹا
clot *n* گاڑھا منجمد مادہ	cobblestone *n* گول پتھر
cloth *n* کپڑا	cobweb *n* مکڑی کا جالا
clothe *v* ڈھانپنا	cocaine *n* کوکین
clothes *n* سلے ہوۓ کپڑے	cock *n* مرغا
clothing *n* پوشاک	cockroach *n* لال بیگ
cloud *n* بادل	cocktail *n* مشربات کا آمیزہ
cloudless *adj* صاف مطلع	cocky *adj* مغرور بانکا
cloudy *adj* ابر آلود	cocoa *n* کوکو
clown *n* مسخرہ	coconut *n* کھوپرا
club *n* کلب؛ ڈنڈھ	cod *n* کوڈ مچھلی
club *v* ڈنڈے سے پیٹنا	code *n* کوڈ
clue *n* اشارہ	codify *v* ضوابط بندی کرنا
clumsiness *n* بھدہ پن	coefficient *n* تعاونی
clumsy *adj* بھدہ	coerce *v* دبائو ڈالنا
cluster *n* جھرمٹ	coercion *n* دبائو
cluster *v* جھرمٹ بنانا	coexist *v* اکٹھے رہنا
clutch *v* پکڑنا	coffee *n* کافی
coach *v* تربیت کرنا	coffin *n* تابوت
coach *n* اتالیق	coherent *adj* متصل
coaching *n* اتالیقی	cohesion *n* پیوستگی
coagulate *v* گاڑھا ہونا	coin *n* سکہ
coagulation *n* جماوٹ	coincidence *n* اتفاق
coal *n* کوئلہ	coincidental *adj* اتفاقی
coalition *n* اتحاد	cold *adj* سرد
coarse *adj* کھردرہ؛ خام	coldness *n* سردی
coast *n* ساحل	colic *n* قولنج
coastal *adj* ساحلی	collaborate *v* تائید کرنا

collaboration *n* تائید	combine *v* ملانا
collaborator *n* تائید کندہ	combustible *n* آتش پذیر
collapse *v* گرانا	combustion *n* سلگن
collapse *n* ضعف	come *iv* آنا
collar *n* کالر	come about *v* وقوع پذیر ہونا
collateral *adj* متوازی	come across *v* اچانک ملنا
colleague *n* رفیق کار	come apart *v* بکھر جانا
collect *v* جمع کرنا	come back *v* واپس ہونا
collection *n* مجموعہ	come down *v* کم ہونا
collector *n* جمع کرنے والا	come forward *v* آگے آنا
college *n* کالج	come from *v* مطلب ہونا
collide *v* ٹکرنا	come in *v* اندر آنا
collision *n* ٹکرائو	come out *v* سامنے آنا
cologne *n* کولون	come over *v* آ ملنا
colon *n* آنت؛ وقف توضیحی	come up *v* ترقی کرنا
colonel *n* کرنل	comeback *n* واپسی
colonial *adj* نوآبادیاتی	comedian *n* بھانڈ
colonization *n* استعمار	comedy *n* طربیہ ناٹک
colonize *v* نوآبادی بنانا	comet *n* دم دار ستارہ
colony *n* نوآبادی	comfort *n* راحت
color *n* رنگ	comfortable *adj* آرام دہ
color *v* رنگنا	comforter *n* لحاف
colorful *adj* رنگین	comical *adj* تفریحی
colossal *adj* دیوقامت	coming *n* رسائی
colt *n* بچھڑا	coming *adj* آمدہ
column *n* کالم	comma *n* سکتہ
comb *n* کنگھی	command *v* حکم
comb *v* کنگھی کرنا	commander *n* کمان دار
combat *n* لڑائی	commandment *n* حکم الٰہی
combat *v* لڑنا	commemorate *v* یاد تازہ کرنا
combatant *n* مبازر	commence *v* ابتدا کرنا
combination *n* میل	commend *v* تحسین کرنا

C

commendation n تحسین	compatibility n مطابقت
comment v رائے زنی کرنا	compatible adj موافق
comment n رائے	compatriot n ہم وطن
commerce n تجارت	compel v مجبور کرنا
commercial adj تجارتی	compelling adj جبری
commission n اختیار	compendium n خلاصہ
commit v ارتکاب کرنا	compensate v تلافی کرنا
commitment n سپردگی	compensation n تلافی
committed adj پابند	compete v موزوں بننا
committee n کمیٹی	competence n موزونیت
common adj عام	competent adj اہل
commotion n اضطراب	competition n مقابلہ
communicate v تبادلہ خیال	competitive adj مسابقتی
communication n ابلاغ	competitor n مسبق
communion n اشتراک	compile v تالیف کرنا
communism n اشتراکیت	complain v شکایت کرنا
communist adj اشتراک پسند	complaint n شکایت
community n گروہ	complement n تکملہ
commute v لین دین کرنا	complete adj مکمل
compact adj منضبط	complete v مکمل کرنا
compact v پرکار بنانا	completely adv مکمل طور پر
companion n ساتھی	completion n تکمیل
companionship n ساتھ	complex adj پیچیدہ
company n کمپنی	complexion n رنگت
comparable adj قابلِ موازنہ	complexity n پیچیدگی
comparative adj تقابلی	compliance n تعمیلِ حکم
compare v موازنہ کرنا	compliant adj مطیع
comparison n موازنہ	complicate v پیچیدہ بنانا
compartment n ڈبہ	complication n پیچیدگی
compass n پرکار	complicity n سازباز
compassion n دردمندی	compliment n آداب
compassionate adj دردمند	complimentary adj اعزازی

C

comply v حکم ماننا	conception n خیال
component n ترکیبی جزو	concern v متعلق ہونا
compose v ترکیب دینا	concern n تعلق
composed adj مطمئن؛ پرسکون	concerning pre بابت
composer n نغمہ ساز	concert n محفل موسیقی
composition n تالیف	concession n رعایت
compost n ملغوبہ	conciliate v منانا
composure n دماغی سکون	conciliatory adj مصالحتی
compound n مرکب	conciousness n ہوش
compound v ملانا	concise adj بلیغ
comprehend v سمجھنا	conclude v نتیجہ نکالنا
comprehensive adj وسیع	conclusion n انجام
compress v دبانا	conclusive adj آخری
compression n دبائو	concoct v گھڑنا
comprise v مشتمل ہونا	concrete n پتھریلامسالہ
compromise n سمجھوتہ	concrete adj ٹھوس
compromise v سمجھوتہ کرنا	concur v ہم آہنگ ہونا
compulsion n مجبوری	concurrent adj ہم آہنگ
compulsive adj جبری	concussion n صدمہ
compulsory adj لازمی	condemn v ملامت کرنا
compute v حساب کرنا	condemnation n ملامت
computer n حساب کرنیوالا	condensation n عمل تکثیف
comrade n ساتھی	condense v گاڑھا بنانا
con man n بھیدی	condescend v انکسار کرنا
conceal v چھپانا	condiment n گرم مسالہ
concede v تسلیم کرنا	condition n حالت
conceited adj خود پسند	conditional adj مشروط
conceive v تشکیل دینا	condo n مشترکہ جائیداد
concentrate v مرتکز کرنا	condolences n تعزیت
concentration n ارتکاز	condone v معاف کرنا
concentric adj ہم مرکز	conducive adj راجع
concept n تصور	conduct n چال چلن

C

conduct v رہبری کرنا	**congenial** adj موافق
conductor n موصل	**congested** adj پُربجوم
cone n مخروطہ	**congestion** n بجوم
confer v عطاکرنا	**congratulate** v مبارک باد کہنا
conference n کانفرنس	**congratulations** n مبارک باد
confess v اعتراف کرنا	**congregate** v مجتمع ہونا
confession n اعتراف	**congregation** n اجتماع
confessional n اعترافی	**congress** n کانگرس
confessor n اعتراف کرنیوالا	**conjecture** n قیاس
confidant n معتمد	**conjugal** adj ازدواجی
confide v راز بتانا	**conjugate** v گردان کرنا
confidence n اعتماد	**conjunction** n اتصال
confident adj پر اعتماد	**conjure up** v دہائی دینا
confidential adj خفیہ	**connect** v جوڑنا
confine v حدود میں رکھنا	**connection** n جوڑ
confinement n قید	**connive** v چشم پوش ہونا
confirm v تصدیق کرنا	**connote** v ثانوی معنی دینا
confirmation n تصدیق	**conquer** v فتح کرنا
confiscate v ضبط کر لینا	**conqueror** n فاتح
confiscation n ضبطی	**conquest** n فتح
conflict n کشمکش	**conscience** n ضمیر
conflict v لڑائی	**conscious** adj باخبر
conflicting adj متضاد	**conscript** n بیگار کا سپاہی
conform v قبول کرنا	**consecrate** v مقدس قرار دینا
conformist adj مقلد	**consecration** n تقدیس
conformity n مطابقت	**consecutive** adj متواتر
confound v منتشر	**consensus** n اتفاقِ رائے
confront v سامنا کرنا	**consent** v منظر کرنا
confrontation n سامنا	**consent** n رضامندی
confuse v تذبذب میں پڑنا	**consequence** n نتیجہ
confusing adj الجھانے والا	**consequent** adj منتج
confusion n الجھاءو	**conservation** n تحفظ

C

conservative *adj*	جدت کا مخالف	**consume** *v*	خرچ کرنا
conserve *v*	رکھنا	**consumer** *n*	استعمال کرنا
conserve *n*	مربہ	**consumption** *n*	خرچ
consider *v*	غور کرنا	**contact** *v*	رابطہ کرنا
considerable *adj*	قابل غور	**contact** *n*	رابطہ
considerate *adj*	قدردان	**contagious** *adj*	متعدی
consideration *n*	ملاحظہ	**contain** *v*	بند رکھانا
consignment *n*	کھیپ	**container** *n*	پیپا
consistency *n*	استواری	**contaminate** *v*	آلودہ کرنا
consistent *adj*	استوار؛ ثابت قدم	**contamination** *n*	آلودگی
consolation *n*	تسلی	**contemplate** *v*	مراقبہ کرنا
console *v*	تسلی دینا	**contemporary** *adj*	ہم عصر
consolidate *v*	ٹھوس بنانا	**contempt** *n*	نفرت
consonant *n*	حرفِ صحیح	**contend** *v*	مقابلہ کرنا
conspicuous *adj*	نمایاں	**contender** *n*	مقابلہ کرنیوالا
conspiracy *n*	سازش	**content** *adj*	مطمئن
conspirator *n*	سازشی	**content** *v*	اطمنان دینا
constancy *n*	ثبات	**contentious** *adj*	جدال پسن
constant *adj*	راسخ	**contents** *n*	مندرجات
consternation *n*	اضطراب	**contestant** *n*	مبازر
constipation *n*	قبض	**context** *n*	سیاق
constitute *v*	تشکیل دینا	**continent** *n*	بر اعظم
constitution *n*	دستور	**continental** *adj*	براعظمی
constrain *v*	مجبور کرنا	**contingency** *n*	امکان
constraint *n*	دبائو؛ بندش	**contingent** *adj*	اتفاقی
construct *v*	تعمیر کرنا	**continuation** *n*	سلسلہ
construction *n*	تعمیر	**continue** *v*	جاری رکھنا
constructive *adj*	تعمیری	**continuity** *n*	تسلسل
consul *n*	قونصل	**continuous** *adj*	جاری
consulate *n*	قونصلیٹ	**contour** *n*	خاکہ
consult *v*	مشورہ کرنا	**contraband** *n*	ممنوعہ شے
consultation *n*	مشاورت	**contract** *v*	مختصر کرنا

C

contract n معاہدہ	convince v قائل کرنا
contraction n سکڑائو	convincing adj قابل یقین
contradict v تردید کرنا	convoluted adj ملفف
contradiction n اختلاف	convoy n کانوائے
contrary adj برخلاف	convulse v تشنج پیدا کرنا
contrast v موازنہ کرنا	convulsion n اینٹھن
contrast n تفریق	cook v پکانا
contribute v حصہ ڈالنا	cook n باورچی
contribution n چندہ؛ حصہ	cookie n خطائی
contributor n حصہ ڈالنے والا	cooking n کھانا پکانا
contrition n سرمساری	cool adj ٹھنڈا
control n ضبط	cool v ٹھنڈا کرنا
control v قابو میں رکھنا	cool down v دھیما ہونا
controversial adj اختلافی	cooling adj ٹھنڈک بخش
controversy n اختلاف	coolness n ٹھنڈک
convalescent adj روبہ صحت	cooperate v تعاون کرنا
convene v جمع ہونا	cooperation n تعاون
convenience n سہولت	cooperative adj تعاون کرنیوالا
convenient adj با سہولت	coordinate v بم ربط بنانا
convent n کانونٹ سکول	coordination n بم ربطگی
convention n اجتماع	coordinator n رابط
conventional adj رواجی	cop n سپاہی
conversation n گفتگو	cope v نمٹنا
converse v گفتگو کرنا	copier n عکسی مشین
conversely adv معکوس طور پر	copper n تانبا
conversion n تبدیلی	copy v نقل کرنا
convert v بدلنا	copy n نقل
convert n نو مذہب	copyright n کاپی رائٹ
convey v پہنچانا	cord n ڈوری
convey v منتقل کرنا	cordial adj خوشگوار
convict v مجرم ٹھہرانا	cordless adj بے تار
conviction n اثباتِ جرم	cordon n فیتہ

cordon off v بند کر دینا	cost n قیمت
core n گری	costly adj قیمتی
cork n کارک	costume n پوشاک
corn n مکئی	cottage n کٹیا
corner n نکڑ	cotton n کپاس
corner n خطہ	couch n صوفہ
cornerstone n بنیادی پتھر	cough n کھانسی
cornet n قرنا	cough v کھانسی کرنا
corollary n بالہ	council n مجلس
coronation n تاج پوشی	counsel v مشورہ دینا
corporal adj جسمانی	counsel n وکیل
corporal n دفعدار فوجی	counsel n مشیر
corporation n کارپوریشن	counselor n مشیر قانونی
corpse n لاش	count v شمار کرنا
corpulent adj فربہ	count n شمار
corpuscle n جسمیہ	count n تعداد
correct v اصلاح کرنا	countdown n الٹی گنتی
correct adj صحیح	countenance n حلیہ
correction n تصحیح	counter n ٹھہرا
correspond v مشابہ ہونا	counteract v توڑ کرنا
correspondent n نامہ نگار	counterfeit v جعل سازی کرنا
corresponding adj مشابہ	counterfeit adj جعلی
corridor n برآمدہ	counterpart n ہم منصب
corroborate v تائید کرنا	countess n کائونٹس
corrode v گھسنا	countless adj بے شمار
corrupt v رشوت لینا	country n ملک
corrupt adj بدعنوان	country n دیہات
corruption n بدعنوانی	countryman n دیہاتی
cosmetic n سنگھار	countryside n دیہاتی علاقہ
cosmic adj کائناتی	county n کائونٹی
cosmonaut n خلانورد	coup n کارگر ضرب
cost iv قیمت ہونا	couple n جوڑا؛ کم تعداد

C

coupon n	کوپن	craftsman n	دستکار
courage n	جرات	cram v	رٹا لگانا
courageous adj	جرات مند	cramp n	اکڑن
courier n	کورئیر	cramped adj	مفلوج
course n	راستہ؛ نصاب	crane n	کونج
court n	عدالت؛ احاطہ	crank v	کج دھرا
court v	رجھانا	cranky adj	بدمزاج
courteous adj	خوش خلق	crap n	ردی
courtesy n	خوشخلقی	crappy adj	بکواس
courtship n	معاشقہ	crash n	ٹکراءو؛ دھماکا
courtyard n	صحن	crash v	ٹکرانا؛ تباہ ہو جانا
cousin n	کزن	crass adj	دبیز
cove n	آدمی	crater n	دہانہ آتش فشاں
covenant n	عہدوپیمان	crave v	خواستگار ہونا
cover n	ڈھکنا؛ پردہ	craving n	خواہش
cover v	ڈھانپنا	crawl v	رینگنا
cover up v	چھپانا	crayon n	رنگین چاک
coverage n	اشاعت	craziness n	جنون
covert adj	خفیہ	crazy adj	جنونی
coverup n	آڑ	creak v	چرمرانا
covet v	لالچ کرنا	creak n	چرمراہٹ
cow n	گائے	cream n	کریم
coward n	بزدل	creamy adj	ملائی دار
cowardice n	بزدلی	crease n	شکن
cowardly adv	بزدلانہ	crease v	شکن ڈالنا
cowboy n	کائو بوائے	create v	تخلیق کرنا
cozy adj	محفوظ	creation n	تخلیق
crab n	کیکڑا	creative adj	تخلیقی
crack n	شگاف	creator n	خالق
crack v	بریک لگانا	creature n	مخلوق
cradle n	پنگھوڑا	credibility n	ساکھ
craft n	مہارت؛ پیشہ	credible adj	قابلِ یقین

credit *n* ساکھ	**cross** *v* پار کرنا
creditor *n* قرض خواہ	**cross out** منسوخ کردینا
creed *n* عقائد	**crossing** *n* پارکرنا
creek *n* ندی	**crossroads** *n* چورابا
creep *v* رینگنا	**crosswalk** *n* عبور پٹی
creepy *adj* پراسرار	**crossword** *n* لفظی معما
crematorium *n* شمشان	**crouch** مائل کرنا
crest *n* فراز	**crow** *n* کوا
crevice *n* درز	**crow** *v* کاییں کاییں کرنا
crew *n* عملہ	**crowbar** *n* کروبار
crib *n* کھٹولا	**crowd** *n* ہجوم
cricket *n* کرکٹ	**crowd** *v* مجمع لگانا
crime *n* جرم	**crowded** *adj* پرہجوم
criminal *adj* مجرم	**crown** *n* تاج
cripple *adj* مفلوج	**crown** *v* تاج پاشی کرنا
cripple *v* مفلوج کرنا	**crowning** *n* تاج پوشی
crisis *n* بحران	**crucial** *adj* قطعی
crisp *adj* خستہ	**crucifix** *n* صلیب
crispy *adj* کرکرا	**crucifixion** *n* تصلیب
criterion *n* کسوٹی	**crucify** *v* مصلوب کرنا
critical *adj* تنقیدی	**crude** *adj* خام
criticism *n* تنقید	**cruel** *adj* جھگڑالو
criticize *v* تنقید کرنا	**cruelty** *n* ظلم
critique *n* فنِ تنقید	**cruise** بحری گشت کرنا
crockery *n* مٹی کے ظروف	**crumb** *n* چورا
crocodile *n* مگرمچھ	**crumble** *v* چورا چورا کرنا
crony *n* لنگوٹیا یار	**crunchy** *adj* مرمری
crook *n* ٹیڑھا	**crusade** *n* صلیبی جنگ
crooked *adj* خمیدہ؛ چالباز	**crush** *v* پیسنا
crop *n* کاٹنا	**crushing** *adj* رگڑائو
cross *n* کانٹا	**crust** *n* قشر؛ پرت
cross *adj* بدمزاج	**crusty** *adj* چھلکے دار

C

crutch *n* بیساکھی	**curfew** *n* کرفیو
cry *n* چیخ	**curiosity** *n* تجسس
cry *v* چلانا	**curious** *adj* متجسس
cry out *v* پکارنا	**curl** *v* چھلا بنانا
crying *n* رونا دھونا	**curl** *n* چھلا
crystal *n* بلور	**curly** *adj* گھونگھریالا
cub *n* شیر کا بچہ	**currency** *n* کرنسی
cube *n* مکعب	**current** *adj* مروجہ
cubic *adj* مکعب جیسا	**currently** *adv* فی الحال
cubicle چھوٹامکعب کمرہ	**curse** *v* بددعا دینا
cucumber *n* کھیرا	**curtail** *v* مختصر کرنا
cuddle *v* بغل گیری	**curtain** *n* پردہ
cuff *n* کف؛ سلوٹ	**curve** *n* اخط منحنی
cuisine *n* کھانا پکانا	**curve** *v* جھکا ہونا
culminate *v* اوج پر ہونا	**cushion** *n* گدی
culpability *n* مجرمیت	**cushion** *v* گدی رکھنا
culprit *n* مجرم	**cuss** *v* کوسنا
cult *n* مسلک	**custard** *n* کسٹرڈ
cultivate *v* کاشت کرنا	**custodian** *n* نگہبان
cultivation *n* کاشت	**custody** *n* تحویل
culture *n* کلچر	**custom** *n* رواج؛ عادت
cumbersome *adj* بوجھل	**customary** *adj* رواجی
cunning *adj* مکار	**customer** *n* گاہک
cup *n* پیالی	**customs** *n* محاصل
cupboard *n* الماری	**cut** *n* چیرا
curable *adj* قابل علاج	**cut** *iv* کاٹنا
curator *n* ہدایت کار	**cut back** *v* تخفیف
curb *v* مجبور کرنا	**cut down** *v* گھٹانا
curb *n* روک	**cut out** *v* کاٹ کر نکالنا
curdle *v* دودھ کا جمنا	**cute** *adj* حسین
cure *v* تندرست کرنا	**cutlery** *n* چھری کانٹے
cure *n* شفا	**cutter** *n* کاٹنے کا آلہ

cyanide *n* سایاناءڈ
cycle *n* چکر
cyclone *n* بگولا
cylinder *n* سلنڈر
cynic *adj* سنکی
cynicism *n* سنکمزاجی
cypress *n* صنوبر
cyst *n* آبلہ
czar *n* زارِ روس

D

dad *n* والد
dagger *n* خنجر
daily *adv* برروز
dairy farm *n* ڈیری فارم
daisy *n* گل دائودی
dam *n* ڈیم
damage *n* نقصان
damage *v* نقصان پہنچانا
damaging *adj* نقصان دہ
damn *v* پھٹکارنا
damnation *n* لعنتِ ابدی
damp *adj* سیلا
dampen *v* گیلا کرنا
dance *n* رقص
dance *v* رقص کرنا
dancing *n* رقص

dandruff *n* سکری
danger *n* خطرہ
dangerous *adj* خطرناک
dangle *v* جھولنا
dare *v* جرات کرنا
dare *n* جرات
daring *adj* جرات مند
dark *adj* تاریک
darken *v* تاریک بنانا
darkness *n* اندھیرہ
darling *adj* پیارا
darn *v* رفو کرنا
dart *n* چھوٹی برچھی
dash *v* دھکا دینا
dashing *adj* بہادر
data *n* معلومات
database *n* ڈیٹابیس
date *n* تاریخ؛ کھجور
date *v* تاریخ ڈالنا
daughter *n* بیٹی
daughter-in-law *n* بہو
daunt *v* ڈرانا
daunting *adj* حوصلہ شکن
dawn *n* سحر
day *n* دن
daydream *v* خیالی پلاءو
daze *v* بکابکا کر دینا
dazzle *v* چندھیا جانا
dazzling *adj* خیرہ کن
de luxe *adj* اعلی
deacon *n* چھوٹا پادری
dead *adj* مردہ

dead end *n* بند رستہ

deaden *v* بے حس کر دینا

deadline *n* حتمی وقت

deadlock *adj* تعطل

deadly *adj* مہلک

deaf *adj* بہرہ

deafen *v* بہرہ کر دینا

deafening *adj* کان پھاڑنے والا

deafness *n* بہرہ پن

deal *iv* معاملہ کرنا

deal *n* سودا

dealer *n* سوداگر

dealings *n* لین دین

dean *n* سربراہ شعبہ

dear *adj* پیارا

dearly *adv* پیار سے

death *n* موت

deathbed *n* بستر مرگ

debase *v* بے قدر کرنا

debatable *adj* قابلِ بحث

debate *v* بحث کرنا

debate *n* بحث

debit *n* ادھار

debrief *v* سوال کرنا

debris *n* ملبہ

debt *n* ادھار

debtor *n* قرض دار

debunk *v* پول کھولنا

debut *n* آغازِ کار

decade *n* دبائی

decadence *n* گراوٹ

decapitate *v* سر قلم کرنا

decay *v* گلنا سرنا

decay *n* زوال

deceased *adj* متوفی

deceit *n* دھوکا

deceitful *adj* دغا باز

deceive *v* دھوکا دینا

December *n* دسمبر

decency *n* شائستگی

decent *adj* شائستہ

deception *n* دھوکا

deceptive *adj* گمراہ کن

decide *v* فیصلہ کرنا

deciding *adj* فیصلہ کن

decimal *adj* اعشاری

decimate *v* قتل کرنا

decipher *v* رمز کشائی

decision *n* فیصلہ

decisive *adj* فیصلہ کن

deck *n* چبوترہ

declaration *n* اعلان

declare *v* اعلان کرنا

declension *n* ڈھلان

decline *v* زوال پذیر ہونا

decline *n* زوال

decompose *v* سڑنا گلنا

décor *n* زیبائش

decorate *v* سجانا

decorative *adj* سجاوٹی

decorum *n* ادب آداب

decrease *v* کم کرنا

decrease *n* کمی

decree *n* حکم

decree v	حکم دینا	defile v	میلا کرنا
decrepit adj	خستہ حال	define v	تعریف کرنا
dedicate v	انتساب کرنا	definite adj	معین
dedication n	انتساب	definition n	تعریف
deduce v	نتیجہ نکالنا	definitive adj	قطعی
deduct v	منہا کرنا	deflate v	ہوا نکالنا
deductible adj	قابلِ منہائی	deform v	صورت بگاڑنا
deduction n	کٹوتی	deformity n	بد شکلی
deed n	عمل	defraud v	ٹھگنا
deem v	سوچنا	defray v	رقم چکانا
deep adj	گہرا	defrost v	پگھلانا
deepen v	گہرا کرنا	deft adj	منجھا ہوا
deer n	ہرن	defuse v	فیوز نکالنا
deface v	مسخ کرنا	defy v	مقابلہ کرنا
defame v	بدنام کرنا	degenerate v	بگڑنا
defeat v	شکست دینا	degenerate adj	بگڑا ہوا
defeat n	شکست	degeneration n	بگاڑ
defect n	عیب	degrade v	درجہ کم کرنا
defect v	غداری کرنا	degrading adj	رسوا کن
defection n	غداری	degree n	سند
defective adj	ناقص	dehydrate v	پانی اڑانا
defend v	دفاع کرنا	deign v	فروتنی کرنا
defendant n	مدعا علیہ	deity n	خدا
defender n	محافظ	dejected adj	افسردہ
defense n	دفاع	delay v	تاخیر کرنا
defenseless adj	نہتا	delay n	تاخیر
defer v	ملتوی کرنا	delegate n	مندوب
defiance n	حکم عدولی	delegation n	وفد
defiant adj	نافرمان	delete v	حذف کرنا
deficiency n	کمی	deliberate v	غور کرنا
deficient adj	نامکمل	deliberate adj	ارادی
deficit n	خسارہ	delicacy n	نزاکت

delicate *adj* نازک	Denmak *n* ڈنمارک
delicious *adj* لذيذ	denominator *n* نسب نما
delight *n* مسرت	denote *v* تعبير ہونا
delight *v* مسرور کرنا	denounce *v* کھلی ملامت کرنا
delightful *adj* مسرت بخش	dense *adj* گنجان؛ گھنا
delinquency *n* غفلت	density *n* کثافت
delinquent *adj* غافل	dent *v* چپ پڑنا
deliver *v* حوالے کرنا؛ بچانا	dent *n* چپ
delivery *n* سپردگی؛ ولادت	dentist *n* ماہر دندان
delude *v* بہکانا	dentures *n* بتیسی
deluge *n* طغيانی	deny *v* انکار کرنا
delusion *n* دھوکا	deodorant *n* دافع بد بو
demand *v* تقاضا کرنا	depart *v* روانہ ہونا
demand *n* تقاضا	department *n* شعبہ
demanding *adj* زيادہ طلب والا	departure *n* روانگی
demean *v* درجہ کم کرنا	depend *v* منحصر ہونا
demeaning *adj* رسوا کن	dependable *adj* قابل بھروسہ
demeanor *n* برتائو	dependence *n* انحصار
demented *adj* مجنون	dependent *adj* منحصر
demise *n* رحلت	depict *v* بيان کرنا
democracy *n* جمہوريت	deplete *v* خالی کرنا
democratic *adj* جمہوری	deplorable *adj* افسوس ناک
demolish *v* گرانا	deplore *v* افسوس کرنا
demolition *n* مسماری	deploy *v* صف آرائی کرنا
demon *n* شيطان	deployment *n* صف آرائی
demonstrate *v* مظاہرہ کرنا	deport *v* ملک بدر کرنا
demonstrative *adj* اثباتی	deportation *n* ملک بدری
demoralize *v* گيلا کرنا	depose *v* بربادی
demote *v* تنزلی کرنا	deposit *n* جمع کروانا
den *n* کچھار	depot *n* مال خانہ؛ گودام
denial *n* انکار	deprave *adj* بداخلاق کرنا
denigrate *v* بدنام کرنا	depravity *n* بد اخلاقی

D

depreciation *n* فرسودگی	**desist** *v* باز رہنا
depress *v* افسرده کرنا	**desk** *n* چوکی؛ ڈیسک
depressing *adj* افسرده کن	**desolate** *adj* اجاڑ
depression *n* افسردگی	**desolation** *n* ویرانی
deprivation *n* محرومی	**despair** *n* ناامیدی
deprive *v* محروم کرنا	**desperate** *adj* بے دھڑک
deprived *adj* محروم	**despicable** *adj* قابلِ نفرت
depth *n* گہرائی	**despise** *v* نفرت کرنا
derail *v* پٹڑی سے اترنا	**despite** *c* کے با وجود
deranged *adj* پراگنده	**despondent** *adj* دل شکستہ
derelict *adj* لاوارث	**despot** *n* جابر
deride *v* تمسخر اڑانا	**despotic** *adj* جابرانہ
derivative *adj* مشق	**dessert** *n* میٹھا
derive *v* اخذکرنا	**destination** *n* منزل
derogatory *adj* توہین آمیز	**destiny** *n* تقدیر
descend *v* اترنا	**destitute** *adj* مفلس
descendant *n* آل	**destroy** *v* تباه کرنا
descent *n* اترائی	**destroyer** *n* تباه کننده
describe *v* بیان کرنا	**destruction** *n* تباہی
description *n* بیان	**destructive** *adj* تباه کن
descriptive *adj* بیانیہ	**detach** *v* علیحده کرنا
desert *n* صحرا	**detachable** *adj* قابلِ علیحدگی
desert *v* چھوڑ دینا	**detail** *n* تفصیل
deserted *adj* ویران	**detail** *v* تفصیل بتانا
deserter *n* فراری	**detain** *v* روکنا
deserve *v* مستحق ہونا	**detect** *v* غلطی پکڑنا
deserving *adj* مستحق	**detective** *n* سراغ رساں
design *n* منصوبہ؛ خاکہ	**detention** *n* حراست
designate *v* نامزد کرنا	**deter** *v* باز رکھنا
desirable *adj* پسندیده	**detergent** *n* مصف
desire *n* خواہش	**deteriorate** *v* انحطاط ہونا
desire *v* خواہش کرنا	**deterioration** *n* انحطاط

determination n عزم	**diagram** n شکل
determine v طے کرنا	**dial** n کرّہ
deterrence n تسدید	**dial tone** n ڈائل کی آواز
detest v نفرت کرنا	**dialect** n مقامی لہجہ
detestable adj کریہہ	**dialogue** n مکالمہ
detonate v بم پھٹنا	**diameter** n قطر
detour n پھیرا	**diamond** n ہیرا
detriment n گزند	**diaper** n پوتڑا
detrimental adj ضرر رسا	**diarrhea** n اسہال
devaluation n تخفیفِ قدرِ زر	**diary** n روزنامچہ
devastate v تباہ کرنا	**dice** n مہرہ
devastating adj تباہ کن	**dictate** v حکم دینا
devastation n تبابی	**dictator** n آمر
develop v ترقی دینا	**dictatorial** adj آمرانہ
development n افزائش	**dictatorship** n آمریت
deviation n انحراف	**dictionary** n ڈکشنری
device n آلہ	**die** v مرنا
devil n شیطان	**die out** v معدوم ہو جانا
devious adj پرفریب	**diet** n غذا
devise v تدبیر کرنا	**differ** v مختلف ہونا
devoid adj محروم	**difference** n اختلاف
devote v وقف کرنا	**different** adj مختلف
devotion n جاں نثاری	**difficult** adj مشکل
devour v نگل لینا	**difficulty** n مشکل
devout adj پارسا	**diffuse** v بکھیرنا
dew n شبنم	**dig** iv کھودنا
diabetes n زیابیطس	**digest** v ہضم کرنا
diabetic adj زیابیطسی	**digestion** n انہضام
diabolical adj شیطانی	**digestive** adj ہاضم
diagnose v تشخیص کرنا	**digit** n عدد
diagnosis n تشخیص	**dignify** v عزت بخشنا
diagonal adj قطر سے متعلق	**dignitary** n معزز شخص

D

dignity n عظمت	**disagree** v متفق نہ ہونا
dilapidated adj ٹوٹا پھوٹا	**disagreeable** adj ناخوشگوار
dilemma n دوہری مشکل	**disagreement** n عدم اتفاق
diligence n جانفشانی	**disappear** v غائب ہو جانا
diligent adj جان فشان	**disappearance** n گم شدگی
dilute v پتلا کرنا	**disappoint** v مایوس ہونا
dim adj مدھم	**disappointing** adj مایوس کن
dim v مدھم کرنا	**disappointment** n مایوسی
dimension n سمتی وسعت	**disapproval** n نامنظوری
diminish v کم کرنا	**disapprove** v نامنظور کرنا
dine v کھانا کھانا	**disarm** v غیر مسلح کرنا
diner n ریستوران	**disarmament** n تخفیفِ اسلحہ
dining room n طعام گاہ	**disaster** n آفت
dinner n عشائیہ	**disastrous** adj تباہ کن
dinosaur n ڈائنو سار	**disband** v منتشر کرنا
diocese n پادری کا حلقہ	**disbelief** n عدم یقین
diphthong n دو صوتیہ	**disburse** v رقم تقسیم کرنا
diploma n ڈپلومہ؛ سند	**discard** v ترک کر دینا
diplomacy n سفارت	**discern** v ادراک کرنا
diplomat n سفیر	**discharge** v بجا لانا؛ نکالنا
diplomatic adj سفارتی	**discharge** n ربائی؛ اخراج
dire adj ہولناک	**disciple** n مرید
direct adj براہِ راست	**discipline** n نظم و ضبط
direct v رخ کرنا	**disclaim** v انکار کرنا
direction n سمت	**disclose** v افشاء کرنا
director n ہدایت کار	**discomfort** n بے آرامی
directory n ڈائریکٹری	**disconnect** v رابطہ منقطع ہونا
dirt n کوڑا کرکٹ	**discontent** adj غیر قانع
dirty adj گندہ	**discontinue** v بند کر دینا
disability n معذوری	**discord** n عدم اتفاق
disabled adj معذور	**discordant** adj بے محل
disadvantage n عدم فائدہ	**discount** v کم کرنا

discouragement n حوصلہ شکنی	disillusion n ازالہءِ التباس
discourtesy n کج خلقی	disinfectant n عفونت ربا
discover v دریافت کرنا	disinherit v عاق کرنا
discovery n دریافت	disintegrate v پارہ پارہ کرنا
discredit v رسوائی	disintegration n پارگی
discreet adj ہوشیار	disinterested adj غیر جانبدار
discrepancy n تضاد	disk n قرص
discretion n صوابدید	dislike v ناپسند کرنا
discriminate v تمیز کرنا	dislike n ناپسندیدگی
discrimination n تمیز	dislocate v سرکانا
discuss v گفتگو کرنا	dislodge v ہٹانا
discussion n گفتگو	disloyal adj غیر وفادار
disdain n تحقیر	disloyalty n غیروفاداری
disease n بیماری	dismal adj تاریک
disembark v جہاز سے اترنا	dismantle v منہدم کرنا
disenchanted adj طلسم سے آزاد	dismay n ہمت شکنی
disentangle v چھڑانا	dismay v ہمت توڑنا
disfigure v بدشکل بنانا	dismiss v برطرف کرنا
disgrace n بے عزتی	dismissal n برطرفی
disgrace v توہین کرنا	dismount v تباہ کر دینا
disgraceful adj باعثِ ذلت	disobedience n حکم عدولی
disgruntled adj شاکی	disobedient adj نافرمان
disguise v بھیس بدلنا	disorder n بد نظمی
disguise n بھیس	disorganized adj بے ترتیب
disgust n نفرت	disown v قبول نہ کرنا
disgusting adj قابل نفرت	disparity n تفاوت
dish n قاب	dispatch v ارسال کرنا
dishonest adj بد دیانت	dispel v زائل کرنا
dishonesty n بد دیانتی	dispensation n بانٹ
dishonor n بے حرمتی	dispersal n انتشار
dishonorable adj قابلِ شرم	disperse v منتشر کرنا
dishwasher n برتن دھونے والا	displace v سرکانا

D

display n مظاہرہ
display v مظاہرہ کرنا
displease v ناخوش
displeasing adj ناراضی کا سبب
displeasure n ناراضی
disposable adj قابلِ نکاسی
disposal n نکاسی
dispose v تلف کرنا
disprove v باطل ثابت کرنا
dispute n مباحثہ
dispute v مباحثہ کرنا
disqualify v نااہل قرار دینا
disregard v نظر انداز کرنا
disrepair n فقدانِ مرمت
disrespect n بے ادبی
disrespectful adj گستاخ
disrupt v خلل ڈالنا
disruption n خلل
dissatisfied adj غیر مطمئن
disseminate v بکھیرنا
dissent v متفق نہ ہونا
dissident adj مختلف الرائے
dissimilar adj غیر مشابہ
dissipate v منتشر کرنا
dissolute adj بدکار
dissolution n تحلیل
dissolve v تحلیل ہونا
dissonant adj ناہموار
dissuade v مزحمت کرنا
distance n فاصلہ
distant adj دور
distaste n ناگواری

distasteful adj ناگوار
distill v کشید کرنا
distinct adj جدا
distinction n امتیاز
distinctive adj امتیازی
distinguish v امتیاز کرنا
distort v توڑنا مروڑنا
distortion n بگاڑ
distract v موڑنا
distraction n انتشار توجہ
distraught adj پریشان حال
distress n کرب
distress v اداس کرنا
distressing adj اذیت ناک
distribute v تقسیم کرنا
distribution n تقسیم
district n ڈسٹرکٹ
distrust n بے اعتمادی
distrust v اعتماد نہ کرنا
distrustful adj ناقابلِ بھروسہ
disturb v خلل ڈالنا
disturbance n خلل
disturbing adj خلل ڈالنے والا
disunity n عدم اتحاد
disuse n عدم استعمال
ditch n کھڈّا
dive v غوطہ لگانا
diver n غوطہ خور
diverse adj متعدد
diversify v متنوع بنانا
diversion n موڑ
diversity n تنوع

D

divert v موڑنا	**domineering** adj جابرانہ
divide v تقسیم کرنا	**dominion** n عملداری
dividend n مقسوم	**donate** v عطیہ کرنا
divine adj خدائی	**donation** n عطیہ
diving n غوطہ خوری	**donkey** n گدھا
divinity n الوہیت	**donor** n دہندہ
divisible adj قابلِ تقسیم	**doom** n تباہی
division n تقسیم	**doomed** adj تباہ شدہ
divorce n طلاق	**door** n دروازہ
divorce v طلاق دینا	**doorstep** n زینہ در
divulge v افشا کرنا	**dope** n گاڑھا سیال
dizziness n چکر	**dope** v لینا
do iv کرنا	**dormitory** n بڑا شبستان
docile adj اصیل	**dosage** n مقدار خوراک
docility n اطاعت پسندی	**dossier** n مسل
dock n گھاٹ	**dot** n نقطہ
doctor n حکیم	**double** adj دبرا
doctrine n نظریہ	**double** v دگنا کرنا
document n دستاویز	**double-check** v دبری پڑتال
documentary n دستاویزی چیز	**double-cross** v دھوکا دبی
dodge v کترانا	**doubt** n شک
dog n کتا	**doubt** v شبہ ہونا
dole out v دینا	**doubtful** adj مشتبہ
doll n گڑیا	**dough** n گندھا ہوا آٹا
dollar n ڈالر	**dove** n فاختہ
dolphin n ڈولفن	**down** adv نیچے
dome n گنبد	**downcast** adj پژمردہ
domestic adj خانگی	**downfall** n زوال
domestic adj اندرونی	**downhill** adv نیچے کی طرف
domesticate v گھریلو بنانا	**downstairs** adv نچلی منزل
dominate v حکمرانی کرنا	**down-to-earth** adj حقیقت پسند
domination n غلبہ	**downtown** n اندرون شہر

downtrodden *adj* پسماندہ	drift *v* بہہ جانا
downturn *n* مندے کا رحجان	drift apart *v* علیحدہ
dowry *n* جہیز	drill *v* مشق کرنا؛ کھودنا
doze *n* اونگھ	drill *n* مشق
doze *v* اونگھنا	drink *iv* مشروب پینا
dozen *n* درجن	drink *n* مشروب
draft *n* مسودہ	drinkable *adj* پینے کے قابل
draft *v* مسودہ تیار کرنا	drinker *n* پینے والا
draftsman *n* نقشہ نویس	drip *v* قطرہ قطرہ گرنا
drag *v* گھسیٹنا	drip *n* ڈرپ
dragon *n* ڈریگن	drive *n* ہانکنا؛ گاڑی چلانا
drain *v* نکاسی آب کرنا	drive *iv* دھکیل
drainage *n* نکاسی	drive away *v* دور چلے جانا
dramatic *adj* ڈرامائی	driver *n* ڈرئیور
dramatize *v* مبالغہ کرنا	drizzle *v* بوندا باندی ہونا
drape *n* پردہ	drizzle *n* بوندا باندی
drastic *adj* شدید	drop *n* قطرہ؛ گرنے کا عمل
draw *n* قرعہ	drop *v* گرنا
draw *iv* کھینچنا	drop in *v* دورہ کرنا
drawback *n* نقص	drop out *v* چھوڑ دینا
drawer *n* دراز	drought *n* خشک سالی
drawing *n* نقشہ کشی	drown *v* ڈوبنا
dread *v* خوف	drowsy *adj* نیم خوابیدہ
dreaded *adj* خوفزدہ	drug *n* دوا
dreadful *adj* خوفناک	drug *v* دوا یا نشہ لینا
dream *iv* خواب دیکھنا	drugstore *n* دواخانہ
dream *n* خواب	drum *n* ڈھول
dress *n* لباس	drunk *adj* مخمور
dress *v* لباس پہننا	drunkenness *n* بدمستی
dresser *n* کپڑوں کی دراز	dry *v* خشک کرنا
dressing *n* مرہم پٹی	dry *adj* خشک
dried *adj* خشک	dryer *n* خشک ساز

dual *adj* دوہرا	dwindle *v* گھٹنا
dubious *adj* مشتبہ	dye *v* رنگنا
duck *n* بطخ	dye *n* خضاب
duck *v* غوطہ لگانا	dying *adj* مرتا ہوا
duct *n* نالی	dynamic *adj* متحرک
due *adj* واجب	dynamite *n* ڈائنامائٹ
duel *n* دنگل	
dues *n* واجب الادا رقم	
duke *n* ڈیوک	
dull *adj* کند ذہن	
duly *adv* باقاعدہ طور پر	
dumb *adj* گونگا	# E
dummy *n* نقل	
dummy *adj* ڈمی	each *adj* ہر ایک
dump *v* پھینکنا	each other *adj* ایک دوسرے کو
dump *n* انبار	eager *adj* مشتاق
dung *n* گوبر	eagerness *n* اشتیاق
dungeon *n* جیل	eagle *n* عقاب
dupe *v* الو بنانا	ear *n* کان
duplicate *v* نقل کرنا	earache *n* کان درد
duplication *n* مثنی سازی	eardrum *n* کان کا پردہ
durable *adj* دیرپا	early *adv* جلدی
duration *n* دورانیہ	earmark *v* نشانِ شناخت
during *pre* کے دوران	earn *v* کمانا
dusk *n* دھندلکا	earnestly *adv* سنجیدگی سے
dust *n* گرد	earnings *n* کماءی
dusty *adj* گردآلود	earphones *n* ائیر فون
Dutch *adj* ولندیزی	earring *n* بندا
duty *n* فرض	earth *n* زمین
dwarf *n* بونا	earthquake *n* زلزلہ
dwell *iv* رہائش پذیر ہونا	earwax *n* کان کا میل
dwelling *n* رہائش	ease *v* سہولت پہنچانا

easily adv آسانی سے	**effigy** n پُتلا
east n مشرق	**effort** n کوشش
Easter n ایسٹر	**effusive** adj پرجوش
eastern adj مشرقی	**egg** n انڈہ
easy adj آسان	**egoism** n انانیت
eat iv کھانا	**egoist** n انانیت پسند
eat away v چٹ کر جانا	**eight** adj آٹھ
eavesdrop v جاسوسی کرنا	**eighteen** adj اٹھاره
ebb v بھاٹا؛ جذر	**eighth** adj آٹھواں
eccentric adj انوکھاہ	**eighty** adj اسی
echo n گونج	**either** adj ایک یا دوسرا
eclipse n گہن	**either** adv کوئی نہ کوئی
ecology n مطالعہ ماحول	**eject** v نکال پھینکنا
economical adj کفایتی	**elapse** v گزرنا
economize v باکفیت بنانا	**elastic** adj لچکیلا
economy n معیشیت	**elated** adj خوش
ecstasy n وجد	**elbow** n کہنی
ecstatic adj وجدآور	**elder** n بڑا
edge n کناره	**elderly** adj بزرگ
edgy adj تیز دھار والا	**elect** v منتخب کرنا
edible adj قابل خوردنی	**election** n انتخاب
edifice n حویلی	**electric** adj برقی
edit v مرتب کرنا	**electrician** n ماہر آلات برق
edition n ایڈیشن	**electricity** n بجلی
educate v تعلیم دینا	**elegance** n حسن
educational adj تعلیمی	**elegant** adj حسین
eerie adj پر اسرار	**element** n عنصر
effect n اثر	**elementary** adj بنیادی
effective adj پر اثر	**elephant** n ہاتھی
effectiveness n تاثیر	**elevate** v اٹھانا
efficiency n کاکردگی	**elevation** n رفعت
efficient adj ابل	**elevator** n آلہ ارتفاع

E

E

eleven *adj* گیاره	emission *n* اخراج
eleventh *adj* گیارواں	emit *v* خارج ہونا
eligible *adj* ابل	emotion *n* جذبہ
eliminate *v* حذف کرنا	emotional *adj* جذباتی
elm *n* ایلم	emperor *n* شہنشاہ
eloquence *n* فصاحت	emphasis *n* تاکید
else *adv* کوئی اور	emphasize *v* تاکید کرنا
elsewhere *adv* کہیں اور	empire *n* سلطنت
elude *v* بچ نکلنا	employ *v* کام میں لانا
emaciated *adj* لاغر	employee *n* ملازم
emanate *v* خارج ہونا	employer *n* آجر
emancipate *v* آزادی دلانا	employment *n* ملازمت
embalm *v* حنوط کرنا	emptiness *n* خالی پن
embark *v* سوار ہونا	empty *adj* خالی
embarrass *v* پریشان کرنا	empty *v* خالی کرنا
embassy *n* سفارت خانہ	enable *v* قابل بنانا
embellish *v* سنگارنا	enchant *v* مسحور کرنا
embers *n* انگارے	enchanting *adj* مسحور کن
embezzle *v* غبن کرنا	encircle *v* حلقہ بنانا
embitter *v* تلخی پیدا کرنا	enclose *v* ملفوف کرنا
emblem *n* علامت	enclosure *n* احاطہ
embody *v* مجسم کرنا	encompass *v* حلقے میں لینا
embrace *v* بغلگیر ہونا	encounter *v* ملنا
embrace *n* بغل گیری	encounter *n* مڈبھیڑ
embroidery *n* کشیدہ کاری	encourage *v* حوصلہ بڑھانا
embroil *v* فساد پیدا کرنا	encroach *v* تجاوز کرنا
embryo *n* جنین	encyclopedia *n* انسائیکلوپیڈیا
emerald *n* زمرد	end *n* آخر
emerge *v* ظاہر ہونا	end *v* ختم کرنا/ہونا
emergency *n* ہنگامی حالت	end up پر خاتمہ ہونا
emigrant *n* مہاجر	endanger *v* خطرہ مول لینا
emigrate *v* ہجرت کرنا	endeavor *v* سعی کرنا

endeavor n سعی	**enrich** v ملامال کرنا
ending n اختتام	**enroll** v میٹرک کرنا
endless adj لامحدود	**enrollment** n اندراج
endorse v توثیق کرنا	**ensure** v یقینی بنانا
endorsement n توثیق	**entail** v مشروط بیمہ کرنا
endure v برداشت کرنا	**entangle** v الجھانا
enemy n دشمن	**enter** v داخل ہونا
energetic adj پر قوت	**enterprise** n کاروباری مہم
energy n قوت	**entertain** v خاطرمدارت کرنا
enforce v نافذ کرنا	**entertaining** adj باعث تفریح
engage v منگنی کرنا	**entertainment** n تفریح
engaged adj مشغول	**enthrall** v شیدا کرنا
engagement n منگنی	**enthralling** adj فریفتہ کرنیوالا
engine n انجن	**enthuse** v گرما دینا
engineer n انجینئر	**enthusiasm** n جوش و خروش
England n انگلینڈ	**entice** v ورغلانا
English adj انگریزی	**enticement** n تحریص
engrave v کنندہ کرنا	**enticing** adj ترغیب آمیز
engraving n کنندہ کاری	**entire** adj سارا
engrossed adj منہمک ہونا	**entirely** adv مکمل طور پر
engulf v محیط ہو جانا	**entrance** n داخلہ
enhance v بڑھانا	**entreat** v عرض کرنا
enjoy v لطف اندوز ہونا	**entree** n حق داخلہ
enjoyable adj پر لطف	**entrenched** adj مورچہ بند
enjoyment n لطف	**entrepreneur** n انٹرپرنیور
enlarge v بڑا کرنا	**entrust** v سپرد کرنا
enlargement n توسیع	**entry** n داخلہ
enlighten v روشنی ڈالنا	**enumerate** v شمار کرنا
enlist v بھرتی کرنا	**envelop** v لپیٹ کر ڈھانپنا
enormous adj ضخیم	**envelope** n لفافہ
enough adv کافی	**envious** adj حاسد
enrage v مشتعل کردینا	**environment** n ماحول

E

envisage v تصور کرنا	escape v فرار ہونا
envoy n لطف اندوز ہونا	escort n بدرقہ
envy n حسد	esophagus n غذاءی نالی
envy v حسد کرنا	especially adv خاص طور پر
epidemic n وبا	espionage n جاسوسی
epilepsy n مرگی	essay n مضمون
episode n قسط	essence n جوہر
epistle n مراسلہ	essential adj اساسی
epitaph n سنگ مزار	establish v قاءم کرنا
epitomize v خلاصہ کرنا	estate n جاٸیداد
epoch n عہد	esteem v توقیر
equal adj برابر	estimate v اندازہ لگانا
equality n مساوات	estimation n اندازہ
equation n مساوات	estranged adj کشیدہ
equator n خط استوا	estuary n دریا کا چوڑا دہانہ
equilibrium n توازن	eternity n ابدیت
equip v لیس کرنا	ethical adj اخلاقی
equipment n سامان	ethics n اخلاقیات
equivalent adj مساوی	etiquette n آداب
era n زمانہ	euphoria n بشاشت
eradicate v بیخ کنی کرنا	Europe n یورپ
erase v مٹا دینا	European adj یورپی
erect v کھڑا کرنا	evacuate v خالی کرنا
erect adj سیدھا کھڑا	evade v ٹالنا
err v غلطی کرنا	evaluate v تشخیص کرنا
errand n دورہ	evaporate v بخارات بن جانا
erroneous adj غلط	evasion n ٹال مٹول
error n غلطی	evasive adj گریز کرنیوالا
erupt v پھٹ پڑنا	eve n شام
escalate v وسعت دینا	even adj حتٰی کہ
escalator n چلتا زینہ	even if c حتٰی کہ اگر
escapade n فرار	evening n شام

event *n* واقعہ	excerpt *n* اقتباس
eventuality *n* احتمال	excess *n* زیادتی
eventually *adv* آخر کار	excessive *adj* متجاوز
ever *adv* ہمیشہ	exchange *v* تبادلہ کرنا
everlasting *adj* لافانی	excite *v* جوش دلانا
every *adj* ہر ایک	excitement *n* جوش
everybody *pro* ہر شخص	exciting *adj* پرجوش
everyday *adj* ہر روز	exclaim *v* پکار اٹھنا
everyone *pro* ہر کوئی	exclude *v* شامل نہ کرنا
everything *pro* ہر شے	excruciating *adj* دکھ دینا
evict *v* نکال باہر کرنا	excursion *n* تفریحی سفر
evidence *n* شہادت	excuse *v* معافی چاہنا
evil *n* شر	excuse *n* معذرت خواہی
evil *adj* بد	execute *v* تعمیل کرنا
evolution *n* ارتقا	executive *n* انتظامی
evolve *v* بتدریج تیار کرنا	exemplary *adj* مثالی
exact *adj* ٹھیک ٹھیک	exemplify *v* مثال پیش کرنا
exaggerate *v* مبالغہ کرنا	exempt *adj* مبرا
exalt *v* سرفراز کرنا	exemption *n* استثنا
examination *n* امتحان	exercise *n* مشق
examine *v* معائنہ کرنا	exercise *v* مشق کرنا
example *n* مثال	exert *v* تگ و دو کرنا
exasperate *v* بے حد خفا کرنا	exertion *n* جانفشانی
excavate *v* کھدائی کرنا	exhaust *v* خالی کرنا
exceed *v* حد سے گزر جانا	exhausting *adj* تھکا دینے والا
exceedingly *adv* بدرجہ اتم	exhaustion *n* ناتوانی
excel *v* سبقت لے جانا	exhibit *v* نمائش کرنا
excellence *n* فضیلت	exhibition *n* نمائش
excellent *adj* شاندار	exhilarating *adj* فرحت بخشنا
except *pre* سوائے	exhort *v* بھیک مانگنا
exception *n* استثناء	exile *v* جلاوطن کرنا
exceptional *adj* استثنائی	exile *n* جلاوطنی

وجود رکھنا exist v	کھوجی explorer n
وجود existence n	دھماکا explosion n
خروج کا رستہ exit n	آتش گیر explosive adj
نقل مکانی exodus n	استحصال explotation n
بے خطا ٹھہرانا exonerate v	برآمد کرنا export v
بہت بڑا exorbitant adj	افشا کرنا expose v
عامل exorcist n	منکشف exposed adj
بدیسی exotic adj	واضع express adj
پھیلانا expand v	اظہار کرنا express v
پھیلائو expansion n	اظہار expression n
توقع رکھنا expect v	صراحتاً expressly adv
امید expectancy n	ضبط کر لینا expropriate v
توقع expectation n	اخراج expulsion n
مصلحت expediency n	نہایت عمدہ exquisite adj
مفید expedient adj	بڑھانا extend v
مہم expedition n	اضافہ extension n
نکال باہر کرنا expel	وسعت extent n
اخراجات expenditure n	بیرونی exterior adj
لاگت expense n	تباہ کر ڈالنا exterminate v
مہنگا expensive adj	خارجی external adj
تجربہ experience n	معدوم extinct adj
آزمائش experiment n	آگ بجھانا extinguish v
ماہر expert adj	اینٹھ لینا extort v
تلافی کرنا expiate v	اضافی extra adv
تلافی expiation n	کشید کرنا extract v
ختم ہو جانا expire v	ملزم سپرد کرنا extradite v
وضاحت کرنا explain v	تحویل extradition n
واضع explicit adj	خارج از extraneous adj
پھٹنا explode v	فضول خرچی extravagance n
تصرف میں لانا exploit v	فضول خرچ extravagant adj
مہم exploit n	انتہائی extreme adj
کھوج لگانا explore v	انتہا پسند extremist adj

extremities *n* ہاتھ پائوں	factual *adj* اصلی
extricate *v* آزاد کرنا	faculty *n* شعبہ
extroverted *adj* دوستانہ	fad *n* وقتی فیشن
exude *v* رسنا	fade *v* پھیکا پڑنا
exult *v* شادمان ہونا	faded *adj* پھیکا
eye *n* آنکھ	fail *v* ناکام ہونا
eyebrow *n* ابرو	failure *n* ناکامی
eye-catching *adj* دیدہ کش	faint *v* بے ہوش ہونا
eyeglasses *n* چشمہ	faint *n* وقتی بے ہوشی
eyelash *n* پلک	faint *adj* بے ہوش
eyelid *n* پیوٹا	fair *n* میلہ
eyesight *n* بینائی	fair *adj* بے عیب؛خوب
eyewitness *n* عینی شاہد	fairness *n* انصاف پسندی
	fairy *n* پری
	faith *n* ایمان
	faithful *adj* وفادار

fable *n* قصہ	fake *v* جعلی روپ دینا
fabric *n* بناوٹ	fake *adj* جعلی
fabricate *v* بنانا	fall *n* زوال؛ انحطاط
fabulous *adj* بہت ہی خوب	fall *iv* گرنا
face *n* چہرہ	fall back پسپا ہونا
face up to *v* سامنا کرنا	fall behind پیچھے رہ جانا
facet *n* پہلو	fall down ناکام ہونا
facilitate *v* سہولت پہنچانا	fall through بے نتیجہ رہنا
facing *pre* سجاوٹ	fallacy *n* مغالطہ
fact *n* حقیقت	fallout *n* دھماکے کا غبار
factor *n* عامل	falsehood *n* باطل
factory *n* کارخانہ	falsify غلط ردوبدل کرنا
	falter لڑکھڑانا
	fame *n* مقبولیت
	familiar *adj* آشنا
	family *n* خاندان

famine n قحط	**faucet** n ٹونٹی
famous adj نامور	**fault** n قصور
fan n پنکھا؛ پرستار	**faulty** adj قصور وار
fanatic adj کٹر	**favor** n عنایت
fancy adj خیال آفرینی	**favorable** adj مفید
fantastic adj انوکھا	**favorite** adj پسندیدہ
fantasy n تخیل کی تخلیق	**fear** n خوف
far adv دور	**fearful** adj خوف زدہ
faraway adj دور دراز	**feasible** adj مکن
farce n سوانگ	**feast** n ضیافت
fare n کرایہ	**feat** n کرتب
farewell n الوداع	**feather** n پر
farm n کھیت	**feature** n خدوخال
farmer n دہقان	**February** n فروری
farming n کھیتی باڑی	**fed up** adj بیزار
farther adv دور	**federal** adj وفاقی
fascinate v مسحور کرنا	**fee** n فیس
fashion n فیشن	**feeble** adj ضعیف
fast adj تیز	**feed** iv خوراک دینا
fasten v باندھنا	**feedback** n جوابی رائے
fat n چکنائی	**feel** iv محسوس کرنا
fat adj موٹا	**feeling** n احساس
fatal adj مہلک	**feelings** n احساسات
fate n تقدیر	**feet** n پائوں
fateful adj فیصلہ کن	**feign** v جھوٹ موٹ بننا
father n والد	**fellow** n ساتھی
fatherhood n والدیت	**fellowship** n شراکت
father-in-law n سسر	**felon** n نمک حرام
fatherly adj پدرانہ	**female** n مادہ
fatigue n تھکن	**feminine** adj مادینی
fatten v فربہ کرنا	**fence** n جنگلا
fatty adj چربی دار	**fencing** n تلوار بازی

F

fend v ٹال دینا

fend off v پرے ہٹا دینا

fender n روک

ferment v خمیر اٹھانا

ferment n خمیر

ferocious adj خون خوار

ferocity n خون خواری

ferry n کشتی

fertile adj زرخیز

fertility n زرخیزی

fertilize v زرخیز بنانا

fervent adj سرگرم

fester v پیپ پڑنا

festive adj تیوہاری

festivity n بشاشت

fetid adj متعفن

feud n خاندانی رقابت

fever n بخار

feverish adj بخار زدہ

few adj چند

fewer adj کم تعداد کا

fiancé n منگیتر

fiber n ریشہ

fickle adj متلون

fiction n افسانہ

fictitious adj غیر حقیقی

fiddle n سارنگی

fidelity n وفاداری

field n میدان

fierce adj تندخو

fiery adj شعلہ فشاں

fifteen adj پندرہ

fifth adj پانچواں

fifty adj پچاس

fifty-fifty adv برابر برابر

fig n انجیر

fight iv لڑنا

fight n لڑائی

fighter n جنگ جو

figure n چہرہ مہرہ

figure out v حل کر لینا

file v درج کرنا

file n مسل؛ فائل

fill v بھرنا

filling n بھرائی

film n فلم

filter n چھلنی

filter v چھاننا

filth n نجاست

filthy adj نجس

fin n فن

final adj حتمی

finalize v نتیجہ نکالنا

financial adj مالیاتی

find iv پانا

find out v تلاش کرنا

fine n جرمانہ

fine v جرمانہ کرنا

fine adv ٹھیک ہے

fine adj عمدہ

finger n انگلی

fingernail n ناخن

fingerprint n انگلی کا نشان

fingertip n سرِ انگشت

F

اختتام کرنا v finish	بھڑک n flare
فن لینڈ n Finland	بھڑکنا v flare-up
فن لینڈ کا adj Finnish	چمک n flash
آگ لگانا v fire	بھڑک دار adj flashy
آگ n fire	فلیٹ n flat
آتشیں اسلحہ n firearm	چپٹا adj flat
پٹاخہ n firecracker	ہموار بنانا v flatten
آگ بجھانے والا n firefighter	خوشامد کرنا v flatter
آگ بجھانے والا n fireman	خوشامد n flattery
انگیٹھی n fireplace	شیخی بھگارنا v flaunt
سوختی لکڑی n firewood	مزا n flavor
آتش بازی n fireworks	نقص n flaw
بے لچک adj firm	بے عیب adj flawless
فرم n firm	پسو n flea
مضبوطی n firmness	بھاگ کھڑا ہونا iv flee
پہلا adj first	پشم n fleece
مچھلی n fish	بحری بیڑا n fleet
ماہی گیر n fisherman	عارضی adj fleeting
مبہم adj fishy	گوشت/ماس n flesh
مکہ n fist	خم دینا v flex
دورہ n fit	لچک دار adj flexible
موزوں v fit	جھلمل کرنا v flicker
اچھی صحت n fitness	جہاز کا رہنما n flier
موزوں adj fitting	پرواز n flight
پانچ adj five	کمزور adj flimsy
پکا کرنا v fix	ہوا میں اچھالنا v flip
چٹانی کھاڑی n fjord	تیرنا v float
جھنڈا n flag	گلہ n flock
بھڑکیلا adj flamboyant	کوڑے مارنا v flog
شعلہ n flame	سیلاب v flood
آتش پذیر adj flammable	آب بند پھاٹک n floodgate
کوکھ n flank	سیلابی n flooding

floodlight *n* تیز روشنی	folly *n* حماقت
floor *n* فرش	fond *adj* مشتاق
flop *n* ناکامی	fondle *v* پیار کرنا
floss *n* کچا ریشم	fondness *n* شوق
flour *n* آٹا	food *n* غذا
flourish *v* فخر سے لہرانا	foodstuff *n* اشیائے خوردنی
flow *v* بہنا	fool *v* بیوقوف بنانا
flow *n* روانی	fool *adj* نادان
flower *n* پھول	foolproof *adj* بے خطا
flowerpot *n* گلدان	foot *n* پاؤں
flu *n* نزلہ	football *n* فٹ بال
fluctuate *v* کم زیادہ ہونا	footnote *n* حاشیہ
fluently *adv* روانی سے	footprint *n* نقشِ پا
fluid *n* سیال	footstep *n* قدم
flunk *v* ناکام ہونا	footwear *n* جوتا
flush *v* پانی کا ریلا بہانا	for *pre* برائے
flute *n* بانسری	forbid *iv* ممانت کرنا
flutter *v* پھڑپھڑانا	force *n* قوت
fly *iv* اڑنا	force *v* مجبور کرنا
fly *n* مکھی	forceful *adj* زور دار
foam *n* فوم	forcibly *adv* طاقت سے
focus *n* ماسکہ	forecast *iv* پیشگوئی کرنا
focus on مرتکز کرنا	forefront *n* اگلا حصہ
foe *n* دشمن	foreground *n* پیش منظر
fog *n* دھند	forehead *n* پیشانی
foggy *adj* کہرآلود	foreign *adj* غیرملکی
foil *v* رکاوٹ ڈالنا	foreigner *n* غیرملکی شخص
fold *v* تہ کرنا	foreman *n* پیش دست
folks *n* لوگ	foremost *adj* اولین
folksy *adj* خوش خلق	foresee *iv* پیش بینی کرنا
follow *v* پیچھے چلنا	foreshadow *v* جھلک دکھانا
follower *n* پیروکار	foresight *n* عاقبت اندیشی

forest n جنگل	**fortunate** adj خوش قسمت
foretaste n توقع	**fortune** n قسمت
foretell v پیش گوئی کرنا	**forty** adj چالیس
forever adv ہمیشہ کے لیے	**forward** adv آگے کو
forewarn v پہلے متنبہ کرنا	**fossil** n سنگوارہ
foreword n پیش لفظ	**foster** v پرورش کرنا
forfeit v حق کھو دینا	**foul** adj غلیظ
forge v جعل سازی کرنا	**foundation** n بنیاد
forgery n جعل سازی	**founder** n بانی
forget v بھول جانا	**fountain** n چشمہ
forgivable adj قابلِ معافی	**four** adj چار
forgive v معاف کرنا	**fourteen** adj چودہ
forgiveness n معافی	**fourth** adj چوتھا
fork n کانٹا	**fox** n لومڑ
form n بنانا	**foxy** adj عیار
formal adj رسمی	**fraction** n کسر
formality n رسمی بات	**fracture** n شکستگی
formalize v رسمی بنانا	**fragile** adj بھربھرا
formally adv رسمی طور پر	**fragment** n ٹکڑا
format n ہیئت	**fragrance** n خوشبو
formation n بناوٹ	**fragrant** adj خوشبودار
former adj پچھلا	**frail** adj کمزور
formerly adv عہدِ ماضی میں	**frailty** n حرص
formidable adj بھیانک	**frame** n چوکھٹا
formula n نسخہ	**framework** n قالب؛ ڈھانچہ
forsake iv چھوڑ دینا	**France** n فرانس
fort n قلعہ	**frank** adj بے جھجھک
forthcoming adj اگلا	**frankly** adv بلا جھجھک
forthright adj بے جھجھک	**frankness** n بے تکلفی
fortify v حصاربندی کرنا	**frantic** adj بدحواس
fortitude n مضبوطی	**fraternal** adj برادرانہ
fortress n قلعہ	**fraternity** n اخوت

F

fraud n دغا	**fringe** n جھالر
fraudulent adj دغاباز	**frivolous** adj نکما
freckle n جھائی	**frog** n مینڈک
freckled adj نشان زدہ	**from** pre من جانب
free v آزاد کرنا	**front** n محاذ
free adj آزاد	**frontage** n سامنا
free adj مفت	**frontier** n سرحد
freedom n آزادی	**frost** n کہر
freeway n کھلا راستہ	**frostbite** n کہر زدگی
freeze iv منجمد کرنا	**frostbitten** adj کہر زدہ
freezing adj ٹھنڈا	**frosty** adj کہر آلود
freight n فریٹ	**frown** v تیوری چڑھانا
French adj فرانسیسی	**frozen** adj منجمد
frenetic adj شوریدہ سر	**frugal** adj باکفایت
frenzy n ذہنی انتشار	**frugality** n کفایت شعاری
frequency n تعدد	**fruit** n پھل
frequent adj بکثرت ہونیوالا	**fruitful** adj مفید
frequent v چکر لگانا	**fruity** adj ثمردار
fresh adj تازہ	**frustrate** v مایوس کرنا
freshen v تازہ بنانا	**frustration** n مایوسی
freshness n تازگی	**fry** v تلنا
friar n راہب	**frying pan** n تلنے کا برتن
friction n رگڑ	**fuel** n ایندھن
Friday n جمعہ	**fuel** v برقرار رکھنا
fried adj تلا ہوا	**fugitive** n مفرور
friend n دوست	**fulfill** v پورا کرنا
friendship n دوستی	**fulfillment** n تکمیل
frigate n فریگیٹ	**full** adj بھرا ہوا
fright n خوف	**fully** adv مکمل طور پر
frighten v خوفزدہ کرنا	**fumes** n دھواں
frightening adj خوفناک	**fumigate** v دھونی دینا
frigid adj ٹھنڈا	**fun** n کھیل تماشا

F
G

function n عمل

fund n سرمایا

fund v سرمایا مہیا کرنا

fundamental adj بنیادی

funds n سرمایا

funeral n جنازہ

fungus n کھمبی

funny adj پرمذاق

fur n سمور

furious adj غصیلا

furiously adv غصے سے

furnace n بھٹی

furnish v کمی پوری کرنا

furnishings n لوازمات

furniture n فرنیچر

furor n غیظ

furrow n لیکھ

furry adj سموری

further adv آگے کو

furthermore adv مزید

fury n طیش

fuse n برقی فیوز

fusion n پگھاءو

fuss n ہلچل

fussy adj چڑچڑا

futile adj بے مصرف

future n مستقبل

fuzzy adj مبہم

G

gadget n کل پرزہ

gag n زبان بندی

gag v خاموش کرانا

gage v گنجائش ناپنا

gain v نفع حاصل کرنا

gain n مفعت

gal n لڑکی

galaxy n کہکشاں

gale n جھکڑ

gall bladder n مثانہ

gallant adj بہادر

gallery n دالان

gallon n گیلن

gallop v سرپٹ دوڑنا

gallows n سولی

gamble v جوا کھیلنا

game n شکار

gang n ٹولہ

gangrene n مرتا ہوا بافت

gangster n داداگیر

gap n داداگیر ؛ اچکا

garage n گیراج

garbage n کوڑاکرکٹ

garden n باغ

gardener n مالی

gargle v غرارے کرنا

garland n ہار

garlic n لہسن

garment n پوشاک

garnish v آراستہ کرنا	gentleness n حلیمی
garnish n آراستگی	genuflect v مائل کرنا
garrison n چھاونی	genuine adj اصلی
garrulous adj باتونی	geography n جغرافیہ
gas n گیس	geology n ارضیات
gash n گھائو	geometry n جیومیٹری
gasoline n گیسولین	germ n جرثومہ
gasp v ہانپنا	German adj جرمن
gastric adj شکمی	Germany n جرمنی
gate n پھاٹک	germinate v نمو پانا
gather v اکٹھا کرنا	gerund n اسمِ مصدر
gathering n اکٹھ	gestation n زمانہء حمل
gauge v ناپنا	gesture n اشارہ
gauze n جالی	get iv حاصل کرنا
gaze v گھورنا	get along v ترقی کرنا
gear n گیءر	get away v فراز ہو جانا
geese n ہنس	get back v واپس آنا
gem n جوہر	get by v زندہ رہنا
gender n صنف	get down v اترنا
gene n جین	get down to v کام شروع کرنا
general n عام	get in v گھر آنا
generalize v تعمیم کرنا	get off v اترنا
generate v پیدا کرنا	get out v باہر چلے جانا
generation n نسل	get over v تلافی کر لینا
generator n جنریٹر	get together v میل ملاقات کرنا
generosity n سخاوت	get up v تیار کرنا
genetic adj جینی	geyser n گرم چشمہ
genial adj فرحت افزا	ghastly adj بھیانک
genocide n نسل کشی	ghost n بھوت
genteel adj نفیس	giant n دیو
gentle adj بامروت	gift n تحفہ
gentleman n شریف آدمی	gifted adj چست

G

gigantic *adj*	دیوقامت	gloomy *adj*	غمگین
giggle *v*	ہنسنا	glorify *v*	تکریم دینا
gimmick *n*	انوکھا دائو	glorious *adj*	عظمت والا
ginger *n*	ادرک	glory *n*	عظمت
giraffe *n*	زرافہ	gloss *n*	چمک دمک
girl *n*	لڑکی	glossary *n*	فرہنگ
girlfriend *n*	دوست خاتون	glossy *adj*	زرق برق
give *iv*	دینا	glove *n*	دستانہ
give away *v*	ہدیہ کرنا	glow *v*	چمکنا
give back *v*	واپس کرنا	glucose *n*	گلوکوز
give in *v*	دب جانا	glue *n*	گوند
give up *v*	ترک کر دینا	glue *v*	لیٹی لگانا
glacier *n*	گلیشینر	glut *n*	بہتات
glad *adj*	خوش	glutton *n*	پرخور شخص
gladiator *n*	گلیڈی ایٹر	gnaw *v*	کترنا
glamorous *adj*	مسحور کن	go *iv*	جانا
glance *v*	نگاہ ڈالنا	go ahead *v*	آگے بڑھنا
glance *n*	نگاہ	go away *v*	روانہ ہو جانا
gland *n*	غدہ	go back *v*	واپس جانا
glare *n*	چندھیا دینا	go down *v*	کم ہونا
glass *n*	شیشہ	go in *v*	شامل ہونا
glasses *n*	عینک	go on *v*	جاری رکھنا
gleam *n*	دمک	go out *v*	متروک ہو جانا
gleam *v*	دمکنا	go over *v*	معائنہ کرنا
glide *v*	پھسلنا	go through *v*	مکمل کرنا
glimmer *n*	جھلمل کرنا	go under *v*	ڈوبنا
glimpse *n*	جھلک	go up *v*	اوپر چڑھنا
glimpse *v*	جھلک دکھانا	goal *n*	منزل؛ گول
glitter *v*	درخشاں ہونا	goalkeeper *n*	گولی
globe *n*	ارض نما کرہ	goat *n*	بکری
globule *n*	گلوبچہ	gobble *v*	لپ لپ کھانا
gloom *n*	تاریکی	God *n*	خدا

G

goddess *n* ديوى	graft *v* پيوند لگانا
godless *adj* كافر	graft *n* پيوند
goggles *n* دهوپ عينک	grain *n* بيج
gold *n* سونا	gram *n* چنا
golden *adj* سنهرى	grammar *n* گرامر
good *adj* اچها	grand *adj* اعظم
good-looking *adj* خوش شکل	grandchild *n* پوتا
goodness *n* اچهائى	granddad *n* دادا
goods *n* سامان	grandfather *n* دادا
goodwill *n* خير سگالى	grandmother *n* دادى
goof *v* کام بگاڑ لينا	grandparents *n* دادا دادى
goof *n* بدهو	grandson *n* پوتا
goose *n* بنس	granite *n* گرينائٹ
gorge *n* گهاٹى	granny *n* نانى دادى
gorgeous *adj* شوخ	grant *v* عطيہ دينا
gorilla *n* گوريلا	grant *n* عطيہ
gory *adj* خونى	grape *n* انگور
gospel *n* انجيل	grapefruit *n* گريپ فروٹ
gossip *v* گپ لگانا	grapevine *n* انگورى بيل
gossip *n* گپ شپ	grasp *n* پکڑ
gout *n* گٹهيا	grasp *v* سمجهنا؛ پکڑنا
govern *v* حکومت کرنا	grass *n* گهاس
government *n* حکومت	grateful *adj* ممنون
governor *n* گورنر	gratify *v* اطمنان بخشنا
gown *n* چوغہ	gratifying *adj* تسکين دہ
grab *v* اچک لينا	gratitude *n* تشکر
grace *n* خوبصورتى	gratuity *n* انعاميہ
graceful *adj* خوش وضع	grave *adj* انتہائى ابم
gracious *adj* مهربان	grave *n* قبر
grade *n* درجہ	gravestone *n* سنگ مزار
gradual *adj* بتدريج	graveyard *n* قبرستان
graduate *v* سند دينا	gravity *n* کششِ ثقل

G

gravy *n* شوربہ	**grip** *n* گرفت
gray *adj* سرمئی	**gripe** *n* خفا کرنا
grayish *adj* خاکستری سا	**grisly** *adj* ہیبت ناک
graze *v* چرنا	**groan** *v* کراہنا
graze *n* رگڑ؛ لمس	**groan** *n* کراہ
grease *v* چکنا کرنا	**groceries** *n* کریانہ
grease *n* گریس	**groin** *n* چڈا
greasy *adj* چکنا	**groom** *n* دولہا
great *adj* عظیم	**groove** *n* جھری
greatness *n* عظمت	**gross** *adj* کل؛ مجموعی
Greece *n* یونان	**grossly** *adv* کلی طور پر
greed *n* لالچ	**grotesque** *adj* بیہودہ
greedy *adj* لالچی	**grotto** *n* کھوہ
Greek *adj* یونانی	**grouch** *v* افسردہ
green *adj* سبز	**grouchy** *adj* بے اطمنان
green bean *n* ریشہ دار لوبیہ	**ground** *n* زمین
greenhouse *n* سبز خانہ	**ground floor** *n* نچلی منزل
Greenland *n* گرین لینڈ	**groundless** *adj* بے سبب
greet *v* آداب کرنا	**groundwork** *n* بنیاد
greetings *n* آداب	**group** *n* گروہ
gregarious *adj* مجلس پسند	**grow** *iv* اگنا
grenade *n* دستی بم	**grow up** *v* بالغ ہونا
greyhound *n* گرے ہائونڈ	**growl** *v* غرانا
grief *n* رنج	**grown-up** *n* جوان
grievance *n* شکوہ	**growth** *n* نمو
grieve *v* رنج دینا	**grudge** *n* حسد
grill *v* سیخ پر بھوننا	**grudgingly** *adv* بے دلی سے
grill *n* سیخ	**gruelling** *adj* ہمت شکن
grim *adj* گھمبیر	**gruesome** *adj* ہولناک
grime *n* کالک	**grumble** *v* شکایت کرنا
grind *iv* پیسنا	**grumpy** *adj* چڑچڑا آدمی
grip *v* گرفت میں لینا	**guarantee** *v* گارنٹی دینا

G

guarantee n گارنٹی	**gust** n تند ہوا
guarantor n گارنٹی دینے والا	**gusto** n ذوق
guard n محافظ	**gusty** adj پرجوش
guardian n سرپرست	**gut** n آنت
guerrilla n چھاپہ مار	**guts** n ہمت
guess v قیاس کرنا	**gutter** n گٹر؛ نالہ
guess n قیاس	**guy** n کوئی شخص
guest n مہمان	**guzzle** v بہت زیادہ پینا
guidance n رہنمائی	**gymnasium** n جمنازیم
guide v رہنمائی کرنا	**gypsy** n خانہ بدوش
guide n رہبر	
guidebook n رہنما کتاب	
guidelines n رہنما اصول	
guild n گلڈ	
guile n فریب	
guillotine n گلوٹین	
guilt n جرم	
guilty adj قصور وار	
guise n ظاہری وضع	
guitar n گٹار	
gulf n خلیج	**habit** n عادت
gull n مرغابی	**habitable** adj قابلِ سکونت
gullible adj سادہ مزاج	**habitual** adj عادی
gulp v ہڑپ کر جانا	**hack** v چیرنا
gulp n نگلنے کاعمل	**haggle** v مول تول کرنا
gulp down v نگلنا	**hail** n اولہ
gum n مسوڑا	**hail** v اولے پڑنا
gun n بندوق	**hair** n بال
gun down v گولی مارنا	**hairbrush** n کنگھا
gunman n بندوقچی	**haircut** n حجامت
gunpowder n بارود	**hairdresser** n مشاطہ
gunshot n توپ گولا	**hairpiece** n جوڑا
	hairy adj بال دار
	half n آدھا حصہ
	half adj آدھا

G
H

hall n بال	**hang up** v لٹکانا,
hallway n برآمدہ	**hanger** n لٹکن
halt v رکنا	**hangup** n دشواری
halve v آدھا کرنا	**happen** v واقع ہونا
ham n سور کا گوشت	**happening** n واقعہ
hamlet n چھوٹا گاءوں	**happiness** n خوشی
hammer n ہتھوڑا	**happy** adj خوش
hammock n جھولن کھٹولا	**harass** v زچ کرناکرنا
hand n ہاتھ	**harassment** n پریشانی
hand down v اگلی نسل کو دینا	**harbor** n بندرگاہ
hand in v دینا	**hard** adj سخت
hand out v تقسیم کرنا	**harden** v سخت بنانا
hand over v حوالے کرنا	**hardly** adv بمشکل
handbag n دستی بیگ	**hardness** n سختی
handbook n چھوٹی کتاب	**hardship** n صعوبت
handcuff v ہتھ کڑی لگانا	**hardware** n دھاتی اشیاء
handcuffs n ہتھکڑی	**hardwood** n سخت لکڑی
handful n مٹھی بھر	**hardy** adj جانفشاں
handgun n دستی اسلحہ	**hare** n خرگوش
handicap n رکاوٹ	**harm** v نقصان پہنچانا
handkerchief n رومال	**harm** n نقصان
handle v نمٹنا	**harmful** adj نقصان دہ
handle n دستہ	**harmless** adj بے ضرر
handout n ہینڈآئوٹ	**harmonize** v ہم آہنگ ہونا
handrail n جنگلہ	**harmony** n ہم آہنگی
handshake n مصافہ	**harp** n ستار
handsome adj خوبرو	**harpoon** n برچھی
handwritting n خط	**harrowing** adj دل خراش
handy adj با سہولت	**harsh** adj کرخت
hang iv لٹکانا	**harshly** adv کرختگی سے
hang around v قیام	**harshness** n کرختگی
hang on v جاری رکھنا	**harvest** n کٹائی

harvest v کٹائی کرنا	**headphones** n سرفون
hashish n حشیش	**headquarters** n صدردفتر
hassle v بحث کرنا	**headway** n ترقی
hassle n بحث	**heal** v مندمل ہونا
haste n عجلت	**healer** n شفابخش
hasten v جلدی کرنا	**health** n صحت
hastily adv عجلت میں	**healthy** adj صحت مند
hasty adj عجلتی	**heap** n ڈھیر
hat n ٹوپی	**heap** v ڈھیر لگانا
hatchet n کلہاڑی	**hear** iv سننا
hate v نفرت کرنا	**hearing** n سماعت
hateful adj نفرت انگیز	**hearsay** n افوہ
hatred n نفرت	**hearse** n جنازہ
haughty adj مغرور	**heart** n دل
haul v گھسیٹنا	**heartbeat** n دل کی دھڑکن
haunt v چکر لگانا	**heartburn** n سوزشِ قلب
have iv رکھنا	**hearten** v دل بڑھانا
have to v کرنا پڑنا	**heartfelt** adj محوس کیاگیا
haven n بندرگاہ	**hearth** n چولھا
havoc n تنابی	**heartless** adj بے حس
hawk n عقاب	**hearty** adj پر تپاک
hay n سوکھی گھاس	**heat** v گرم ہونا/کرنا
haystack n گھاس کا انبار	**heat** n حرارت
hazard n خطرہ	**heater** n گرمالہ
hazardous adj پر خطر	**heathen** n ملحد
haze n کہر	**heatstroke** n لو
hazy adj دھندلا	**heatwave** n گرمی کی لہر
he pro وہ (مرد)	**heaven** n جنت
head n سر	**heavenly** adj آسمانی
headache n سردرد	**heaviness** n بوجھل پن
heading n سرخی	**heavy** adj بھاری
head-on adv سیدھا	**heckle** v مداخلت کرنا

H

H

hectic *adj* مدقوقتعلق	**heresy** *n* بدعت
heed *v* دھیان کرنا	**heretic** *adj* بدعتی
heel *n* ایڑی	**heritage** *n* میراث
height *n* اونچائی	**hermetic** *adj* ہوا بند
heighten *v* بلند تر کرنا	**hermit** *n* راہب
heinous *adj* کریہہ	**hernia** *n* آنت ترنا
heir *n* وارث	**hero** *n* ہیرو
heiress *n* وارثہ	**heroic** *adj* جوانمردانہ
heist *n* نقب زنی کرنا	**heroin** *n* ہیروئین
helicopter *n* ہیلی کاپٹر	**heroism** *n* ہیروکی خصوصیات
hell *n* جہنم	**hers** *pro* کا(عورت)اس
hello *e* ہیلو	**herself** *pro* خود نے (عورت)اس
helm *n* پتوار	**hesitant** *adj* متأمل
helmet *n* ہیلمٹ	**hesitate** *v* ہچکچانا
help *v* مدد کرنا	**hesitation** *n* ہچکچاہٹ
help *n* مدد	**heyday** *n* ترنگ
helper *n* مددگار	**hiccup** *n* ہچکی
helpful *adj* مفید	**hidden** *adj* پوشیدہ
helpless *adj* بے بس	**hide** *iv* چھپانا
hem *n* کیڑے کا کنارہ	**hideaway** *n* جائےپناہ جگہ
hemisphere *n* نصف کرہ	**hideous** *adj* مکروہ
hemorrhage *n* جریان خون	**hierarchy** *n* نظام مراتب
hen *n* مرغی	**high** *adj* اونچا
hence *adv* چنانچہ	**highlight** *n* نمایاں کرنا
henchman *n* معتمدِ خاص	**highly** *adv* انتہائی
her *adj* کا (لڑکی) اس	**Highness** *n* عزت مآب
herald *v* نقیب	**highway** *n* شاہراہ
herald *n* پیام دینا	**hijack** *v* طیارہ اغوا کرنا
herb *n* جڑی بوٹی	**hijack** *n* طیارے کا اغوا
here *adv* یہاں	**hike** *v* چال؛ سیر
hereafter *adv* من بعد	**hike** *n* چڑھائی
hereditary *adj* موروثی	**hilarious** *adj* زندہ دل

hill *n* پہاڑی	**hoist** *v* بلند کرنا
hillside *n* ڈھلان	**hoist** *n* چڑھائی
hilltop *n* چوٹی	**hold** *iv* تھامنا
hilly *adj* پہاڑی	**hold on to** *v* چمٹنا
hilt *n* دستہ	**hold out** *v* پیش کرنا
hinder *v* پچھلا	**hold up** *v* برقرار رکھنا
hindrance *n* مزاحمت	**holdup** *n* ڈاکہ
hindsight *n* ادراک	**hole** *n* سوراخ
hinge *v* لٹکانا	**holiday** *n* چھٹی کا دن
hinge *n* چول	**holiness** *n* تقدس
hint *n* اشارہ	**Holland** *n* ہالینڈ
hint *v* اشارہ دینا	**hollow** *adj* کھوکھلا
hip *n* چوتڑ	**holocaust** *n* مکمل تباہی
hire *v* کرائے پر لینا	**holy** *adj* مقدس
his *adj* اس (مرد) کا	**homage** *n* عقیدت
his *pro* اس کا	**home** *n* گھر
Hispanic *adj* ہسپانوی	**homeland** *n* وطن
hiss *v* سسکارنا	**homeless** *adj* بےگھر
historian *n* مورخ	**homely** *adj* گھریلو
history *n* تاریخ	**homemade** *adj* گھر کا بنا ہوا
hit *n* چوٹ	**hometown** *n* آبائی شہر
hit *n* کامیابی	**homework** *n* گھر کا کام
hit *iv* ضرب لگانا	**homicide** *n* مردم کشی
hitch *n* گرہ	**homily** *n* وعظ
hitch up *v* باندھنا	**honest** *adj* دیانت دار
hitherto *adv* ہنوز	**honesty** *n* دیانت داری
hive *n* چھتہ	**honey** *n* شہد
hoard *v* ذخیرہ کرنا	**honeymoon** *n* ماہِ عروسی
hoarse *adj* گلوگرفہ	**honk** *v* ہوں ہوں کرنا
hoax *n* چکمہ	**honor** *v* عزت
hobby *n* مشغلہ	**hood** *n* کلاہ
hog *n* خنزیر	**hoodlum** *n* ٹھگ

hoof *n* سم	housekeeper *n* منتظم خانہ
hook *n* آنکڑا؛ کانٹا	housewife *n* گھریلو خاتون
hooligan *n* ہلڑ باز	housework *n* امورِ خانہ داری
hop *v* پھدکنا	hover *v* منڈلانہ
hope *n* امید	how *adv* کیسے
hopeful *adj* پرامید	however *c* تاہم
hopefully *adv* پرامید طور پر	howl *v* چیخنا
hopeless *adj* ناامید	howl *n* چیخ
horizon *n* افق	hub *n* مدار
horizontal *adj* افقی	huddle *v* انبار لگا دینا
hormone *n* ہارمون	hug *v* بغل گیر ہونا
horn *n* سینگ	hug *n* بغل گیری
horrendous *adj* دہشت ناک	huge *adj* بہت بڑا
horrible *adj* خوفناک	hull *n* پھل کا چھلکا
horrify *v* خوف زدہ کرنا	hum *v* بھنبھنانا
horror *n* دہشت	human *adj* انسانی
horse *n* گھوڑا	human being *n* انسان
hose *n* نالی	humanities *n* بشری علوم
hospital *n* ہسپتال	humankind *n* بنی نوع انسان
hospitality *n* مہمان نوازی	humble *adj* خاکسار
host *n* میزبان	humbly *adv* عاجزی سے
hostage *n* یرغمال	humid *adj* سیلا
hostess *n* خاتون میزبان	humidity *n* نمی
hostile *adj* معاندانہ	humiliate *v* ذلیل کرنا
hostility *n* مخالفت	humility *n* عاجزی
hot *adj* گرم	humor *n* مزاح
hotel *n* ہوٹل	humorous *adj* پرمزاح
hound *n* شکاری کتا	hump *n* کوبان
hour *n* گھنٹا	hunch *n* کب
hourly *adv* ہرگھنٹے بعد	hunchback *n* کبڑا
house *n* گھر	hunched *adj* کب والا
household *n* کنبہ	hundred *adj* سو

hundredth *adj* سواں	
hunger *n* بھوک	**I** *pro* میں
hungry *adj* بھوکا	**ice** *n* برف
hunt *v* شکار کرنا	**ice cream** *n* آئس کریم
hunter *n* شکاری	**ice skate** *v* برف جوتے
hunting *n* شکار	**iceberg** *n* برف کا توده
hurdle *n* رکاوٹ	**icebox** *n* برف دان
hurl *v* پھینکنا	**ice-cold** *adj* سخت ٹھنڈا
hurricane *n* گردباد	**icon** *n* مجسمہ
hurriedly *adv* عجلت میں	**icy** *adj* برفانی
hurry *v* عجلت	**idea** *n* خیال
hurry up *v* جلدی کرنا	**ideal** *adj* خیالی
hurt *iv* زخمی کرنا	**identical** *adj* متماثل
hurt *adj* مجروح	**identify** *v* شناخت کرنا
hurtful *adj* اذیت رساں	**identity** *n* شناخت
husband *n* خاوند	**ideology** *n* نظریہ
hush *n* خاموشی	**idiom** *n* محاوره
hush up *v* خاموش کرانا	**idiot** *n* احمق
husky *adj* چھلکے دار	**idiotic** *adj* بے وقوف
hustle *n* دھکیلنا	**idle** *adj* کابل
hut *n* کٹیا	**idol** *n* بت
hydrogen *n* ہائیڈروجن	**idolatry** *n* بت پرستی
hyena *n* لگڑ بگڑ	**if** *c* اگر
hymn *n* حمد	**ignite** *v* آگ دکھانا
hyphen *n* خطِ ربط	**ignorance** *n* جاہلیت
hypnosis *n* تنویم	**ignorant** *adj* جاہل
hypnotize *v* ہیپناٹاءز کرنا	**ignore** *v* نظر انداز کرنا
hypocrisy *n* منافقت	**ill** *adj* بیمار
hypocrite *adj* منافق	**illegal** *adj* غیر قانونی
hypothesis *n* مفروضہ	**illegitimate** *adj* ناجائز
hysteria *n* ہسٹیریا	
hysterical *adj* ہسٹیریائی	

illicit *adj* خلافِ قانون	**immune** *adj* محفوظ
illiterate *adj* ناخوانده	**immunity** *n* مدافعت
illness *n* بیماری	**immunize** *v* محفوظ بنانا
illogical *adj* غیرمنطقی	**immutable** *adj* تغیر نا پذیر
illuminate *v* منور کرنا	**impact** *n* اثر
illusion *n* فریبِ نظر	**impact** *v* اثر انداز ہونا
illustration *n* مثال	**impair** *v* معیار گھٹانا
illustrious *adj* شاندار	**impartial** *adj* غیر جانبدار
image *n* عکس	**impatience** *n* بے صبری
imagination *n* تصور	**impatient** *adj* بے صبر
imagine *v* تصور کرنا	**impeccable** *adj* بے قصور
imbalance *n* عدم توازن	**impediment** *n* لکنت
imitate *v* نقل کرنا	**impending** *adj* قریب ہونا
imitation *n* نقل	**imperfection** *n* عدم کمال
immaculate *adj* بے عیب	**imperial** *adj* سامراجی
immature *adj* ناپختہ	**imperialism** *n* سامراجیت
immaturity *n* ناپختگی	**impersonal** *adj* لاشخصی
immediately *adv* فوراً	**impertinence** *n* گستاخی
immense *adj* بے انتہا	**impertinent** *adj* گستاخ
immensity *n* وسعت	**impetuous** *adj* تند
immerse *v* بھگونا	**implacable** *adj* کٹھور
immersion *n* ڈباءو	**implant** *v* جمانا
immigrant *n* تارک وطن	**implement** *v* نافذ کرنا
immigrate *v* ترکِ وطن کرنا	**implicate** *v* معنی نکالنا
immigration *n* ترکِ وطن	**implication** *n* مضمر
imminent *adj* متوقع	**implicit** *adj* مضمر
immobile *adj* غیر متحرک	**implore** *v* بھیک مانگنا
immobilize *v* بے حرکت بنانا	**imply** *v* مفہوم ہونا
immoral *adj* غیر اخلاقی	**impolite** *adj* ناشائستہ
immorality *n* بداخلاقی	**import** *v* درآمد کرنا
immortal *adj* غیرفانی	**importance** *n* اہمیت
immortality *n* لایموت	**importation** *n* درآمد کاری

impose v عاید کرنا	inaugurate v افتتاح کرنا
imposing adj متاثر کن	inauguration n افتتاح
imposition n نفاذ	incalculable adj بے شمار
impossibility n عدم امکان	incapable adj ناقابل
impossible adj ناممکن	incapacitate v معذور کرنا
impotent adj نامرد	incarcerate v احاطہ بند کرنا
impound v ضبط کر لینا	incense n لوبان
impoverished adj مفلس کرنا	incentive n ترغیب
impractical adj غیر افادی	inception n ابتدا
imprecise adj نادرست	incessant adj متواتر
impress v نقش کرنا	inch n انچ
impressive adj متاثر کن	incident n واقعہ
imprison v قید میں ڈالنا	incidentally adv اتفاقی طور پر
improbable adj خلافِ قیاس	incision n شگاف
impromptu adv برجستہ	incite v اکسانا
improper adj غیر مناسب	incitement n اکسابٹ
improve v سدھارنا	inclination n ترجیح
improvement n بہتری	incline v میلان ہونا
improvise v بندوبست کرنا	include v شامل کرنا
impulse n قوتِ محرکہ	inclusive adv بشمول
impulsive adj اضطراری	incoherent adj نامربوط
impunity n عافیت	income n آمدنی
impure adj غیر خالص	incoming adj متداخل
in pre اندر	incompatible adj متضاد
in depth adv تفصیل سے	incompetence n نااہلیت
inability n عدم اہلیت	incompetent adj نااہل
inaccessible adj ناقابل رسائی	incomplete adj نامکمل
inaccurate adj نادرست	inconsistent adj غیر مستقیم
inadequate adj ناکافی	incontinence n عدم استقامت
inadmissible adj ناقابلِ قبول	inconvenient adj زحمت دہ
inappropriate adj نامناسب	incorporate v شامل کرنا
inasmuch as c جہاں تک	incorrect adj نادرست

incorrigible *adj* ناقابلِ اصلاح	**indivisible** *adj* ناقابلِ تقسیم
increase *v* بڑھانا	**indoor** *adv* اندرانِ خانہ
increase *n* اضافہ	**induce** *v* ترغیب دینا
increasing *adj* بڑھتا ہوا	**indulge** *v* تسکین کرنا
incredible *adj* ناقابلِ یقین	**indulgent** *adj* مہربان
increment *n* اضافہ	**industrious** *adj* جفاکش
incriminate *v* الزام لگانا	**industry** *n* محنت
incur *v* زمہ ڈالنا	**ineffective** *adj* غیر موثر
incurable *adj* لاعلاج	**inefficient** *adj* ناابل
indecency *n* ناشائستگی	**inept** *adj* بے استعداد
indecision *n* عدم فیصلہ	**inequality** *n* غیرمساوات
indecisive *adj* بےاستقلالی	**inevitable** *adj* ناگزیر
indeed *adv* درحقیقت	**inexcusable** *adj* ناقابلِ عذر
indefinite *adj* غیرمعین	**inexpensive** *adj* ارزاں
indemnify *v* تلافی کرنا	**inexperienced** *adj* ناتجربہ کار
indemnity *n* تاوان	**inexplicable** *adj* ناقابلِ تشریح
independence *n* آزادی	**infamous** *adj* رسوا
independent *adj* آزاد	**infancy** *n* طفولیت
index *n* فہرست	**infant** *n* شیرخوار
indicate *v* دکھانا	**infantry** *n* پیادہ فوج
indication *n* علامت	**infect** *v* آلودہ ہونا
indict *v* ملزم قرار دینا	**infection** *n* آلودگی
indifference *n* لاتعلقی	**infectious** *adj* متعدی
indifferent *adj* لاتعلق	**infer** *v* نتیجہ نکالنا
indigent *adj* کنگال	**inferior** *adj* کمتر
indigestion *n* بدہضمی	**infertile** *adj* بانجھ
indirect *adj* بالواسطہ	**infested** *adj* اٹاہونا
indiscreet *adj* ناقابلِ ادراک	**infidelity** *n* بے وفائی
indiscretion *n* نادانی	**infiltrate** *v* مداخلت کرنا
indispensable *adj* ناگزیر	**infiltration** *n* دخول
indisposed *adj* بیزار	**infinite** *adj* لامحدود
indisputable *adj* مسلم	**infirmary** *n* مریض خانہ

inflammation *n* سوزش	initial *adj* ابتدائی
inflate *v* ہوا بھرنا	initially *adv* ابتدائی طور پر
inflation *n* افراطِ زر	initials *n* مختصر دستخط
inflexible *adj* اٹل	initiate *v* آغاز کرنا
inflict *v* عائد کرنا	initiative *n* ابتدائی قدم
influence *n* اثر	inject *v* ٹیکا لگانا
influential *adj* موٴثر	injection *n* ٹیکا
influenza *n* فلو	injure *v* نقصان پہنچانا
influx *n* درآمد	injurious *adj* نقصان دہ
inform *v* اطلاع دینا	injury *n* زخم
informal *adj* غیر رسمی	injustice *n* ناانصافی
informality *n* غیر رسمی پن	ink *n* سیاہی
informant *n* مخبر	inkling *n* اشارہٴ خفیف
information *n* خبر	inlaid *adj* مرصع
informer *n* مخبر	inland *adv* اندرونِ ملک کا
infraction *n* قانون شکنی	inland *adj* اندراونِ ملک
infrequent *adj* شاذ	in-laws *n* سسرال والے
infuriate *v* اشتعال دلانا	inmate *n* اہل خانہ
infusion *n* انڈیلنا	inn *n* سرائے
ingenuity *n* اختراع پسندی	innate *adj* پیدائشی
ingot *n* ڈھیلا	inner *adj* اندرونی
ingrained *adj* پختہ	innocence *n* معصومیت
ingratitude *n* ناشکری	innocent *adj* معصوم
ingredient *n* جز	innovation *n* جدت
inhabit *v* سکونت رکھنا	innuendo *n* کنایہ
inhabitable *adj* قابلِ سکونت	innumerable *adj* لا تعداد
inhabitant *n* ساکن	input *n* لین
inhale *v* سانس لینا	inquest *n* تحقیقات
inherit *v* ورثہ پانا	inquire *v* پوچھنا
inheritance *n* میراث	inquiry *n* تحقیق
inhibit *v* روکنا	inquisition *n* بازپرس
inhuman *adj* غیر انسانی	insane *adj* دیوانہ

insanity n دیوانگی

insatiable adj حریص

inscription n کتبہ

insect n کیڑا

insecurity n عدم تحفظ

insensitive adj غیر حساس

inseparable adj لاینفک

insert v داخل کرنا

insertion n دخول

inside adj اندرونی

inside pre اندر کی طرف

insignificant adj غیر اہم

insincere adj غیر مخلص

insincerity n بے اخلاصی

insinuate v اشارہ دینا

insinuation n اشارہ

insipid adj بے لطف

insist v اصرار کرنا

insistence n اصرار

insolent adj گستاخ

insoluble adj حل ناپذیر

insomnia n بے خوابی

inspect v معاینہ کرنا

inspection n معائنہ

inspector n معائنہ کار

inspiration n تحریک

inspire v تحریک دینا

instability n قیام نا پذیری

install v تنصیب کرنا

installation n تنصیب

installment n قسط

instance n مثال

instant n فوری

instantly adv فوراً

instead adv کی بجائے

instigate v اکسانا

instil v ٹپکانا

instinct n جبلت

institute v قائم کرنا

institution n ادارہ

instruct v ہدایت دینا

instructor n معلم

insufficient adj ناکافی

insulate v جدا کرنا

insulation n غیر موصل کاری

insult v تذلیل کرنا

insult n بے عزتی

insurance n انشورنس

insure v انشورنس کروانا

insurgency n بغاوت

insurrection n فتنہ

intact adj محفوظ

intake n مدخول

integrate v جوڑنا

integration n تکمیل

integrity n سالمیت

intelligent adj ذہین

intend v ارادہ ہونا

intense adj شدید

intensify v شدید تر بنا دینا

intensity n شدت

intensive adj شدید کا حامل

intention n نیت

intercede v بیچ میں پڑنا

intercept v راہ میں لینا	intrepid adj نڈر
intercession n وساطت	intricate adj پیچیدہ
interchange v تبادل کرنا	intrigue n سازش کرنا
interchange n تبادلہ	intriguing adj سازشی
interest n دلچسپی	intrinsic adj اندرونی
interested adj غرضمند	introduce v متعارف کرانا
interesting adj دلچسپ	introduction n تعارف
interfere v مداخلت کرنا	intrude v گھسنا
interference n مداخلت	intruder n گھس بیٹھیا
interior adj اندرونی	intrusion n مداخلت
interlude n وقفہ	intuition n وجدان
intermediary n وسیلہ	inundate v سیلاب
intern v زیرِ تربیت ماہر	invade v حملہ آور ہونا
interpret v تشریح کرنا	invader n حملہ آور
interpretation n تشریح	invalid n اپاہج
interpreter n مترجم	invalidate v باطل کرنا
interrogate v تفتیش کرنا	invaluable adj بیش قدر
interrupt v مداخلت کرنا	invasion n حملہ
interruption n مداخلت	invent v ایجاد کرنا
intersect v قطع کرنا	invention n ایجاد
intertwine v بٹنا	inventory n فہرست سامان
interval n وقفہ	invest v سرمایاکاری کرنا
intervene v حائل ہونا	investigate v تفتیش کرنا
intervention n دخل اندازی	investigation n تفتیش
interview n انٹرویو	investment n سرمایاکاری
intestine n انتڑی	investor n سرمایاکار
intimacy n قربت	invincible adj ناقابلِ تسخیر
intimate adj بے تکلف	invisible adj غیر مرئی
intimidate v دھمکانا	invitation n دعوت نامہ
intolerable adj ناقابلِ برداشت	invite v مدعو کرنا
intolerance n عدم برداشت	invoice n مسودہ قانون
intoxicated adj مخمور	invoke v طلب کرنا

involve v وابستہ ہونا	**Italian** adj اٹلی کا
involved v الجھا ہوا	**italics** adj ترچھا ٹائپ
involvement n وابستگی	**Italy** n اٹلی
inward adj داخلی	**itch** v کھجلانا
inwards adv داخلی طرف	**item** n آیٹم
iodine n آیوڈین	**itinerary** n سفرکا راستہ
irate adj برہم	**ivory** n ہاتھی دانت
Ireland n آئرلینڈ	
Irish adj آئرلینڈ کا	
iron n لوہا	
iron v استری کرنا	
ironic adj طنزیہ	
irony n طنز	
irrational adj نامعقول	
irrefutable adj ناقابل تردید	**J**
irregular adj بے قاعدہ	
irrelevant adj غیر متعلق	**jackal** n گیدڑ
irreparable adj ناقابلِ تلافی	**jacket** n جیکٹ
irresistible adj ناقابلِ مزاحمت	**jackpot** n جیک پاٹ
irrespective adj قطع نظر	**jaguar** n تیندوا
irreversible adj رجعت نا پذیر	**jail** n جیل
irrevocable adj ناقابلِ واپسی	**jail** v جیل بھیجنا
irrigate v آبیاری کرنا	**jailer** n جیلر
irrigation n آبیاری	**jam** n جام؛ پھنس جانا
irritate v مشتعل کرنا	**janitor** n بھنگی
irritating adj اشتعل انگیز	**January** n جنوری
Islamic adj اسلامی	**Japan** n جاپان
island n جزیرہ	**Japanese** adj جاپانی
isle n جزیرہ	**jar** n مٹکا
isolate v تنہا کردینا	**jasmine** n یاسمین
isolation n تنہائی	**jaw** n جبڑا
issue n اجرا	**jealous** adj حاسد
	jealousy n حسد
	jeans n جینز

jeopardize v اندیشہ	jug n جگ
jerk v جھٹکے دینا	juggler n شعبدہ باز
jerk n جھٹکا	juice n عرق
jersey n جرسی	juicy adj رسیلا
Jew n یہودی	July n جولائی
jewel n جوہر	jump v اچھلنا
jeweler n جوہری	jump n چھلانگ
Jewish adj یہودی	jumpy adj کودنے والا
jigsaw n رقصندہ آرا	junction n سنگم؛ اتصال
job n کام	June n جون
jobless adj بے کار	jungle n جنگل
join v شامل ہونا	junior adj جونئیر
joint n جوڑ	junk n کاٹھ کباڑ
jointly adv اکٹھے	jury n جیوری
joke n لطیفہ	just adj انصاف پر مبنی
joke v مذاق کرنا	justice n انصاف
jokingly adv ازراہِ مذاق	justify v صحیح ثابت کرنا
jolly adj ہنس مکھ	justly adv منصفانہ طور پر
jolt v ہچکولے دینا	juvenile n نوعمر شخص
jolt n ہچکولے	juvenile adj کمسن
journal n روزنامچہ	
journalist n صحافی	
journey n سفر	
jovial adj ہنس مکھ	
joy n خوشی	
joyful adj پرمسرت	
joyfully adv خوشی سے	
jubilant adj پرمسرت	
Judaism n یہودیت	
judge n منصف	kangaroo n کینگرو
judgment n فیصلہ	karate n کراٹے
judicious adj سمجھ دار	keep iv رکھنا
	keep on جاری رکھنا
	keep up v برقرار رکھنا

J
K

keg n پیپا	**kneel** iv مائل کرنا
kettle n کیتلی	**knife** n چھری
key n چابی	**knight** n نائٹ
keyboard n کی بورڈ	**knit** v بُننا
kick n ٹھوکر مارنا	**knob** n ناب
kickback n کٹوتی	**knock** n دستک
kid n بچہ؛ نو عمر	**knock** v کھٹکھٹانا
kidnap v اغوا کرنا	**knot** n گرہ
kidnapper n اغوا کار	**know** iv جاننا
kidnapping n اغوا	**know-how** n مہارت
kidney n گردہ	**knowingly** adv دانستہ
kidney bean n لوبیہ	**knowledge** n علم
kill v مار دینا	
killer n قاتل	
killing n قتل	
kilogram n کلوگرام	
kilometer n کلو میٹر	
kilowatt n کلوواٹ	
kind adj شفیق	# L
kindle v سلگانا	
kindly adv مہربانی سے	**lab** n لیبارٹری
kindness n مہربانی	**label** n چٹ
king n بادشاہ	**labor** n مزدوری
kingdom n سلطنت	**laborer** n مزدور
kinship n رشتہ داری	**labyrinth** n بھول بھلیّاں
kiosk n گرمائی گھر	**lace** n تسمہ
kiss v بوسہ لینا	**lack** v کمی ہونا
kiss n بوسہ	**lack** n فقدان
kitchen n باورچی خانہ	**lad** n لڑکا
kite n پتنگ	**ladder** n سیڑھی
kitten n بلی کا بچہ	**laden** adj لدا ہوا
knee n گھٹنا	**lady** n خاتون
	lagoon n ساحلِ جھیل

lake *n* جھیل	late *adv* دیر سے آنیوالا
lamb *n* بھیڑ	lately *adv* حال ہی میں
lame *adj* لنگڑا	later *adv* بعد میں
lament *v* ماتم ہونا	later *adj* بعد کا
lament *n* ماتم	lateral *adj* بغلی
lamp *n* لیمپ	latest *adj* تازہ ترین
land *n* زمین	lather *n* کفِ صابون
land *v* خشکی پر اترنا	latitude *n* عرض بلد
landlady *n* مکان مالکن	latter *adj* تازہ تر
landlord *n* مکان مالک	laugh *v* ہنسنا
landscape *n* ارضی منظر	laugh *n* ہنسی
lane *n* کوچہ	laughable *adj* قہقہہ آور
language *n* زبان	laughter *n* ہنسی
languish *v* سست	launch *n* آغاز
lantern *n* لالٹین	launch *v* دھکیلنا
lap *n* گود؛ جھولی	laundry *n* دھوبی گھر
lapse *n* لغزش؛ غلطی	lavatory *n* طہارت خانہ
lapse *v* غلطی ہونا	lavish *adj* مسرف
larceny *n* سرقہ	lavish *v* کھلا خرچ کرنا
lard *n* سور کی چربی	law *n* قانون
large *adj* بڑا	law-abiding *adj* پابندِ قانون
larynx *n* لیرنکس	lawful *adj* قانونی؛ جائز
laser *n* لیزر	lawmaker *n* قانون ساز
lash *n* تازیانہ؛ کوڑا	lawn *n* لان
lash *v* کوڑے مارنا	lawsuit *n* مقدمہ
lash out *v* پھٹ پڑنا	lawyer *n* وکیل
last *v* برداشت کرنا	lax *adj* ڈھیلا
last *adj* آخری	laxative *adj* قبض کشا
last night *adv* گزشتہ شب	lay *n* گیت
lasting *adj* برقرار رہنے والا	lay *iv* ٹکانا؛ رکھنا
lastly *adv* بالآخر	lay off *v* الگ کرنا
latch *n* چٹخنی	layer *n* تہہ

L

layman n عام آدمی	**leave** iv روانہ ہونا
lay-out n خاکہ	**leave out** v نظر انداز کر دینا
laziness n سستی	**lectern** n رِحل
lazy adj متامل	**lecture** n درس
lead iv رہنمائی کرنا	**ledger** n بہی
lead n سیسا؛ سکہ	**leech** n جونک
leaded adj سیسا ملا ہوا	**leftovers** n باقیات
leader n رہنما	**leg** n ٹانگ
leadership n قیادت	**legacy** n ترکہ
leading adj سرکردہ	**legal** adj قانونی
leaf n پتا	**legality** n قانونیت
league n لیگ	**legalize** v قانونی بنانا
leak v رسنا	**legend** n روایت
leak n سوراخ	**legion** n جمِ غفیر
leakage n خراج	**legislate** v قانون سازی کرنا
lean adj دبلا	**legislation** n قانون سازی
lean adj لاغر	**legitimate** adj جائز
lean iv جھُکنا	**leisure** n فرصت
lean on v اعتبار	**lemon** n لیموں
leaning n جھکائو	**lend** iv ادھار دینا
leap iv چھلانگ لگانا	**length** n لمبا
leap n چھلانگ	**lengthen** v لمبا کرنا
leap year n لوند کا سال	**lengthy** adj لمبا
learn iv سیکھنا	**leniency** n طویل
learned adj عالم	**lenient** adj نرم دل
learner n متعلم	**lense** n لینز
learning n تعلم	**lentil** n مسور
lease v پٹہ پر لینا	**leopard** n بڑا چیتا
lease n پٹہ	**leper** n کوڑھی
leash n پٹی	**leprosy** n کوڑھ
least adj کم ازکم	**less** adj کم تر
leather n چمڑا	**lessee** n کرایہ دار

L

lessen v کم کرنا	**lid** n ڈھکنا
lesser adj کم تر	**lie** iv لیٹنا
lesson n سبق	**lie** v جھوٹ بولنا
lessor n پٹا دہندہ	**lie** n جھوٹ
let iv اجازت دینا	**lieu** n جگہ
let down v مایوس کرنا	**lieutenant** n لیفٹیننٹ
let go v جانے دینا	**life** n زندگی
let in v اندر آنے دینا	**lifeguard** n محافظِ زندگی
let out v اظہار کرنا	**lifeless** adj بے جان
lethal adj مہلک	**lifestyle** n انداز زندگی
letter n خط؛ مکتوب	**lifetime** adj مدت العمر
lettuce n کاہو	**lift** v اٹھانا
leukemia n سرطانِ خون	**lift off** v ہوا میں اٹھنا
level n سطح؛ سطح پیما	**ligament** n رباط
lever n لیور	**light** iv روشن ہونا
leverage n بیرمی نظام	**light** adj ہلکا
levy v محصول	**light** n روشنی
lewd adj غنڈہ	**lighter** n لائٹر
liability n جواب دہی	**lighthouse** n مینارہء نور
liable adj ذمہ دار	**lighting** n چراغاں
liaison n رابطہ	**lightning** n بجلی
liar adj جھوٹا	**likable** adj پسندیدہ
libel n توہین	**like** pre اسی انداز میں
liberate v آزاد کرانا	**like** v پسند کرنا
liberation n آزادی	**likelihood** n امکان
liberty n آزادی	**likely** adv موقع
librarian n لائبریرین	**likeness** n مشابہت
library n کتب خانہ	**likewise** adv اسی طرح
lice n جوں (جمع)	**liking** n پسند
licence n اجازت	**limb** n عضو
license v اجازت دینا	**limestone** n چونا پتھر
lick v چاٹنا	**limit** n حد

L

limit v قابو میں رکھنا	**litre** n لیٹر
limitation n حد	**litter** n کوڑا کرکٹ
limp v لنگڑا کر چلنا	**little** adj چھوٹا
limp n لنگڑا	**live** adj زندہ
linchpin n میخ محور	**live** v زندہ رہنا
line n خط	**livelihood** n روزی
linen n لینن	**lively** adj زندہ دل
linger v لٹکنا	**liver** n جگر
lingering adj لٹکا ہوا	**livestock** n مال مویشی
lining n استر	**livid** adj کبود
link v جوڑنا	**living room** n دیوان خانہ
link n تعلق	**lizard** n گرگٹ
lion n شیر	**load** v وزن اٹھانا
lioness n شیرنی	**load** n وزن
lip n ہونٹ	**loaded** adj لدا ہوا؛ بوجھل
liqueur n شراب	**loaf** n چپاتی
liquid n مائع	**loan** v قرض دینا
liquidate v اختتام کرنا	**loan** n ادھار
liquidation n کاروبار کا خاتمہ	**loathe** v نفرت کرنا
liquor n شراب	**loathing** n گھن
list v فہرست بنانا	**lobby** n ہال
list n فہرست	**lobby** v ترغیب دینا
listen v سننا	**lobster** n جھینگا
listener n سامع	**local** adj مقامی
litany n وظیفہ	**localize** v دھب لگنا
liter n لیٹر	**locate** v رکھنا
literal adj لفظی	**located** adj واقع
literally adv لفظی طور پر	**location** n مقام بندی
literate adj پڑھا لکھا	**lock** v تالا لگا
literature n ادب	**lock** n تالا
litigate v مقدمہ بازی کرنا	**lock up** v جیل بھیجنا
litigation n مقدمہ بازی	**locksmith** n قفل ساز

L

locust n ٹڈی	**looks** n شکل
lodge v رہائش مہیا کرنا	**loom** n کھڈی
lodging n مسکن	**loom** v خوفناک لگنا؛ ڈرانا
lofty adj بلند	**loophole** n تنگ سوراخ
log n گولا؛ لٹھا	**loose** v کھولنا
log n گولا	**loose** adj ڈھیلا
log v لکھنا	**loosen** v ڈھیلا کرنا
log in داخل ہونا	**loot** v لتھیانا
log off v چھوڑ دینا	**loot** n مالِ غنیمت
logic n منطق	**lord** n آقا
logical adj منطقی	**lordship** n سرداری
loin n شیر	**lose** iv ہارنا
loiter v ٹہلنا	**loser** n ہارنے والا
loneliness n تنہائی	**loss** n نقصان
lonely adv تنہا	**lot** adv قرعہ اندازی
lonesome adj تنہا	**lotion** n لوشن
long adj طویل	**lots** adj متعدد
long for آرزو کرنا	**lottery** n لاٹری
longing n شوق	**loud** adj اونچا
longitude n طول بلد	**loudly** adv بلند آواز سے
long-term adj طویل مدتی	**loudspeaker** n لاؤڈ سپیکر
look n ظاہری حلیہ	**louse** n جوں
look v دیکھنا؛ متوجہ ہونا	**lousy** adj قابلِ نفرت
look after v دیکھ بھال کرنا	**lovable** adj قابلِ محبت
look at v دیکھنا	**love** v پیار کرنا
look down v نفرت کرنا	**love** n پیار
look for v تلاش کرنا	**lovely** adj پیارا
look forward v منتظر ہونا	**lover** n عاشق
look into v معائنہ کرنا	**loving** adj محبت آمیز
look out v ہوشیار ہونا	**low** adj نشیبی
look over v بغور جائزہ لینا	**lower** adj کم تر
looking glass n آئینہ	**lowly** adj غیر اعلیٰ

L

loyal *adj* وفادار
loyalty *n* وفاداری
lubricate *v* تیل دینا
lubrication *n* چکنائو
lucid *adj* واضح
luck *n* قسمت
lucky *adj* خوش قسمت
lucrative *adj* نفع آور
ludicrous *adj* مضحکہ خیز
luggage *n* سامان
lukewarm *adj* نیم گرم
lumber *n* کٹے شہتیر
luminous *adj* تاباں
lump *n* ڈلا؛ ڈھیلا
lump together *v* اکٹھے کرنا
lunacy *n* دیوانگی
lunatic *adj* دیوانہ آدمی
lunch *n* ظہرانہ
lung *n* پھیپھڑا
lure *v* پھسلانا
lurid *adj* بہت نمایاں
lush *adj* شاداب
lust *v* ہوس ہونا
lust *n* ہوس
lustful *adj* آرزومند
luxurious *adj* فراواں
luxury *n* عیش پسندی
lynx *n* جنگلی بلا

M

machine *n* مشین
machine gun *n* مشین گن
mad *adj* پاگل
madam *n* مادام
madden *v* پاگل بنانا
madly *adv* دیوانگی سے
madman *n* پاگل
madness *n* دیوانگی
magazine *n* میگزین
magic *n* جادو
magical *adj* جادوئی
magician *n* جادوگر
magistrate *n* مجسٹریٹ
magnet *n* مقناطیس
magnetic *adj* مقناطیسی
magnetism *n* مقناطیسیت
magnificent *adj* عظیم الشان
magnify *v* بڑا کرنا
magnitude *n* عظمت
maid *n* نوکرانی
maiden *n* کنواری
mail *n* ڈاک
mailbox *n* ڈاک کا ڈبہ
mailman *n* ڈاکیا
maim *v* مثلہ کرنا
main *adj* بڑا
mainland *n* براعظم
mainly *adv* زیادہ تر
maintain *v* برقرار رکھنا

maintenance *n* دیکھ بھال	mangle *v* کاٹنا
majestic *adj* پروقار	manhandle *v* برا سلوک کرنا
majesty *n* وقار	manhunt *n* آدم کھوج
major *n* میجر	maniac *adj* جنونی
major *adj* بڑا	manifest *v* صاف ظاہر
majority *n* اکثریت	mankind *n* نوعِ انسانی
make *n* بناوٹ	manliness *n* مردانگی
make *iv* بنانا	manly *adj* مردانہ
make up *v* مکل کرنا	manner *n* طریقہ
make up for *v* تلافی کرنا	mannerism *n* خاص ڈھب
maker *n* بنانے والا	manners *n* آداب
makeup *n* میک اپ	manpower *n* افرادی قوت
malaria *n* ملیریا	mansion *n* حویلی
male *n* نر	manslaughter *n* غیرقانونی قتل
malevolent *adj* بدخواہ	manual *n* رہنما کتابچہ
malice *n* کینہ	manual *adj* دستی
malign *v* بدنام کرنا	manufacture *v* بنانا
malignancy *n* بَیر	manure *n* کھاد ڈالنا
malignant *adj* مہلک	manuscript *n* مسودہ
mall *n* خیابان	many *adj* متعدد
malnutrition *n* ناقص غذا	map *n* نقشہ
malpractice *v* ناجائز فعل	marble *n* سنگِ مرمر
mammal *n* میمل	march *v* پیدل چلنا
mammoth *n* میمتھ	march *n* پیدل سفر
man *n* انسان	March *n* مارچ
manage *v* چلانا	mare *n* گھوڑی
management *n* بندوبست	margin *n* حاشیہ
manager *n* منتظم	marginal *adj* کنارے کا
mandate *n* حکم	marine *adj* بحری
mandatory *adj* لازم	marital *adj* ازدواجی
maneuver *n* ماہرانہ انتظام	mark *n* نشان
manger *n* کھرلی	mark *v* نشان لگانا

M

mark down v قیمت کم کردینا	mastery n دسترس
marker n مارکر	mat n چٹائی
market n منڈی	match n دیا سلائی؛ مقابلہ
marksman n نشانہ باز	match v میل کرنا؛ جوڑ بنانا
marmalade n مارملیڈ	mate n ساتھی
marriage n شادی	material n مادہ؛ مسالا
married adj شادی شدہ	materialism n مادیت
marrow n گودا	maternal adj مادرانہ
marry v شادی کرنا	maternity n امومت
Mars n مریخ	math n ریاضی
marshal n مارشل	matriculate v میٹرک کرنا
martyr n شہید	matrimony n بیاہ
martyrdom n شہادت	matter n معاملہ؛ مادہ
marvel n حیران ہونا	mattress n گدا
marvelous adj بہت عجیب	mature adj بالغ
marxist adj مارکسی	maturity n پختگی
masculine adj نَر کا	maul v پیٹنا
mash v ملانا	maxim n مسلمہ اصول
mask n نقاب	maximum adj زیادہ سے زیادہ
mason n معمار	May n مئی
masquerade v سوانگ میلہ	may iv ہو سکتا ہے
mass n ڈھیر؛ انبار	may-be adv شاید
massacre n قتلِ عام	mayhem n شدید ضرب
massage n مالش	mayor n میئر
massage v ماش کرنا	maze n بھول بھلیاں
masseur n مساج کرنیوالا	meadow n چراگاہ
massive adj جسیم	meager adj حقیر
mast n مستول	meal n اناج
master n مالک	mean iv مطلب ہونا
mastermind n شہ عقل	mean adj کمینہ
mastermind v رخ کرنا	meaning n معنی
masterpiece n شاہکار	meaningful adj بامعنی

meaningless *adj* بے معنی	**member** *n* رکن
meanness *n* کمینگی	**membership** *n* رکنیت
means *n* ذرائع	**membrane** *n* جھلی
meantime *adv* اس دوران	**memento** *n* یادگاری نشانی
meanwhile *adv* اس اثنا میں	**memo** *n* یاداشت
measles *n* خسرہ	**memoirs** *n* یاداشت
measure *v* پیمائش کرنا	**memorable** *adj* یادگار
measurement *n* پیمائش	**memorize** *v* یاد کرنا
meat *n* گوشت	**memory** *n* حافظہ
mechanic *n* مستری	**men** *n* لوگ
mechanism *n* میکانیہ	**menace** *n* نقصان
mechanize *v* میکانی بنانا	**mend** *v* مرمت کرنا
medal *n* تمغا	**meningitis** *n* ورم
medallion *n* بڑا تمغا	**menopause** *n* انقطاعِ حیض
meddle *v* دخل دینا	**menstruation** *n* حیض
mediator *n* ثالث	**mental** *adj* ذہنی
medication *n* علاج	**mentality** *n* ذہنیت
medicine *n* دوا	**mentally** *adv* ذہنی طور پر
meditate *v* غوروخوض کرنا	**mention** *v* ذکر کرنا
meditation *n* تفکر	**mention** *n* ذکر
medium *adj* اوسط	**merchandise** *n* سامان
meek *adj* مسکین	**merchant** *n* تاجر
meekness *n* عاجزی	**merciful** *adj* کریم
meet *iv* ملنا	**merciless** *adj* بے رحم
meeting *n* ملاقات	**mercury** *n* پارہ
melancholy *n* دل شکستگی	**mercy** *n* رحم
mellow *adj* دھیما	**merely** *adv* محض
mellow *v* دھیما کرنا	**merge** *v* ضم کرنا؛ ملانا
melodic *adj* نغمگین	**merger** *n* انضمام
melody *n* راگ	**merit** *n* اہلیت
melon *n* خربوزہ	**merit** *v* قابل ہونا
melt *v* پگھلنا	**mermaid** *n* جل پری

M

merry adj خوش	**migraine** n سردرد
mesh n جال	**migrant** n تارک وطن
mesmerize v تنویم کرنا	**migrate** v ہجرت کرنا
mess n گندگی	**mild** adj نرم
mess around v گندہ کرنا	**mildew** n پھپھوندی
mess up v الجھانا	**mile** n میل
message n پیغام	**militant** adj جنگجو
messenger n پیامبر	**milk** n دودھ
Messiah n مسیح	**milky** adj دودھیا
messy adj بے ترتیب	**mill** n چکی
metal n دھات	**millennium** n ہزاریہ
metallic adj دھاتی	**milligram** n ملی گرام
metaphor n استعارہ	**millimeter** n ملی میٹر
meteor n شہابیہ	**million** n ملین
meter n میٹر	**millionaire** n لاکھ پتی
method n طریقہ کار	**mime** v نقل اتارنا
methodical adj باضابطہ	**mince** v قیمہ کرنا
meticulous adj محتاط	**mincemeat** n قیمہ
metric adj اعشاری	**mind** v دھیان کرنا
metropolis n بڑا یا اہم شہر	**mind** n ذہن
mice n چوہے (جمع)	**mindful** adj متوجہ
microbe n جرثومہ	**mindless** adj کوڑھ مغز
microphone n مائیکروفون	**mine** n کان
microscope n مائیکروسکوپ	**mine** pro میرا
midday n دوپہر	**minefield** n سرنگ علاقہ
middle n وسط	**miner** n کان کن
middleman n بچولیا	**mineral** n کانی
midget n بونا	**mingle** v ملانا
midnight n نصف شب	**miniature** n مصغر
midsummer n وسطِ گرما	**minimize** v کم کرنا
midwife n دایہ	**minimum** n کم از کم
mighty adj طاقت ور	**miniskirt** n منی سکرٹ

M

minister *n* وزیر	**mismanage** *v* بد انتظامی کرنا
minister *n* پادری	**misplace** *v* کھو دینا
minister *v* خدمت کرنا	**misprint** *n* غلط چھپائی کرنا
ministry *n* وزارت؛ کلیسا	**miss** *v* غلطی کرنا
minor *adj* چھوٹا	**miss** *n* کنواری لڑکی
minority *n* اقلیت	**missile** *n* میزائل
mint *n* پودینہ	**missing** *adj* گمشدہ
minus *adj* تفریق	**mission** *n* خاص مقصد
minute *n* منٹ	**missionary** *n* مبلغ
miracle *n* معجزہ	**mist** *n* دھند
miraculous *adj* معجزاتی	**mistake** *iv* غلطی کرنا
mirage *n* سراب	**mistake** *n* غلطی
mirror *n* آئینہ	**mistaken** *adj* غلط
misbehave *v* بدتمیزی کرنا	**mister** *n* مسٹر
miscalculate *v* غلط حساب لگانا	**mistreat** *v* بدسلوکی کرنا
miscarriage *n* اسقاط حمل	**mistreatment** *n* بدسلوکی
miscarry *v* اسقاط حمل ہونا	**mistress** *n* مالکن
mischief *n* شرارت	**mistrust** *n* بے اعتمادی
mischievous *adj* شرارتی	**mistrust** *v* شبہ کرنا
misconstrue *v* غلط تعبیر کرنا	**misty** *adj* کہر آلود
misdemeanor *n* نا مناسب رویہ	**misunderstand** *v* غلط سمجھنا
miser *n* کنجوس	**mitigate** *v* کم کرنا
miserable *adj* مصیبت زدہ	**mix** *v* ملانا
misery *n* خستہ حالی	**mixed-up** *adj* گڈمڈ
misfit *adj* ناموزوں	**mixer** *n* ملانے والا
misfortune *n* بد قسمتی	**mixture** *n* آمیزہ
misgiving *n* وسوسہ	**mix-up** *n* خلط ملط
misguided *adj* گمراہ	**moan** *v* کراہنا
misinterpret *v* جھوٹی تعبیر کرنا	**moan** *n* کراہ
misjudge *v* غلط اندازہ لگانا	**mob** *v* ہجوم کرنا
mislead *v* گمراہ کرنا	**mob** *n* ہجوم
misleading *adj* گمراہ کن	**mobile** *adj* متحرک

M

متحرک بنانا	**mobilize** v	نگرانی کرنا	**monitor** v
تمسخر اڑانا	**mock** v	راہب	**monk** n
تضحیک	**mockery** n	بندر	**monkey** n
انداز	**mode** n	یک زوجی	**monogamy** n
نمونہ	**model** n	واحد کلامی	**monologue** n
اعتدال پسند	**moderate** adj	قابو میں رکھنا	**monopolize** v
اعتدال	**moderation** n	اجارہ داری	**monopoly** n
جدید	**modern** adj	اکتابٹ بھرا	**monotonous** adj
جدید بنانا	**modernize** v	یک اسلوبی	**monotony** n
منکسر	**modest** adj	عفریت	**monster** n
پاکدامنی	**modesty** n	دیوقامت	**monstrous** adj
ردوبدل کرنا	**modify** v	مہینہ	**month** n
مقاسیہ	**module** n	ماہوار	**monthly** adv
نمدار بنانا	**moisten** v	یادگار	**monument** n
نمی	**moisture** n	یادگاری	**monumental** adj
ڈاڑھ	**molar** n	کیفیتِ مزاج	**mood** n
سانچہ	**mold** n	روٹھا ہوا	**moody** adj
پھپھوندی لگا	**moldy** adj	چاند	**moon** n
تِل؛ چھچھوندر	**mole** n	لنگر انداز کرنا	**moor** v
مالیکیول	**molecule** n	صاف کرنا	**mop** v
ستانا	**molest** v	اخلاقی	**moral** adj
ماں	**mom** n	اخلاقی سبق	**moral** n
لمحہ	**moment** n	اخلاقیات	**morality** n
لمحہ بھر کو	**momentarily** adv	مزید	**more** adj
بہت اہم	**momentous** adj	مزید برآں	**moreover** adv
سلطان	**monarch** n	صبح	**morning** n
ملوکیت	**monarchy** n	طفل دماغ	**moron** adj
خانقاہ	**monastery** n	مارفین	**morphine** n
راہبانہ	**monastic** adj	نوالہ	**morsel** n
پیر	**Monday** n	فانی	**mortal** adj
رقم	**money** n	شرح اموات	**mortality** n
منی آرڈر	**money order** n	کھرل	**mortar** n

M

mortgage n رہن	**move back** v واپس لے لینا
mortification n نفس کشی	**move out** v روانہ ہونا
mortuary n مردہ خانہ	**move up** v چڑھنا
mosaic n پچی کاری	**movement** n حرکت
mosque n مسجد	**movie** n متحرک فلم
mosquito n مچھر	**mow** v کاٹنا
moss n کائی	**much** adv زیادہ
most adj سب سے زیادہ	**mucus** n لعاب
mostly adv زیادہ تر	**mud** n مٹی
motel n موٹل	**muddle** n گدلا کرنا
moth n پروانہ	**muddy** adj گدلا
mother n ماں	**muffle** v ڈھانپنا
motherhood n ممتا	**muffler** n مفلر
mother-in-law n ساس	**mug** n پیالہ
motion n حرکت	**mug** v حملہ کرنا
motionless adj بے حرکت	**mugging** n منہ چڑانا
motivate v تحریک دینا	**mule** n خچر
motive n محرک	**multiple** adj کثیرالعناصر
motor n موٹر	**multiplication** n ضرب
motorcycle n موٹر سائیکل	**multiply** v تعداد بڑھانا
motto n مقولہ	**multitude** n کثرتِ تعداد
mouldy adj پھپھوندی لگا	**mumble** v بڑبڑانا
mount n پہاڑی	**mummy** n ممی
mount v چڑھنا	**mumps** n کن پیڑے
mountain n پہاڑ	**munch** v چبانا
mountainous adj پہاڑی	**munitions** n گولہ بارود
mourn v ماتم کرنا	**murder** n قتل
mourning n ماتم	**murderer** n قاتل
mouse n چوہا	**murky** adj تاریک
mouth n مونہہ	**murmur** v سرسرانا
move n حرکت	**murmur** n سرسرہٹ
move v حرکت کرنا	**muscle** n پٹھہ

M

museum n عجائب گھر

mushroom n کھمبی

music n موسیقی

musician n موسیقار

Muslim adj مسلمان

must iv چاہیے

mustache n مونچھ

mustard n سرسوں

muster v اکٹھا کرنا

mutate v بدلنا

mute adj خاموش

mutilate v مسخ کرنا

mutiny n سرکشی

mutually adv باہمی طور پر

muzzle v زبان بندی کرنا

muzzle n تھوتھنی

my adj میرا

myopic adj فریب نظر

myself pro میں خود

mysterious adj پر اسرار

mystery n راز

mystic adj عارفانہ

mystify v مخفی کرنا

myth n داستان

N

nag v ٹٹو

nail n ناخن

naive adj سادہ لوح

naked adj ننگاہ

name n نام

namely adv یعنی

nap n اونگھ

napkin n دست رومال

narcotic n نشہ آور

narrate v بیان کرنا

narrow adj تنگ

narrowly adv بمشکل

nasty adj غلیظ

nation n قوم

national adj قومی

nationality n قومیت

nationalize v قومیانہ

native adj مقامی

natural adj قدرتی

naturally adv قدرتی طور پر

nature n فطرت

naughty adj شرارتی

nausea n متلی

nave n نافِ چرخ

navel n ناف

navigate v جہازرانی کرنا

navigation n جہازرانی

navy n بحریہ

navy blue adj گہرا نیلا رنگ

near *pre* قریب	**Netherlands** *n* نیدرلینڈز
nearby *adj* متصل	**network** *n* جال
nearly *adv* قریباً	**neutral** *adj* غیر جانبدار
nearsighted *adj* قریب نظر	**neutralize** *v* غیرجانبدار بنانا
neat *adj* صاف ستھرا	**never** *adv* کبھی نہیں
neatly *adv* ستھرائی سے	**nevertheless** *adv* باوجود اس کے
necessary *adj* ضروری	**new** *adj* نیا
necessitate *v* ضرورت ہونا	**newborn** *n* نومولود
necessity *n* ضرورت	**newcomer** *n* نووارد
neck *n* گردن	**newly** *adv* حال ہی میں
necklace *n* گلوبند	**newlywed** *adj* نوبیاہتا
necktie *n* ٹائی	**news** *n* خبر
need *v* ضرورت ہونا	**newscast** *n* خبر نامہ
need *n* ضرورت	**newsletter** *n* اطلاع نامہ
needle *n* سوئی	**newspaper** *n* اخبار
needless *adj* غیر ضروری	**newsstand** *n* اخباری دکان
needy *adj* ضرورت مند	**next** *adj* اگلا
negative *adj* منفی	**nibble** *v* کترنا
neglect *v* نظر انداز کرنا	**nice** *adj* عمدہ
neglect *n* صرفِ نظر	**nicely** *adv* عمدگی سے
negligence *n* غفلت	**nickel** *n* نکل
negligent *adj* لاپرواہ	**nickname** *n* عرف
negotiate *v* مول تول کرنا	**nicotine** *n* نکوٹین
negotiation *n* مذاکرات	**niece** *n* بھتیجی
neighbor *n* ہمسایہ	**night** *n* رات
neighborhood *n* ہمسائیگی	**nightfall** *n* دھندلکا
neither *adv* نہ یہ نہ وہ	**nightingale** *n* بلبل
nephew *n* بھتیجا	**nightmare** *n* ڈرائونا خواب
nerve *n* عصب	**nine** *adj* نو
nervous *adj* عصبی	**nineteen** *adj* انیس
nest *n* گھونسلا	**ninety** *adj* نوے
net *n* جال	**ninth** *adj* نواں

N

nip n چٹکی	**nostril** n نتھنا
nip v دبانا	**not** adv نہیں
nipple n بھٹنی	**notable** adj نامور
nitrogen n نائٹروجن	**notary** n مصدق الاسناد
no one pro کوئی بھی نہیں	**notation** n علامتی ترقیم
nobility n طبقہ امرا	**note** v لکھنا
noble adj معزز	**notebook** n کتاب یادداشت
nobleman n امیرزادہ	**noteworthy** adj توجہ کے قابل
nobody pro کوئی نہیں	**nothing** n کچھ نہیں
nocturnal adj شبانہ	**notice** v توجہ میں لانا
noise n شور	**notice** n اطلاع نامہ
noisily adv شر مچاکر	**noticeable** adj لائقِ توجہ
noisy adj شور مچانے والا	**notification** n اعلان
nominate v نامزد کرنا	**notify** v مطلع کرنا
none pre کوئی نہیں	**notion** n خیال
nonetheless c باوجود اس کے	**notorious** adj بدنام
nonsense n مبهم	**noun** n اسم
nonstop adv بلا توقف	**nourish** v پرورش کرنا
noon n دوپہر	**nourishment** n پرورش
noose n کمند	**novel** n عجیب
nor c نہ ہی	**novelist** n ناول نگار
norm n معیار	**novelty** n ندرت
normal adj حسب قاعدہ	**November** n نومبر
normalize v نارمل بنانا	**novice** n نوآموز
normally adv عام طور پر	**now** adv اب
north n شمال	**nowadays** adv آجکل
northeast n شمال مشرق	**nowhere** adv کہیں نہیں
northern adj شمالی	**noxious** adj فاسد
Norway n ناروے	**nozzle** n ٹونٹی
nose n ناک	**nuance** n درجہ
nosedive v ناک ڈُبکی	**nuclear** adj نیوکلیائی
nostalgia n عارضہ یاد وطن	**nude** adj ننگا

N

nudism n عریانیت	**obedient** adj اطاعت شعار
nudist n عریانیت پسند	**obese** adj توندل
nudity n عریانیت	**obey** v حکم ماننا
nuisance n مخل	**object** v اعتراض کرنا
null adj معدوم	**object** n اعتراض
nullify v منسوخ کرنا	**objection** n اعتراض
numb adj سن	**objective** n مقصد
number n تعداد	**obligate** v پابند کرنا
numbness n بے حسی	**obligation** n پابندی
numerous adj بے شمار	**obligatory** adj قابل پابندی
nun n نن	**oblige** v احسان کرنا
nurse n نرس	**obliged** adj ممنون
nurse v تیمارداری کرنا	**oblique** adj آڑا
nursery n نرسری؛ گہوارہ	**obliterate** v چھیل دینا
nurture v پالنا پوسنا	**oblivion** n نسیان
nut n گری	**oblivious** adj نسیانی
nutrition n تغذیہ	**oblong** adj لمبوترا
nut-shell n خلاصہ	**obnoxious** adj بےہودہ
nutty adj جوز دار	**obscene** adj فحش
	obscenity n فحاشی
	obscure adj غیر واضع
	obscurity n ابہام

O

	observation n مشاہدہ
	observatory n رصد گاہ
	observe v دیکھنا
	obsession n وہم کا تسلط
oak n شاہ بلوط	**obsolete** adj متروک
oar n چپو	**obstacle** n رکاوٹ
oasis n نخلستان	**obstinacy** n ڈھیٹ پن
oath n حلف	**obstinate** adj ڈھیٹ
oatmeal n جئی کا کھانا	**obstruct** v روڑے اٹکانا
obedience n اطاعت شعاری	**obstruction** n رکاوٹ

N O

obtain v حاصل کرنا	**offset** v متوازن/برابر کرنا
obvious adj واضح	**offspring** n اولاد
obviously adv واضح طور پر	**often** adv اکثر
occasion n موقع	**oil** n تیل
occasionally adv کبھی کبھار	**ointment** n مرہم
occult adj پراسرار	**okay** adv اوکے
occupant n قابض	**old** adj پرانا
occupation n پیشہ	**old age** n بڑھاپا
occupy v قبضہ کرنا	**old-fashioned** adj پرانے انداز کا
occur v واقع ہونا	**olive** n زیتون
ocean n سمندر	**olympics** n اولمپک کھیل
October n اکتوبر	**omelette** n آملیٹ
octopus n آکٹوپس	**omen** n شگون
ocurrence n وقوع	**ominous** adj بدشگونی والا
odd adj بے جوڑ	**omission** n حذف
odds n تفاوت	**omit** v حذف کرنا
odious adj نفرت انگیز	**on** pre پر
odometer n مسافت پیما	**once** c ایک مرتبہ
odor n بو	**one** adj ایک
odyssey n اوڈیسی	**oneself** pre آپ
of pre کا	**ongoing** adj جاری
off adv پرے	**onion** n پیاز
offend v مجروح کرنا	**onlooker** n دیکھنے والا
offense n جرم	**only** adv صرف
offensive adj ناگوار	**onset** n دھاوا
offer v پیش کرنا	**onslaught** n بلا
offer n پیشکش	**opaque** adj گدلا
offering n چڑھاوا	**open** v کھولنا
office n دفتر	**open** adj کھلا
officer n افسر	**open up** v لڑنے لگنا
official adj اہلکار دفتری	**opening** n آغاز
officiate v قائم مقامی کرنا	**open-minded** adj کشادہ دل

openness n کھلاپن	orchestra n آرکسٹرا
opera n اوپیرا	ordeal n آزمائش
operate v چلانا	order n حکم
operation n آپریشن	ordinarily adv عام طور پر
opinion n رائے	ordinary adj عام
opinionated adj ضدی	ordination n نفاذ فرمان
opium n افیون	ore n لید
opponent n مخالف	organ n آرگن
opportune adj برمحل	organism n عضو
opportunity n موقع	organist n آرگن بجانیوالا
oppose v مخالفت کرنا	organization n تنظیم
opposite adj متضاد	organize v منظم ہونا یا کرنا
opposite adv بر عکس	orient n قیمتی
opposite n متضاد	oriental adj مشرقی
opposition n مخالفت	orientation n تعین رخ
oppress v مغلوب کرنا	origin n ابتدا
oppression n دبائو	original adj اصلی
opt for v انتخاب کرنا	originally adv اصل میں
optical adj بصری	originate v وجود میں لانا
optician n عینک ساز	ornament n زیور
optimism n رجائیت	ornamental adj زیبائشی
optimistic adj پر امید	orphan n یتیم
option n راستہ	orphanage n یتیمی
optional adj اختیاری	orthodox adj دقیانوسی
opulence n کثرت	ostentatious adj نمائشی
or c یا	ostrich n شتر مرغ
oracle n غیبی آواز	other adj دوسرا
orally adv زبانی طور پر	otherwise adv بصورتِ دیگر
orange n سنگترہ	otter n اود بلائو
orangutan n انسان نما بندر	ought to iv چاہیے
orbit n مدار	ounce n اونس
orchard n باغ	our adj ہمارا

O

ours pro ہمارا	**outside** adv بیرونی سطح
ourselves pro ہم خود	**outsider** n باہر کا
oust v نکال باہر کرنا	**outskirts** n گردونواح
out adv باہر	**outspoken** adj صاف گو
outbreak n وبا کی پھوٹ	**outstanding** adj نمایاں
outburst n ہیجان	**outstretched** adj پھیلانا
outcast adj خارج شدہ	**outward** adj باہر کی جانب
outcome n نتیجہ	**outweigh** v زیادہ بھاری ہونا
outcry n چیخ	**oval** adj بیضوی
outdated adj پرانا	**ovary** n بیضہ دانی
outdo v بہتر کام کرنا	**ovation** n پرجوش استقبال
outdoor adv بیرونی	**oven** n اون
outdoors adv بیرون خانہ	**over** pre کے اوپر
outer adj خارجی	**overall** adv مجموعی طور پر
outfit n لباس	**overbearing** adj زیر کرنا
outgoing adj دوستانہ	**overcast** adj بادل چھانا
outing n سیر سپاٹا	**overcharge** v زیادہ قیمت لینا
outlast v زیادہ کام کرنا	**overcoat** n اوورکوٹ
outlaw v ممانعت کرنا	**overcome** v قابو پانا
outlet n نکاس؛ ذریعہ اظہار	**overdone** adj زیادہ پکا ہوا
outline n خاکہ؛ خلاصہ	**overdue** adj زائد المعیاد
outline v خاکہ بیان کرنا	**overflow** v چھلکنا
outlive v زندہ بچ رہن	**overhaul** v مرمت کرنا
outlook n نظریہ	**overlap** v اوپر چڑبنا
outmoded adj متروک شدہ	**overlook** v دھیان نہ دینا
outpatient n بیرونی مریض	**overnight** adv رات رات میں
outpouring n انڈیلنا	**overpower** v مغلوب کرلینا
output n ماحصل	**overrate** v زیادہ دام لگانا
outrage n انتہائی ظلم	**override** v کچل ڈالنا
outrageous adj سخت ظالمانہ	**overrule** v رد کرنا
outright adj صاف صاف	**overrun** v دوڑ جانا
outset n شروعات کرنا	**overseas** adv سمندر پار

نگرانی کرنا v oversee	چپو چلانا v paddle
غلطی n oversight	قفل n padlock
بڑھا کر کہنا v overstate	بت پرست adj pagan
پکڑ لینا v overtake	خدمت گار، غلام n page
شکست دینا v overthrow	پیالہ n pail
بربادی n overthrow	درد pain
فتح کرنا v overturn	غم آلودہ adj painful
زیادتی وزن adj overweight	درد بغیر adj painless
مغلوب کرنا v overwhelm	رنگنا v paint
مالک ہونا owe	رنگ روغن n paint
الو n owl	رنگ روغن کا برش n paintbrush
اپنا ذاتی v own	مصور n painter
حقدار ہونا adj own	رنگ آمیزی n painting
مالک n owner	جوڑا n pair
ملکیت n ownership	پجامہ n pajamas
بیل n ox	دوست n pal
آکسیجن n oxygen	محل شاہی n palace
کستورا مچھلی n oyster	تالو n palate
	زرد adj pale
	زردی n paleness
	کھجور کا درخت n palm
P	کمینہ adj paltry
	خوب کھلانا v pamper
	رسالہ n pamphlet
پانچ فٹ کا پیمانہ v pace	جسم کل عضو پتہ n pancreas
ٹہلنا n pace	دلالی کرنا v pander
ٹھنڈا کرنا pacify	تکلیف n pang
گٹھڑی v pack	ناگہانی خوف n panic
پارسل n package	تیندوا n panther
بندش n pact	نعمت خانہ n pantry
بھر دینا pad	دل کی حرکت n pants
	کاغذ n paper

parable *n* مثال

parade *n* صف آرائی

paradise *n* بہشت

paradox *n* بعیدالعقل بات

paragraph *n* فقرہ

parallel *n* متوازی

paralysis *n* قوت حرکت کا زوال

paralyze *v* فالج کرنا

paramount *adj* بلند مرتبہ

paranoid *adj* مالیخولیا

parasite *n* آکاش بیل

paratrooper *n* چھتر سپاہی

parcel *n* تودہ گٹھری

parcel post *n* پارسل ڈاک

parch *v* بھوننا، خشک کرنا

pardon *v* معاف کرنا

pardon *n* عفو

parenthesis *n* جملہ متعرضہ

parents *n* والدین

parish *n* پادری کا علاقہ

parity *n* یکسانیت

park *v* گاڑی کھڑی کرنا

park *n* احاطہ

parliament *n* مقننہ

parochial *adj* مقامی

parrot *n* طوطا

parsley *n* اجمود

parsnip *n* گاجر کی قسم

part *v* حصے بخرے کرنا

part *n* حصہ

partial *adj* جزوی

partially *adv* جزوی طور پر

participate *v* حصہ لینا

participation *n* حصہ داری

particle *n* ذرہ

particular *adj* مخصوص

particularly *adv* تاکید سے

parting *n* علیحدگی

partisan *n* طرفدار

partition *n* تقسیم

partly *adv* کسی قدر

partner *n* شریک

partnership *n* شراکت

partridge *n* تیتر

party *n* جماعت، فرقہ

pass *n* حالت

pass *v* تقسیم کرنا

pass around *v* چھوڑ جانا

pass away *v* چھوڑ جانا

pass out *v* تقسیم کرنا

passage *n* راستہ

passenger *n* مسافر

passion *n* جوش

passionate *adj* پرجوش

passive *adj* صابر

passport *n* پروانہ راہ داری

password *n* پہچان کا لفظ

past *adj* ماضی

paste *v* لیٹی لگانا

paste *n* گوندھا ہوا آٹا

pastime *n* شغل

pastor *n* پادری

pastoral *adj* پادری سے متعلق

pastry *n* چراگاہ

pat *n* درست	**peak** *n* پہاڑ کی چوٹی
patch *v* پیوند لگانا	**peanut** *n* موم پھلی
patch *n* قطعہ زمین	**pear** *n* ناشپاتی
patent *n* سند حق ایجاد	**pearl** *n* موتی
patent *adj* عام	**peasant** *n* دیہاتی
paternity *n* پدری رشتہ	**pebble** *n* گول کنکر
path *n* راستہ	**peck** *v* دانہ چگنا
pathetic *adj* پر اثر	**peck** *n* ایک پیمانہ
patience *n* صبر	**peculiar** *adj* نادر
patient *adj* مستقل مزاج	**pedagogy** *n* فن تعلیم
patrimony *n* میراث	**peel** *v* چھلنا
patriot *n* وطن پرست	**peel** *n* چھلکا
patrol *n* فوجی گشت	**peep** *v* تاکنا
patron *n* حامی، پشت پناہ	**peer** *n* ہم مرتبہ
patronage *n* سرپرستی	**pellet** *n* غلیلہ
patronize *v* حمایت کرنا	**pen** *n* قلم
pattern *n* نمونہ	**penalize** *v* سزا دینا
pavilion *n* گبند دار عمارت	**penalty** *n* سزا، جرمانہ
paw *n* پنجہ	**penance** *n* کفارہ
pawn *v* رہن رکھنا	**penchant** *n* میلان طبع
pay *n* تنخواہ	**pencil** *n* سرمی قلم
pay *iv* معاوضہ	**pendant** *n* لٹکن
pay back *v* منافع	**pending** *adj* زیر تجویز
pay off *v* فائدہ پہنچانا	**pendulum** *n* لنگر
payable *adj* واجب الادا	**penetrate** *v* مداخلت کرنا
payee *n* وصول کنندہ	**peninsula** *n* جزیرہ نما
payment *n* ادائے قرض	**penitent** *n* نادم
pea *n* مٹر	**penniless** *adj* محتاج
peace *n* امن	**penny** *n* ولایت کا پیسہ
peaceful *adj* پر امن	**pension** *n* پنشن
peach *n* آڑو	**pent-up** *adj* محبوس ہونا
peacock *n* مور	**people** *n* افراد

P

pepper *n*	مرچ
per *pre*	فی
perceive *v*	محسوس کرنا
percent *adv*	فی صدی
perception *n*	قیاس
perennial *adj*	دائمی؛ سال بھر
perfect *adj*	مکمل
perfection *n*	کمال
perforate *v*	سوراخ کرنا
perforation *n*	سوراخ
perform *v*	انجام دینا
perform *v*	انجام دینا، پورا کرنا
performance *n*	عمل،کام
perfume *n*	خوشبو
perhaps *adv*	شاید
peril *n*	ڈر
perilous *adj*	خوفناک
period *n*	معیاد
perish *v*	نیست و نابود ہونا
perishable *adj*	فانی
permanent *adj*	پرثبات
permeate *v*	نفوذ کرنا
permission *n*	اجازت
permit *v*	اجازت دینا
pernicious *adj*	مضر
perpetrate *v*	مرتکب ہونا
persecute *v*	ستانا
persevere *v*	مستقل رہنا
persist *v*	ثابت قدم رہنا
persistence *n*	ثابت قدمی
persistent *adj*	مستقل مزاج
person *n*	شخص

personal *adj*	ذاتی
personality *n*	شخصیت
personify *v*	وجود قرار دینا
personnel *n*	زمرہ ملازمان
perspective *n*	ہیئت
perspiration *n*	پسینہ
perspire *v*	پسینہ نکلنا
persuade *v*	باور کرنا
persuasion *n*	ترغیب
persuasive *adj*	پھسلانے والا
pertain	علاقہ رکھنا
pertinent *adj*	مناسب
perturb *v*	تکلیف دینا
perverse *adj*	ضدی
pervert *v*	گمراہ کرنا
pervert *adj*	منحرف؛ گمراہ
pessimism *n*	قنوطیت
pessimistic *adj*	یاسیت پسند
pest *n*	مہلک بیماری
pester *v*	تکلیف دینا
pesticide *n*	کیڑے مار دوائی
pet *n*	پالتو جانور
petal *n*	پھول کی پتی
petite *adj*	حقیر
petition *n*	عرضی
petrified *adj*	سخت ہو جانا
petroleum *n*	مٹی کا تیل
pettiness *n*	کمینہ پن
petty *adj*	چھوٹا ، ادنی
pew *n*	بینچ
phantom *n*	تصور
pharmacist *n*	دوا ساز؛ عطارد

pharmacy *n* دوا سازی	piercing *n* تیز
phase *n* صورت	piety *n* خدا ترسی
pheasant *n* تیتر	pig *n* سور
phenomenon *n* عجیب واقعہ	pigeon *n* کبوتر
philosopher *n* فلسفہ دان	pile *v* ڈھیر لگانا
philosophy *n* فلسفہ	pile *n* ڈھیر
phobia *n* خوف	pile up *v* جمع کرنا
phone *n* ٹیلی فون کا آلہ	pilfer *v* ضائع کرنا
phoney *adj* صوتیاتی	pilgrim *n* حاجی
phosphorus *n* گندھک	pilgrimage *n* حج
photo *n* عکس	pill *n* گولی
photocopy *n* فوٹو کاپی	pillage *v* لوٹ مار
photograph *v* عکسی تصویر	pillar *n* ستون
photographer *n* عکس بنانے والا	pillow *n* تکیہ
phrase *n* محاورہ	pillowcase *n* تکیہ کا غلاف
physically *adv* جسمانی طور پر	pilot *n* جہاز کا رہنما
physician *n* طبیب	pimple *n* مہاسا
physics *n* علم مادیات	pin *n* کیل
pianist *n* پیانو باجا بجانے والا	pincers *n* دست پناہ
piano *n* پیانو	pinch *v* تنگ کرنا
pick *v* پسند کرنا، اچکنا	pinch *n* چٹکی
pick up *v* اٹھنا	pine *n* چیل کا درخت
pickpocket *n* جیب تراش	pineapple *n* انناس
pickup *n* اٹھان	pink *adj* گلابی رنگ
picture *n* تصویر	pinpoint *v* انگی اٹھانا
picture *v* تصویر کینچھنا	pioneer *n* رہنما
picturesque *adj* تصویر کی ماندد	pious *adj* دیندار
pie *n* کچوری	pipe *n* پیپا،حقہ
piece *n* ٹکڑا	pipeline *n* پائپ لائن
piecemeal *adv* الگ الگ کرکے	piracy *n* ڈکیتی
pier *n* گھاٹ	pirate *n* سمندری چور
pierce *v* گڑھا کھودنا	pistol *n* پستول

P

pit n گڑھا	**plea** n دلیل
pitch-black adj تاریکی	**plead** v وکالت کرنا
pitfall n دھوکے کی جگہ	**pleasant** adj خوش طبع
pitiful adj حقیر	**please** v خوش کرنا
pity n ہمدردی	**pleasing** adj پسندیدہ
placard n اشتہار	**pleasure** n خوشی
placate v تسلی دینا	**pleat** n چنت ڈالنا
place n جگہ	**pleated** adj شکن زدہ
placid adj متحمل	**pledge** v رہن رکھنا
plague n وبا	**pledge** n ضامن
plain n ہموار	**plentiful** adj زرخیز
plain adj کھرا، ظاہر	**plenty** n کثرت
plainly adv سچائی سے	**pliable** adj لچکدار
plaintiff n مدعی	**pliers** n چمٹا؛ چمٹی
plan v تدبیر کرنا	**plot** v تدبیر کرنا
plan n ترکیب	**plot** n ہموار قطع زمین
plane n ہموار	**plow** v ہل چلانا
planet n سیارہ	**ploy** n مشغلہ
plant v بونا	**pluck** v چننا
plant n پودا	**plug** v ڈاٹ لگانا
plaster n پلستر	**plug** n ڈاٹ
plaster v پلستر لگانا	**plum** n آلو بخارہ
plastic n پلاسٹک بنانا	**plumbing** n نل کاری
plate n رکابی	**plummet** v تھاہ لینے کا لنگر
plateau n بلند ہموار میدان	**plump** adj یک بیک
platform n چبوترہ	**plunder** v خیانت کرنا
plausible adj نمائشی	**plunge** v ڈبونا
play v کھیلنا	**plunge** n غوطہ
play n بازی لگانا	**plural** n جمع
player n کھلاڑی	**plus** adj زائد
playful adj شوخ	**plush** adj نرم روادار کا کپڑا
playground n کھیل کا میدان	**plutonium** n جہنمی؛ آتشی

pneumonia *n* نمونیا	pomposity *n* شان و شکوہ
pocket *n* جیب	pond *n* جوہڑ
poem *n* نظم	ponder *v* غورو حوض کرنا
poet *n* شاعر	pontiff *n* بڑا پادری
poetry *n* شاعری	pool *n* نلیا،ساکن پانی
poignant *adj* تلخ ذائقہ	pool *v* روپیہ اکٹھا کرنا
point *n* نقطہ	poor *n* غریب
point *v* تیز کرنا	poorly *adv* مفلسی سے
pointed *adj* نوکدار؛ نوکیلا	popcorn *n* مکی بھوننا
pointless *adj* بے معنی؛ کند	poppy *n* پوست
poise *n* وزن کرنا	popular *adj* بردلعزیز
poison *v* زبر ملا دینا	popularize *v* عام پسند کرنا
poison *n* زہر	populate *v* آباد کرنا
poisoning *n* زہریلا	population *n* آبادی
poisonous *adj* زہریلا	porch *n* ڈیوڑھی
Poland *n* پولینڈ	porcupine *n* خارپشت
pole *n* قطب	pore *n* مسام
police *n* پولیس	pork *n* سور کا گوشت
policeman *n* پولیس کا سپاہی	porous *adj* مسام دار
policy *n* حکمت عملی	port *n* بندرگاہ
Polish *adj* پولینڈ کا باشندہ	portable *adj* بلکا
polish *n* چکنی سطح	portent *n* منحوس
polish *v* چمکیلا کرنا	porter *n* دربان
polite *adj* مہذب	portion *n* حصہ
politeness *n* شائستگی	portrait *n* تصویر
politician *n* سیاستدان	portray *v* تصویر کھینچنا
politics *n* علم سیاست	pose *n* طرز
poll *n* سر کا پچھلا حصہ	posh *adj* شاندار
pollen *n* پھولوں کی خاک	position *n* حالت
pollute *v* گندہ کرنا	positive *adj* صریح
pollution *n* آلودگی	possess *v* ملکیت رکھنا
pomegranate *n* انار	possession *n* قبضہ

P

possibility n امکان	**prawn** n جھینگا مچھلی
possible adj ممکن	**pray** v دعا ماگنا
post n ڈاک، کھمبا	**prayer** n نماز
post office n ڈاکخانہ	**preach** v وعظ کرنا
postage n محصول ڈاک	**preacher** n واعظ
postcard n پوسٹ کارڈ	**preamble** n دیباچہ
poster n اشتہار	**precarious** adj مشکوک
posterity n نسل	**precaution** n احتیاط
postman n چھٹی رساں	**precede** v مقدم ہونا
postpone v التوا کرنا	**precedent** n مثال
postponement n توقف	**preceding** adj تبلیغ
potato n آلو	**precept** n فرمان
potent adj طاقت ور	**precious** adj قیمتی
potential adj امکان	**precipice** n ڈھال
poultry n مرغی	**precise** adj باریک بین
pound v احاطہ میں بند کرنا	**precision** n عمدگی
pound n قریباً آدھا کلو	**precocious** adj قبل از وقت
pour v جھڑنا	**precursor** n پیشوا
poverty n مفلسی	**predecessor** n بزرگ مورث
powder n سفوف	**predicament** n آفت
power n طاقت	**predict** v پشین گوئی کرنا
powerful adj طاقتور	**prediction** n پشین گوئی
powerless adj کمزور	**predilection** n طرفداری
practical adj عملی	**predisposed** adj رغبت
practice n ہنر	**predominate** v غالب ہونا
practise v عادت ڈالنا	**preface** n دیباچہ
practising adj مشاق	**prefer** v فوقیت دینا
prairie n گھاس کا میدان	**preference** n ترجیح
praise v تعریف کرنا	**prefix** n پیشتر درج کرنا
praise n ثنا	**pregnancy** n حمل
praiseworthy adj قابل تحسین	**pregnant** adj حاملہ
prank n مزاق	**prehistoric** adj قبل از تاریخ

prejudice n تعصب	**presumption** n قیاس
preliminary adj ابتدائی	**presuppose** v اخَذ کَرنا
prelude n عنوان	**presupposition** n گمان
premature adj قبل از وقت	**pretend** v بهانہ کرنا
premeditate v پیش بندی کرنا	**pretense** n بهانہ
premeditation n عاقبت اندیشی	**pretension** n مفروضہ
premier adj اعلی	**pretty** adj نفیس
premise n مفروضہ	**prevail** v فوقیت رکھنا
premonition n اگاہی	**prevalent** adj مروج
preoccupation n محویت	**prevent** v باز رکھنا
preoccupy v پریشانی	**prevention** n ممانعت
preparation n تیاری	**preview** n پیشگی مشاہدہ
prepare v تیار کرنا	**previous** adj سابقہ
preposition n حرف اضافت	**previously** adv گذشتہ
prerequisite n ضروری شے	**prey** n شکار
prerogative n استحقاق کامل	**price** n قیمت
prescription n نسخہ،حق قدامت	**pricey** adj قیمتی
presence n موجودگی	**prick** v چبهنا
present adj حاضر	**pride** n غرور
present v پیش کرنا	**priest** n پادری
presentation n نمائش	**priestess** n پجارن
preserve v محفوظ کرنا	**priesthood** n پجاری کا عہدہ
preside v صدارت کرنا	**primarily** adv ابتدائ طور پر
presidency n حاکم کا علاقہ	**prime** adj اول درجے کی
president n حاکم	**primitive** adj قدیم
press n چھاپہ خانہ	**prince** n شہزادہ
press v دبانا، مجبور کرنا	**princess** n شہزادی
pressing adj ناگزیر	**principal** adj اول
pressure v وڈالنادبا	**principle** n اصول
pressure n دباؤ	**print** v چھپنا
prestige n مقبولیت	**print** n نقش
presume v فرض کرنا	**printer** n چھاپنے والا

P

printing *n* چھاپنے کا ہنر	produce *n* پیداوار
prior *adj* اولین	product *n* پیداوار
priority *n* ترجیح دینا	production *n* پیداواری/نتیجہ
prism *n* مخروط	productive *adj* پیدا کرنے والا
prison *n* جیل خانہ	profane *adj* ناپاک
prisoner *n* قیدی	profess *v* اقرار کرنا
privacy *n* پوشیدگی	profession *n* پیشہ/نوکری
private *adj* پوشیدہ	professor *n* استاذ
privilege *n* اختیار	proficiency *n* استعداد
prize *n* انعام	proficient *adj* ماہر
probability *n* قیاس	profile *n* خاکہ
probable *adj* ممکن	profit *v* نفع اٹھانا
probe *v* تفتیش کرنا	profit *n* منافع
probing *n* چھان بین	profitable *adj* مفید
problem *n* مسلہ	profound *adj* فاضل
problematic *adj* مشتبہ	progress *v* ترقی کرنا
procedure *n* طریق طرز	progress *n* لیاقت
proceed *v* آگے جانا	progressive *adj* ترقی کرنے والا
proceedings *n* کاروائی	prohibit *v* ممانعت کرنا
proceeds *n* آمدنی	prohibition *n* ممانعت
process *v* عمل کرنا	project *v* منصوبہ
process *n* کاروائی	project *n* تجویز
procession *n* جلوس	prologue *n* مقدمہ
proclaim *v* اعلان کرنا	prolong *v* ملتوی کرنا
proclamation *n* اشتہار	promenade *n* چہل قدمی
procrastinate *v* ٹالنا	prominent *adj* نامی گرامی
procreate *v* جننا	promiscuous *adj* مخلوط
procure *v* پانا	promise *n* قول
prod *v* چبھونا	promote *v* ترقی دینا
prodigious *adj* عجیب	promotion *n* ترقی
prodigy *n* عجب	prompt *adj* مستعد
produce *v* حاضر کرنا	prone *adj* منہ کے بل

P

pronoun n ضمير	**protrude** v زبردستی گھسنا
pronounce v حتمی طور پر کہنا	**proud** adj مغرور
proof n ثبوت	**proudly** adv فخریہ
propaganda n اِشتہار بازی	**prove** v ثبوت دینا
propagate v پھیلانا	**proven** adj ثابت شدہ
propel v دھکیلنا	**proverb** n ضرب المثل
propensity n چسکا	**provide** v مہیا کرنا
proper adj مناسب	**providence** n دور اندیشی
properly adv بخوبی	**providing that** c بشرطیکہ
property n ملکیت	**province** n صوبہ
prophecy n پیش گوئی	**provision** n فراہمی
prophet n خدا کا رسول	**provisional** adj عارضی
proportion n مقدار	**provocation** n اشتعال
proposal n تجویز	**provoke** v اکسانا
propose v تجویز کرنا	**prow** n جہاز کا اگلا حصہ
proposition n قول	**prowl** v پھرتے رہنا
prose n نثر	**proximity** n نزدیکی
prosecute v مقدمہ چلانا	**proxy** n مختار
prosecutor n مستغیث	**prudence** n دانائی
prospect n امکان	**prudent** adj دانا
prosper v پھیلنا پھولنا	**prune** v تراشنا
prosperity n کامیابی	**prune** n آلو بخارہ
prosperous adj برا بھرا	**prurient** adj نفس پرست
prostrate adj سجدہ کرنا	**psychic** adj نفسیاتی
protect v محفوظ رکھنا	**psychology** n علم النفس
protection n حفاظت	**psychopath** n نفسیاتی مریض
protein n بیضیہ	**puberty** n بلوغت
protest v احتجاج کرنا	**public** adj عوام
protest n احتجاج	**publication** n اشاعت
prototype n پہلا نمونہ	**publicity** n تشہیر
protract v لمبا کرنا	**publicly** adv اعلانیہ طور پر
protracted adj طویل شدہ	**publish** v شائع کرنا

P

publisher n ناشر	**purge** v صاف کرنا
pudding n حلوہ	**purification** n صفائی
puerile adj طفلانا	**purify** v پاک صاف کرنا
puff n پھونک	**purity** n پاکیزگی
puffy adj پھولا ہوا	**purple** adj ارغوانی
pull v کھینچنا	**purpose** n مقصد
pull down v گرانا	**purposely** adv بالارادہ
pull out v باہر نکالنا	**purse** n بٹوا
pulley n چرخی	**pursue** v تعاقب کرنا
pulp n گودا	**pursuit** n تعاقب؛ جستجو
pulpit n واعظ	**pus** n پیپ
pulsate v نبض کا چلنا	**push** v دھکیلنا
pulse n نبض	**pushy** adj مہم جو
pulverize v پیسنا	**put** iv ڈالنا
pump v خارج کرنا	**put aside** v ایک طرف کر دینا
pump n پمپ	**put away** v بچا کر رکھنا
pumpkin n پیٹھا	**put off** v ٹالنا
punch v مکا مارنا؛ مہر لگانا	**put out** v بجھا دینا
punch n مہر؛ گھونسا	**put up** v کھڑا کرنا
punctual adj وقت کا پابند	**put up with** v برداشت کرنا
puncture n سوراخ	**putrid** adj بدبو دار
punish v سزا دینا	**puzzle** n پہیلی
punishable adj لائقِ سزا	**puzzling** adj الجھانے والا
punishment n سزا	**pyramid** n مخروطی
pupil n شاگرد	**python** n اژدھا
puppet n پتلی	
puppy n پلا	
purchase v خریدنا	
purchase n خریداری	
pure adj خالص	
purgatory n کفارہ گاہ	
purge n صفائی	

Q

quagmire *n* دلدل

quail *n* بٹیر

quake *v* بلنا

qualify *v* اہلیت پر پورا اترنا

quality *n* معیار

qualm *n* ضمیر کی چبھن

quandery *n* گومگو کا عالم

quantity *n* مقدار

quarrel *v* لڑائی کرنا

quarrel *n* لڑائی

quarrelsome *adj* جھگڑالو

quarry *n* کان

quarter *n* چوتھا حصہ

quarterly *adj* سہ ماہی

quarters *n* گروہ

quash *v* خارج کرنا

queen *n* ملکہ

queer *adj* عجیب

quell *v* دبانا

quench *v* پیاس بجھانا

quest *n* تفتیش

question *v* سوال کرنا

question *n* سوال

questionable *adj* قابلِ اعتراض

questionnaire *n* سوال نامہ

queue *n* قطار

quick *adj* سریع

quicken *v* تیز تر کرنا

quickly *adv* جلدی سے

quicksand *n* دلدل

quiet *adj* خاموش

quietness *n* خاموشی

quilt *n* لحاف

quit *iv* چھوڑ دینا

quite *adv* بالکل

quiver *v* تھرتھرانا

quiz *v* سوال

quotation *n* اقتباس

quote *v* حوالہ دینا

quotient *n* خارج قسمت

R

rabbi *n* یہودی فقیہہ

rabbit *n* خرگوش

rabies *n* بائولاپن

raccoon *n* خرسک

race *v* دوڑ لگانا

race *n* دوڑ؛ نسل

racism *n* نسل پرستی

racist *adj* نسل پرست

racket *n* ٹینس کا چھکا

racketeering *n* بددیانتی

radar *n* راڈار

radiation *n* شعاع ریزی

radiator *n* اشعاع کننده

radical *adj* انقلاب پسند

Q
R

radio n ریڈیو	**rank** n عہدہ؛ درجہ
radish n مولی	**rank** v درجہ بندی کرنا
radius n نصف قطر	**ransack** v مکمل تلاشی لینا
raffle n ریفل	**ransom** v تاوان دینا
raft n بیڑی	**ransom** n تاوان
rag n چیتھڑا	**rape** v زنا بالجبر کرنا
rage n سخت غصہ	**rape** n زنا بالجبر
ragged adj پھٹا پرانا	**rapid** adj تیز
raid n چھاپا	**rapist** n زانی
raid v چھا مارنا	**rapport** n مناسبت
raider n چھاپا مار	**rare** adj نایاب
rail n ریل؛ پٹڑی	**rarely** adv کبھی کبھار
railroad n ریل کی پٹڑی	**rascal** n بدقماش
rain n بارش	**rash** v جلدبازی کرنا
rain v بارش ہونا	**rash** n چھپاکی
rainbow n قوس قزع	**raspberry** n رس بھری
raincoat n برساتی	**rat** n چوہا
rainy adj برساتی	**rate** n نرخ؛ شرح
raise n بلندی؛ چبوترا	**rather** adv قدرے
raise v بڑھانا	**ratification** n تصدیق
raisin n کشمش	**ratify** v تصدیق کرنا
rake n جھانپنا	**ratio** n نسبت
rally n مجتمع ہونا	**ration** v راشن دینا
ram n مینڈھا	**ration** n خوراک
ramification n پیچیدگی	**rational** adj استدلالی
ramp n ڈھلان	**rationalize** v تشریح کرنا
rampage v حملہ کرنا	**rattle** v کھڑکھڑانا
rampant adj قابو سے باہر	**ravage** v تباہ کرنا
ranch n مویشی خانہ	**ravage** n تباہ کرنا
rancor n تلخی	**raven** n پہاڑی کوا
randomly adv اٹکل پچو	**ravine** n گھاٹی
range n حد	**raw** adj کچا

R

ray *n* شعاع

raze *v* منہدم کرنا

razor *n* استرا

reach *v* پہنچنا

reach *n* رسائی

react *v* رد عمل دینا

reaction *n* رد عمل

read *iv* پڑھنا

reader *n* قاری

readiness *n* تیاری

reading *n* پڑھائی

ready *adj* تیار

real *adj* اصلی

realism *n* مقیقت بینی

reality *n* حقیقت

realize *v* احساس ہونا

really *adv* حقیقتاً

realm *n* سلطنت

realty *n* غیر منقولہ جائیداد

reap *v* کاٹنا

reappear *v* دوبارہ نمودار ہونا

rear *v* پالنا پوسنا

rear *n* پچھواڑا

rear *adj* عقبی

reason *v* نتیجہ نکالنا

reason *n* وجہ

reasonable *adj* معقول

reasoning *n* استدلال

reassure *v* حوصلہ بڑھانا

rebate *n* تخفیف کرنا

rebel *v* سرکشی کرنا

rebel *n* سرکش

rebellion *n* بغاوت

rebirth *n* نیا جنم

rebound *v* زور سے پلٹنا

rebuff *v* جھڑکنا؛ دھتکارنا

rebuff *n* جھڑکی

rebuild *v* تعمیر نو کرنا

rebuke *v* سرزنش کرنا

rebuke *n* سرزنش

rebut *v* رد کرنا

recall *v* یاد کرنا

recant *v* توبہ کرنا

recap *v* خلاصہ بیان کرنا

recapture *v* مکرر قبضہ کرنا

recede *v* پسپا ہونا

receipt *n* رسید

receive *v* وصول کرنا

recent *adj* حالیہ

reception *n* استقبال

receptionist *n* استقبالی افسر

receptive *adj* ادراک پذیر

recess *n* تعطیل

recession *n* واپسی

recharge *v* بیٹری بھرنا

recipe *n* ترکیب پکوان

reciprocal *adj* معکوسی

recital *n* قراءت

recite *v* پڑھنا

reckless *adj* بے دھڑک

reckon *v* گننا

reclaim *v* اصلاح کرنا

recline *v* تکیہ لگانا

recluse *n* قیدی

R

recognition *n* پہچان	recurrence *n* تکرار
recognize *v* پہچاننا	red *adj* سرخ
recollect *v* یاد کرنا	red tape *n* سرک فیتا
recollection *n* یاد	redden *v* سرخ بنانا
recommend *v* سفارش کرنا	redeem *v* چھڑا لینا
recompense *v* تلافی کرنا	redemption *n* آزادی
recompense *n* تلافی	redo *v* دوبارہ کرنا
reconcile *v* مل جانا	redouble *v* اضافہ کرنا
reconsider *v* دوبارہ غور کرنا	redress *v* داد رسی کرنا
reconstruct *v* دوبارہ تعمیر کرنا	reduce *v* تخفیف کرنا
record *v* قلمند کرنا	redundant *adj* زائد
record *n* ریکارڈ؛ روداد	reed *n* سرکنڈا
recorder *n* ریکارڈ کرنے کا آلہ	reef *n* پتھریلا ساحل
recording *n* صوت بندی	reel *n* پھرکی
recount *n* تفصیل بیان کرنا	reel *n* ایک رقص
recoup *v* کم کر لینا	reelect *v* دوبارہ منتخب ہونا
recourse *v* بدلہ حاصل کرنا	reenactment *n* دوبارہ قانون سازی
recourse *n* استعانت	reentry *n* دوبارہ داخلہ
recover *v* صحت یاب ہونا	refer to *v* تعلق ہونا
recovery *n* بازیابی	referee *n* ریفری
recreate *v* تفریح کرنا	reference *n* حوالہ
recreation *n* تفریح	referendum *n* استصواب
recruit *v* بھرتی کرنا	refill *v* دوبارہ بھرنا
recruit *n* نیا بھرتی شدہ	refinance *v* دوبارہ قرضہ دینا
recruitment *n* بھرتی	refine *v* عمدہ/خالص بنانا
rectangle *n* مستطیل	refinery *n* کارخانہ صاف گری
rectangular *adj* مستطیلی	reflect *v* منعکس کرنا
rectify *v* درست کرنا	reflection *n* عکس
rector *n* ریکٹر	reform *v* اصلاح کرنا
rectum *n* مقعد	reform *n* اصلاح
recuperate *v* صحت یاب ہونا	refrain *v* باز رہنا
recur *v* دوبارہ ہونا	refresh *v* تازگی بخشنا

R

refreshing *adj* تازہ دم کرنے والا

refreshment *n* تفریح

refrigerate *v* ٹھنڈا کرنا

refuel *v* دوبارہ بھرنا

refuge *n* پناہ

refugee *n* پناہ گزین

refund *v* رقم واپس کرنا

refund *n* واپس شدہ رقم

refurbish *v* دوبارہ چمکانا

refusal *n* انکار

refuse *v* انکار کرنا

refuse *n* کوڑا کرکٹ

refute *v* مسترد کرنا

regain *v* دوبارہ حاصل کرنا

regal *adj* شاہانہ

regard *v* سمجھنا

regarding *pre* بلحاظ

regardless *adv* بلا لحاظ

regards *n* آداب

regeneration *n* تجدید

regent *n* نائب السلطنت

regime *n* دورِ حکومت

regiment *n* دستہ

region *n* خطہ

regional *adj* علاقائی

registration *n* اندراج

regret *v* پچھتانا

regret *n* پچھتاوا

regrettable *adj* قابلِ افسوس

regularity *n* باقاعدگی

regularly *adv* باقاعدگی سے

regulate *v* باقاعدہ بنانا

regulation *n* قاعدہ

rehabilitate *v* بحال کرنا

rehearsal *n* دہرائی

rehearse *v* مشق کرنا

reign *v* حکومت کرنا

reign *n* دورِ حکومت

reimburse *v* واپس ادا کرنا

rein *v* لگام سے قابو کرنا

rein *n* لگام

reindeer *n* رینڈئیر

reinforce *v* کمک دینا

reinforcements *n* اضافی دستے

reiterate *v* دہرانا

reject *v* مسترد کرنا

rejection *n* نامنظوری

rejoice *v* خوش ہونا

rejoin *v* دوبارہ شامل ہونا

rejuvenate *v* دوبارہ جوان کرنا

relapse *n* دوبارہ مبتلا ہونا

related *adj* متعلقہ

relationship *n* تعلق

relative *adj* رشتہ دار

relative *n* رشتہ دار

relax *v* ڈھیلا چھوڑنا

relaxation *n* رعایت

relaxing *adj* نرمی برتنے والا

relay *v* بز نشر کرنا

release *v* رہا کرنا

relent *v* پسیج جانا

relentless *adj* سنگ دل

relevant *adj* متعلقہ

reliable *adj* معتبر

R

reliance n اعتماد	remodel v تجدید کرنا
relic n تبرک	remorse n ندامت
relief n آرام	remorseful adj پشیمان
relieve v درد سے خلاصی	remote adj دور افتادہ
religion n مذہب	removal n برطرفی
religious adj مذہبی	remove v ہٹانا
relinquish v ترک کر دینا	remunerate v صلہ دینا
relish v لطف اندوز ہونا	renew v تجدید کرنا
relive v پھر جینا	renewal n تجدید
relocate v نقل مکانی کرنا	renounce v دستبردار ہونا
relocation n نقل مکانی	renovate v تجدید کرنا
reluctant adj متامل	renovation n تجدید
reluctantly adv ہچکچاتے ہوئے	renowned adj مشہور
rely on v انحصار کرنا	rent v کرایہ پر دینا
remain v باقی بچ جانا	rent n کرایہ
remainder n باقیات	reorganize v دوبارہ منظم کرنا
remaining adj باقی کا	repair v مرمت کرنا
remains n باقیات	reparation n مرمت
remake v دوبارہ بنانا	repatriate v وطن واپس آنا/لانا
remark v رائے دینا	repay v واپس ادا کرنا
remark n رائے	repayment n واپس ادائیگی
remarkable adj غیر معمولی	repeal v منسوخ کرنا
remarry v عقد ثانی کرنا	repeal n منسوخی
remedy v علاج کرنا	repeat v دہرانا
remedy n دو	repel v دفع کرنا
remember v یاد رکھنا	repent v پچھتانا
remembrance n یاد	repentance n پچھتاوا
remind v یاد دلانا	repetition n اعادہ
reminder n یاد دہانی	replace v بدل کا کام کرنا
remission n چھوٹ	replacement n تبدیلی
remittance n ترسیلِ زر	replay n دوبارہ بجانا/چلانا
remnant n بقیہ	replenish v پھر سے بھر دینا

R

replete *adj* لبالب	requirement *n* تقاضا
replica *n* نقشِ ثانی	rescue *v* جان بچانا
replicate *v* نقشِ ثانی تیار کرنا	rescue *n* خلاصی
reply *v* جواب دینا	research *v* تحقیق کرنا
reply *n* جواب	research *n* تحقیق
report *v* رپورٹ دینا	resemblance *n* مماثلت
report *n* روداد	resemble *v* مشابہ ہونا
reporter *n* رپورٹر	resent *v* خفا ہونا
repose *v* سستانا	resentment *n* خفگی
repose *n* استراحت	reservation *n* تحفظ
represent *v* نمائندگی کرنا	reserve *v* محفوظ کرنا
repress *v* زیر کر لینا	reservoir *n* ذخیرہ
repression *n* ضبط	reside *v* رہائش پذیر ہونا
reprieve *n* سزا کا التوا	residence *n* رہائش
reprint *v* دوبارہ چھاپنا	residue *n* تلچھٹ
reprint *n* طبع مکرر	resign *v* استعفیٰ دینا
reprisal *n* انتقام	resignation *n* استعفیٰ
reproach *v* برابھلا کہنا	resilient *adj* جفاکش
reproach *n* ڈانٹ ڈپٹ	resist *v* مزحمت کرنا
reproduction *n* تخلیق نو	resistance *n* مزاحمت
reptile *n* رینگنے والا	resolute *adj* پر عزم
republic *n* جمہوریہ	resolution *n* عزم و استقلال
repudiate *v* نامنظور کرنا	resolve *v* پکا ارادہ کرنا
repugnant *adj* بدذائقہ	resort *v* رجوع کرنا
repulse *v* پرے ہٹا دینا	resounding *adj* گونج دار
repulse *n* نامنظوری	resource *n* سہارا
repulsive *adj* دافع	respect *v* عزت کرنا
reputation *n* ساکھ	respect *n* عزت
reputedly *adv* ناموری سے	respectful *adj* باادب
request *v* استدعا کرنا	respective *adj* کھلا
request *n* التجاء	respiration *n* عمل تنفس
require *v* مطالبہ کرنا	respite *n* وقفہ برائے آرام

R

جواب دینا v **respond**	دوباره حاصل کرنا v **retrieve**
جواب n **response**	موڑنا v **return**
ذمہ داری n **responsibility**	واپسی n **return**
ذمہ دار adj **responsible**	دوباره ملاپ n **reunion**
آرام کرنا v **rest**	ظاہر کرنا **reveal**
آرام n **rest**	انکشاف کرنیوالا adj **revealing**
کمرہء آرام n **rest room**	مسرور v **revel**
ریستوران n **restaurant**	انکشاف n **revelation**
آرام دہ adj **restful**	بدلہ لینا v **revenge**
بحالی n **restitution**	بدلہ n **revenge**
بے آرام adj **restless**	آمدنی n **revenue**
بحالی n **restoration**	تکریم n **reverence**
بحال کرنا v **restore**	التائو n **reversal**
روک رکھنا v **restrain**	الٹنا n **reverse**
بندش n **restraint**	قابلِ منسوخی adj **reversible**
محدود کردینا v **restrict**	پلٹ آنا v **revert**
نتیجہ n **result**	جائزہ لینا v **review**
شروع کرنا v **resume**	جائزہ؛ معائنہ n **review**
دوباره قبضہ n **resumption**	نظر ثانی کرنا v **revise**
دوباره ابھرنا v **resurface**	نظر ثانی n **revision**
حشر n **resurrection**	احیا کرنا v **revive**
اوسان بحال کرنا v **resuscitate**	منسوخ کرنا v **revoke**
رکھنا v **retain**	باغی ہونا v **revolt**
جواب دینا v **retaliate**	بغاوت n **revolt**
مکافات n **retaliation**	بغاوت پر آمادہ adj **revolting**
احمق adj **retarded**	گھومنا v **revolve**
حافظہ n **retention**	گھومنے والا v **revolver**
ریٹائر ہونا؛ واپس جانا v **retire**	ریوو n **revue**
ریٹائرمنٹ n **retirement**	نفرت n **revulsion**
پسپا ہونا v **retreat**	اجر دینا v **reward**
پسپائی n **retreat**	اجر n **reward**
دوباره حصول n **retrieval**	صلہ دینے والا adj **rewarding**

R

rheumatism *n* گھنٹھیا	ripe *adj* پکا ہوا
rhinoceros *n* گینڈا	ripen *v* پکنا
rhyme *n* قافیہ	ripple *n* چھوٹی سی موج
rhythm *n* آہنگ	rise *iv* اٹھنا
rib *n* پسلی	risk *v* خطرہ مول لینا
ribbon *n* فیتہ	risk *n* خطرہ
rice *n* چاول	risky *adj* خطرناک
rich *adj* امیر	rite *n* رسم
rid of *iv* چھٹکارہ پانا	rival *n* رقیب
riddle *n* پہیلی	rivalry *n* رقابت
ride *iv* سوری کرنا	river *n* دریا
ridge *n* پشت	riveting *adj* جوڑنے والا
ridicule *v* تمسخر اڑانا	road *n* سڑک
ridicule *n* تمسخر	roam *v* آوارہ گردی کرنا
ridiculous *adj* مضحکہ خیز	roar *v* دھاڑنا
rifle *n* رائفل	roar *n* دھاڑ
rift *n* درز	roast *v* بھوننا
right *adv* دائیں طرف کو	roast *n* بھنا ہوا گوشت
right *adj* صحیح؛ درست	rob *v* لوٹنا
right *n* حق	robber *n* ڈاکو
rigid *adj* سخت	robbery *n* ڈاکہ
rigor *n* تندی	robe *n* جبہ
rim *n* حلقہ؛ چھلا	robust *adj* صحتمند
ring *iv* آواز پیدا ہونا	rock *n* چٹان
ring *n* حلقہ؛ چھلا	rocket *n* راکٹ
ringleader *n* سرغنہ	rocky *adj* متزلزل
rinse *v* کھنگالنا	rod *n* ڈنڈا
riot *v* بلوہ کرنا	roll *v* گھومنا
riot *n* بلوہ	romance *n* رومان
rip *v* پھاڑنا	roof *n* چھت
rip apart *v* آنسو بہانا	room *n* کمرہ؛ جگہ
rip off *v* دھوکا دینا	roomy *adj* کشادہ

R

rooster n مرغ	**ruin** v تباہ کرنا
root n جڑ	**ruin** n تباہی
rope n رسہ	**rule** v حکمرانی کرنا
rosary n گلاب کی سیج	**rule** n قاعدہ
rose n گلاب	**ruler** n حکمران؛ پیمانہ
rosy adj گلابی	**rum** n رم
rot v گلنا	**rumble** v گرجنا
rot n گند	**rumble** n کڑک
rotate v گھومنا	**rumor** n افواہ
rotation n گردش	**run** iv دوڑنا
rotten adj بوسیدہ	**run away** v بھاگ جانا
rough adj کھردرہ	**run out** v ختم کرنا/ہونا
round adj گول	**runner** n بھاگنے والا
roundup n معائنہ	**runway** n رن وے
rouse v جگانا	**rupture** n انشقاق
route n راستہ	**rupture** v پھٹنا
routine n معمول	**rural** adj دیہاتی
row v کشتی چلانا	**ruse** n چال
row n لکیر	**rush** v جلدی کرنا
rowdy adj بدتمیزشخص	**Russia** n روس
royal adj شاہی	**Russian** adj روسی
royalty n حق ملکیت	**rust** v زنگ لگنا
rub v رگڑنا	**rust** n زنگ
rubber n ربڑ	**rustic** adj دیہاتی
rubbish n فضول	**rusty** adj زنگ آلود
rubble n کاٹھ کباڑ	**ruthless** adj بے رحم
ruby n لعل	**rye** n تلخہ
rudder n پتوار	
rude adj گستاخ	
rudeness n گستاخی	
rudimentary adj بنیادی	
rug n قالین	

R

S

sabotage v سبو تاژ کرنا
sabotage n سبوتاژی
sack v لوٹ مار کرنا
sack n پوری؛ تھیلا
sacred adj مقدس
sacrifice n قربانی
sacrilege n بے حرمتی کرنا
sad adj اداس
sadden v اداس کرنا
saddle n زین
sadist n سادیت سند
sadness n اداسی
safe adj محفوظ
safeguard n حفاظت
safety n حفاظت
sail v سفر کرنا
sail n بادبان
sailboat n بادبانی کشتی
sailor n ملاح
saint n ولی
salad n سلاد
salary n تنخواہ
sale n فروخت
sale slip n فروخت کی پرچی
salesman n بیچنے والا
saliva n لعاب
salmon n سامن مچھلی
saloon n سیلون
salt n نمک

salty adj نمکین
salvage v نجات
salvation n نجات
same adj وہی
sample n نمونہ
sanctify v تطہیر کرنا
sanction v پابندی لگانا
sanction n پابندی
sanctity n حرمت
sanctuary n حرم
sand n ریت
sandal n سینڈل
sandpaper n ریگ مال
sandwich n سینڈوچ
sane adj عاقل
sanity n دانائی
sap n عرق
sap v رس نکالنا
saphire n یاقوت
sarcasm n طنز
sarcastic adj طنزیہ
satanic adj شیطانی
satellite n سیٹلائٹ
satire n طنز
satisfaction n تسلی
satisfactory adj تسلی بخش
satisfy v مطمئن کرنا
saturate v سیراب کرنا
Saturday n بفتہ
sauce n چٹنی
saucepan n کڑاہی
saucer n طشتری

S

sausage *n* ساسيج	scenario *n* منظرنامہ
savage *adj* جنگلی	scene *n* منظر؛ نظارہ
savagery *n* جنگلی پن	scenery *n* نظارہ
save *v* بچانا؛ محفوظ کرنا	scent *n* عطر
savings *n* بچت	sceptic *adj* شک پرست
savior *n* نجات دہندہ	schedule *v* جدول
savor *v* ذائقہ	schedule *n* کام کی ترتیب بنانا
saw *iv* آری سے کاٹنا	scheme *n* منصوبہ
saw *n* آری	schism *n* تفرقہ
say *iv* کہنا	scholar *n* سکالر
saying *n* کہاوت	scholarship *n* تعلیمی وظیفہ
scaffolding *n* مچان	school *n* سکول
scald *v* جلانا	science *n* سائنس
scale *v* تولنا	scientific *adj* سائنسی
scale *n* میزان؛ ترازو	scientist *n* سائنسدان
scale *n* پیمانہ	scissors *n* قینچی
scalp *n* کاسہ	scoff *v* دہتکارنا
scam *n* دھوکا	scold *v* جھڑکنا
scan *v* سکین کرنا	scolding *n* ڈانٹ ڈپٹ
scandal *n* بدنامی کا واقعہ	scooter *n* سکوٹر
scandalize *v* رسواکرنا	scope *n* گنجائش
scapegoat *n* قربانی کا بکرا	scorch *v* جھلسانا
scar *n* داغ	score *n* حاصل کردہ نمبر
scarce *adj* کمیاب	score *v* سکور کرنا
scarcely *adv* بمشکل	scorn *v* تحقیر
scarcity *n* کمیابی	scornful *adj* حقارت آمیز
scare *v* ڈرانا	scorpion *n* بچھو
scare *n* خوف	scoundrel *n* لچا
scare away *v* ڈرا کر بھگا دینا	scour *v* مانجھنا
scarf *n* سکارف	scourge *n* چابک
scary *adj* ڈرائونا	scout *n* سکائٹ
scatter *v* بکھیرنا	scramble *v* ہاتھ پائوں پر چلنا

S

scrambled *adj* خلط ملط	search *n* تلاش
scrap *n* ریزہ	seashore *n* ساحل
scrap *v* ٹکڑے کرنا	seasick *adj* سمندر زدہ
scrape *v* کھرچنا	seaside *adj* ساحل سمندر
scratch *v* کھریدنا	season *n* موسم
scream *v* چیخنا	seasonal *adj* موسمی
scream *n* چیخ	seasoning *n* گرم مسالہ
screech *v* چلّانا	seat *n* بیٹھنے کی جگہ
screen *n* پردہ؛ آڑ	seated *adj* بیٹھا ہوا
screen *v* جالی لگانا	secede *v* علیحدہ ہونا
screw *v* پیچ لگانا؛ کسنا	secluded *adj* الگ تھلگ
screw *n* پیچ	seclusion *n* خانہ نشینی
screwdriver *n* پیچ کس	second *n* سیکنڈ
script *n* رسم الخط	secondary *adj* ثانوی
scroll *n* مرغولا	secrecy *n* رازداری
scrub *v* رگڑنا	secret *n* راز
scruples *n* احساسِ اضطراب	secretary *n* سیکریٹری
scrupulous *adj* متامل	secretly *adv* رازداری سے
scrutiny *n* جانچ	sect *n* فرقہ
scuffle *n* گتھم گتھا ہونا	section *n* حصہ
sculptor *n* مجسمہ ساز	sector *n* قطعہ
sculpture *n* مورت	secure *v* محفوظ بنانا
sea *n* سمندر	secure *adj* محفوظ
seafood *n* آبی غذا	security *n* حفاظت
seagull *n* بحری بگلا	sedate *v* غیر مضطرب
seal *v* مہر لگانا	seduce *v* گمراہ کرنا
seal *n* مہر؛ سیل	seduction *n* گمرابی
seal off *v* گھیرا ڈالنا	see *iv* دیکھنا
seam *n* سلائی	seed *n* بیج
seamless *adj* بے جوڑ	seedless *adj* بے بیج
seamstress *n* درزن	seedy *adj* بیجدار
search *v* تلاش کرنا	seek *iv* طلب کرنا،رنا

S

seem *v* لگنا

see-through *adj* باریک

segment *n* حصہ

segregate *v* علیحدہ کرنا

segregation *n* تنہاسازی

seize *v* پکڑنا

seize *v* گرفت میں لینا

seizure *n* پکڑنے کا عمل

seldom *adv* کبھی کبھار

select *v* منتخب کرنا

selection *n* انتخاب

self-esteem *n* خود توقیری

self-evident *adj* واضح

self-interest *n* ذاتی مفاد

selfish *adj* خودغرض

selfishness *n* خودغرضی

self-respect *n* عزتِ نفس

sell *iv* بیچنا

seller *n* فروخت کنندہ

semblance *n* مماثلت

semester *n* سمسٹر

seminary *n* مدرسہ

senate *n* سینیٹ

senator *n* سینیٹر

send *iv* بھیجنا

sender *n* بھیجنے والا

senile *adj* بوڑھا

senior *adj* سننیر

seniority *n* تقدم

sensation *n* سنسنی

sense *v* محسوس کرنا

sense *n* حس؛ شعور

senseless *adj* بے حس

sensible *adj* سمجھدار

sensitive *adj* حساس

sentence *v* جملہ

sentence *n* سزا سنانا

sentiment *n* جذبہ

sentimental *adj* جذباتی

sentry *n* سنتری

separate *v* علیحدہ کرنا

separate *adj* علیحدہ

separation *n* علیحدگی

September *n* ستمبر

sequence *n* تسلسل

serenade *n* سریناد

serene *adj* خاموش

serenity *n* طمانیت

sergeant *n* سارجنٹ

series *n* سیریز

serious *adj* سنجیدہ

seriousness *n* سنجیدگی

sermon *n* وعظ

serpent *n* اژدھا

serum *n* سیال مادہ

servant *n* غلام

serve *v* خدمت کرنا

service *n* خدمت؛ نوکری

service *v* مدد کرنا

session *n* اجلاس

set *n* سیٹ

set *iv* مقرر کرنا

set about *v* آمادہ کرنا

set off *v* بھڑکانا

set out v سفر پر روانہ ہونا	shaken adj ہلا ہوا
set up v لگانا	shaky adj متزلزل
setting n ترتیب	shallow adj اتھلا
settle v فیصلہ کرنا؛ مقیم ہونا	sham n بناوٹی
settle down v کام میں لگ جانا	shambles n مذبح
settle for v اقرار کرنا	shame v شرمندہ کرنا
settlement n تصفیہ	shame n شرم
settler n آبادکار	shameful adj شرمناک
setup n ساخت	shameless adj بے شرم
seven adj سات	shape v شکل اختیار کرنا
seventeen adj سترہ	shape n شکل
seventh adj ساتواں	share v حصہ
seventy adj ستر	share n حصہ؛ بخرا
sever v ٹوٹنا	shareholder n حصے دار
several adj کئ	shark n شارک مچھلی
severance n قطع تعلقی	sharp adj تیز دھار؛ نوکدار
severe adj شدید؛ سخت	sharpen v تیز کرنا؛ چمکانا
severity n سختی	sharpener n سان
sew v سینا	shatter v پاش پاش کر دینا
sewage n میل کچیل	shattering adj تباہی
sewer n گند کا نکاس	shave v داڑھی بنانا
sewing n سلائی	she pro (عورت) وہ
sex n جنس	shear iv مونڈنا
sexuality n جنسی کشش	shed iv بہانا
shabby adj گندہ	sheep n بھیڑ
shabby adj گھسنا ہوا	sheets n بستری چادر
shack n کٹھیا	shelf n طاق
shackle n زنجیر	shell n خول
shade n سایہ	shellfish n پترا مچھلی
shadow n پرچھائی	shelter v پناہ دینا
shady adj سایہ دار	shelter n پناہ گاہ
shake iv ہلنا	shelves n (جمع) طاق

S

shepherd *n* گڈریا	shortcoming *n* خامی
sherry *n* شیری	shortcut *n* مختصر راستہ
shield *v* محفوظ رکھنا	shorten *v* چھوٹا کرنا
shield *n* ڈھال	shorthand *n* مختصر نویسی
shift *n* ترتیب؛ باری	shortlived *adj* کم معیا
shift *v* بدلنا؛ باری بدلنا	shortly *adv* کچھ ہی دیر میں
shine *iv* چمکنا	shorts *n* مختصر جامہ
shiny *adj* چمکدار	shortsighted *adj* کوتاہ نظر میں
ship *n* جہاز	shot *n* شاٹ؛ گولہ
shipment *n* جہازی سامان	shotgun *n* دونالی بندوق
shipwreck *n* الثنا	shoulder *n* کندھا
shipyard *n* جہازگاہ	shout *v* چلّانا
shirk *v* جی چرانا	shout *n* چیخ
shirt *n* قمیض	shouting *n* چیخنے کا عمل
shiver *v* کانپنا	shove *v* دھکیلنا
shiver *n* کپکپاہٹ	shove *n* دھکا
shock *v* صدمہ لگنا	shovel *n* بیلچ
shock *n* صدمہ؛ شدید ضرب	show *iv* دکھانا
shocking *adj* صدمہ انگیز	show off *v* دکھاوا کرنا
shoddy *adj* گھٹیا	show up *v* نگاہ میں آنا
shoe *n* جوتا	shower *n* ہلکا چھینٹا
shoelace *n* جوتے کا تسمہ	shrapnel *n* شرپنل
shoepolish *n* جوتے کی پالش	shred *v* پارہ پارہ کرنا
shoestore *n* جوتوں کی دوکان	shred *n* دھجی
shoot *iv* گولی مارنا	shrewd *adj* زیرک
shoot down *v* مار گرانا	shriek *v* چیخنا
shop *v* خریداری کرنا	shriek *n* چیخ
shop *n* دوکان	shrimp *n* جھینگا
shopping *n* خریداری	shrine *n* مزار
shore *n* ساحل	shrink *iv* سکڑنا
short *adj* چھوٹا؛ کم	shroud *n* کفن
shortage *n* کمی	shrouded *adj* ڈھکا ہوا

S

shrub *n* جھاڑی	significance *n* اہمیت
shrug *v* کندھے اچکانا	significant *adj* اہم
shudder *n* کپکی	signify *v* مطلب ہونا
shudder *v* کانپ اٹھنا	silence *n* خاموشی
shuffle *v* باری بدلنا	silence *v* خاموش کرانا
shun *v* احتراز کرنا	silent *adj* خاموش
shut *iv* بند کرنا	silhouette *n* تصویری خاکہ
shut off *v* قریب ہونا	silk *n* ریشم
shut up *v* منہ بند کرنا	silly *adj* نادان
shuttle *v* شٹل	silver *n* چاندی
shy *adj* شرمیلا	silverplated *adj* چاندی چڑھا ہوا
shyness *n* شرمابٹ	silverware *n* چاندی کے برتن
sick *adj* بیمار	similar *adj* مماثل
sicken *v* علیل کرنا	similarity *n* مماثلت
sickening *adj* بیزار کر دینے والا	simmer *v* ابالنا
sickle *n* درانتی	simple *adj* سادہ
sickness *n* بیماری	simplicity *n* سادگی
side *n* طرف	simplify *v* سادہ بنانا
sidestep *v* ایک جانب ہو جانا	simply *adv* سادہ طور پر
sidewalk *n* پگڈنڈی	simulate *v* بہروپ بھرنا
sideways *adv* آڑا ترچھا	simultaneous *adj* ہم آہنگ
siege *n* محاصرہ	sin *v* گناہ کرنا
siege *v* محاصرہ کرنا	sin *n* گناہ
sift *v* چھاننا	since *c* اس وقت سے
sigh *n* آہ	since then *adv* تب سے اب تک
sigh *v* آہ بھرنا	sincere *adj* مخلص
sight *n* بصارت	sincerity *n* اخلاص
sightseeing *v* مناظر بینی	sinful *adj* گناہ گار
sign *v* دستخط کرنا	sing *iv* گانا
sign *n* دستخط؛ نشان	singer *n* گویہ
signal *n* اشارہ	single *n* ایک شخص
signature *n* دستخط	single *adj* کنوارہ؛ اکیلا

S

singleminded *adj* یک رخا	skim *v* بالائی اتارنا
singular *adj* غیر معمولی	skin *v* کھال ادھیڑنا
sinister *adj* منحوس	skin *n* جلد
sink *iv* ڈوبنا	skinny *adj* بہت دبلا
sink in *v* مداخلت کرنا	skip *v* اچھلنا
sinner *n* گنہگار	skip *n* چھلانگ
sip *v* چسکی لینا	skirmish *n* جھڑپ
sip *n* چسکی	skirt *n* سکرٹ
sir *n* سر	skull *n* کھوپڑی
siren *n* سائرن	sky *n* آسمان
sirloin *n* پٹھ کا گوشت	skylight *n* روشن دان
sissy *adj* بزدل	slab *n* سل
sister *n* بہن	slack *adj* ڈھیلا
sister-in-law *n* بھابھی	slacken *v* سست بنانا
sit *iv* بیٹھنا	slacks *n* پاجامہ
site *n* موقع	slam *v* دے مارنا
sitting *n* بیٹھنے کا انداز	slander *n* بہتان
situated *adj* واقع	slanted *adj* ڈھلوانی وضع کا
situation *n* صورتحال	slap *n* چانٹا
six *adj* چھہ	slap *v* تھپڑ مارنا
sixteen *adj* سولہ	slash *n* ضرب
sixth *adj* چھٹا	slash *v* کاٹنا
sixty *adj* ساٹھ	slate *n* سلیٹ
sizable *adj* خاصا بڑا	slaughter *v* ذبح کرنا
size *n* قد	slaughter *n* ذبیحہ
size up *v* بھانپ جانا	slave *n* غلام
skeleton *n* ڈھانچہ	slavery *n* غلامی
skeptic *adj* شک پرست	slay *iv* مار دینا
sketch *v* خاکہ بنانا	sleazy *adj* کمزور
sketch *n* خاکہ	sleep *iv* سونا
skill *n* مہارت	sleep *n* نیند
skillful *adj* ماہر	sleeve *n* آستین

S

sleeveless *adj* بلا آستین	**smash** *v* توڑ پھوڑ دینا
sleigh *n* سلی	**smear** *n* چکنا مواد
slender *adj* دبلا پتلا	**smear** *v* چپکتی چیز مَلنا
slice *v* قاشیں بنانا	**smell** *iv* سونگھنا
slice *n* ٹکڑا	**smelly** *adj* بو دار
slide *iv* پھسلنا	**smile** *v* مسکرانا
slightly *adv* تھوڑا سا	**smile** *n* مسکراہٹ
slim *adj* دبلا پتلا؛ کم	**smith** *n* دھات گر
slip *v* پھسلنا	**smoke** *v* دھواں
slip *n* لغزش؛ غلطی	**smooth** *v* ہموار بنانا
slipper *n* سلیپر	**smooth** *adj* ہموار
slippery *adj* پھسلنی	**smoothness** *n* ہمواری
slob *adj* اجڈ	**smother** *v* دم گھٹنا
slogan *n* نعرہ	**smuggler** *n* سمگلر
slope *n* ڈھلوان	**snail** *n* گھونگھا
sloppy *adj* ڈھوانی	**snake** *n* سانپ
slot *n* جھری	**snapshot** *n* تصویر
slow *adj* آہستہ	**snare** *v* پھانسنا
slow down *v* آہستہ ہو جانا	**snare** *n* پھندا
slow motion *n* سست حرکتی	**snatch** *v* چھیننا
slowly *adv* آہستگی سے	**sneeze** *v* چھینکنا
sluggish *adj* کاہل	**sneeze** *n* چھینک
slum *n* کچی آبادی	**sniff** *v* سڑکنا
slump *v* دھڑام سے گرنا	**snitch** *v* چرا لے جانا
slump *n* دلدل	**snooze** *v* اونگھنا
slur *v* الزام تراشی کرنا	**snore** *v* خراٹے لینا
sly *adj* مکار	**snore** *n* خر خراہٹ
smack *n* چٹخارہ	**snow** *v* برفباری ہونا
smack *v* ہونٹ چٹخارنا	**snow** *n* برف
small *adj* چھوٹا	**snowfall** *n* برف باری
smallpox *n* چیچک	**snowflake** *n* برف کا گالا
smart *adj* چست	**snub** *v* حقارت برتنا

S

snub n دهتکار	**solely** adv بلا شرکتِ غیرے
soak v بھگونا	**solemn** adj سنجیدہ
soak in v ڈوبنا	**solid** adj ٹھوس
soak up v مائع جذب ہونا	**solidarity** n یکجہتی
soar v ہوا میں بلند ہونا	**solitary** adj تنہا
sob v سسکی بھرنا	**solitude** n تنہائی
sob n سسکی	**soluble** adj حل پذیر
sober adj متین	**solution** n محلول
so-called adj نام نہاد	**solve** v حل کرنا
sociable adj ملنسار	**solvent** adj محلل
socialism n اشتراکیت	**somber** adj تاریک
socialist adj اشتراکی	**some** adj کچھ
socialize v میل جول پیدا کرنا	**somebody** pro کوئی شخص
society n معاشرہ	**someday** adv کسی دن
sock n جراب	**somehow** adv کسی طرح
sod n گھاس کا تختہ	**someone** pro کوئی ایک
soda n سوڈا	**something** pro کوئی چیز
sofa n صوفا	**sometimes** adv کسی وقت
soft adj نرم	**someway** adv کسی طور
soften v نرم بنانا	**somewhat** adv کسی قدر
softly adv نرمی سے	**son** n بیٹا
softness n نرمی	**song** n گیت
soggy adj شرابور	**son-in-law** n داماد
soil n مٹی	**soon** adv جلد
soiled adj مٹی سے آلودہ	**soothe** v راحت دینا
solace n راحت	**sorcerer** n ساحر
solar adj شمسی	**sorcery** n جادوگری
solder v ٹانکا لگانا	**sore** n زخم
soldier n سپاہی	**sore** adj دکھنے والا
sold-out adj بکا ہوا	**sorrow** n غم
sole n تَلا	**sorrowful** adj غمناک
sole adj اکیل	**sorry** adj قابلِ افسوس

S

sort *n* قسم	spark off *v* تحریک دینا
sort out *v* حل کر لینا	sparkle *v* شرارے چھوڑنا
soul *n* روح	sparrow *n* چڑیا
sound *n* آواز	sparse *adj* چھدرا
sound *v* آواز پیدا کرنا	spasm *n* تشنج
sound out *v* پکارنا	speak *iv* بولنا
soup *n* شوربہ	speaker *n* مقرر؛ خطیب
sour *adj* کھٹا	spear *n* نیزہ
source *n* مآخذ	spearhead *v* نیزے کی انّی
south *n* جنوب	special *adj* خاص
southeast *n* جنوب مشرق	specialty *n* خصوصیت
southern *adj* جنوبی	species *n* نوع
southerner *n* جنوب کا باسی	specific *adj* مخصوص
southwest *n* جوب مغرب	specimen *n* نمونہ
souvenir *n* یادگار	speck *n* چھوٹا سا دھبہ
sovereign *adj* مقتدر اعلیٰ	spectacle *n* منظر
sovereignty *n* اقتدارِ اعلیٰ	spectator *n* تماشائی
soviet *adj* روسی	speculate *v* قیاس آرائی کرنا
sow *iv* بونا	speculation *n* قیاس آرائی
spa *n* معدنی چشمہ	speech *n* تقریر
space *n* جگہ	speechless *adj* گونگا
spacious *adj* کشادہ	speed *iv* رفتار تیز کرنا
spade *n* پھاوڑا	speed *n* رفتار
Spain *n* سپین	speedily *adv* تیز رفتاری سے
span *v* پاٹنا	speedy *adj* تیز رفتار
span *n* تھوڑا سا عرصہ؛ پاٹ	spell *iv* ہجے کرنا
Spaniard *n* ہسپانوی	spell *n* موسم
Spanish *adj* ہسپانوی	spelling *n* ہجے
spare *v* تھوڑا سا عرصہ؛ پاٹ	spend *iv* خرچ کرنا
spare *adj* فالتو رکھا ہوا	spending *n* خرچہ
sparingly *adv* کبھی کبھار	sperm *n* نرتولیدی مادہ
spark *n* چنگاری	sphere *n* کرّہ

S

spice *n* گرم مسالہ	**spoonful** *n* چمچ بھر
spicy *adj* مسالے دار	**sporadic** *adj* اکا دکا
spider *n* مکڑا	**sport** *n* تفریح
spiderweb *n* مکڑے کا جالا	**sportman** *n* کھلاڑی
spill *iv* گرانا	**sporty** *adj* نمائشی
spill *n* گولی	**spot** *v* دھبہ لگنا
spin *iv* گھمانا	**spot** *n* دھب
spin *iv* کاتنا	**spotless** *adj* بے نشان
spine *n* ریڑھ کی ہڈی	**spotlight** *n* دائرہء نور
spineless *adj* بے ریڑھ	**spouse** *n* خاوند یا بیوی
spinster *n* عمررسیدہ کنواری	**sprain** *v* موچ آنا
spirit *n* نفس	**sprawl** *v* بڑھانا
spiritual *adj* روحانی	**spray** *v* پھوار ڈالنا
spit *iv* تھوکنا	**spread** *iv* پھیلانا
spite *n* کینہ	**spring** *iv* جست لگانا
spiteful *adj* کینہ پرور	**spring** *n* بہار؛ جست
splash *v* چھینٹے اڑانا	**springboard** *n* تختہء جست
splendid *adj* شاندار	**sprinkle** *v* چھڑکنا
splendor *n* درخشانی	**sprout** *v* پھوٹنا
splint *n* چپٹی کھپچی	**spruce up** *v* بنائو سنگھار کرنا
splinter *v* ٹکڑے ٹکڑے کرنا	**spur** *v* ایڑ
split *n* ٹوٹ پھوٹ	**spur** *n* ایڑ؛ مہمیز
split *iv* پھٹنا	**spy** *v* جاسوسی کرنا
split up *v* تقسیم کرنا	**spy** *n* جاسوس
spoil *v* بگاڑنا	**squalid** *adj* غلیظ
spoils *n* مالِ غنیمت	**squander** *v* فضول خرچ کرنا
sponge *n* اسفنج	**square** *adj* مربع
sponsor *n* ضامن	**square** *n* مربع
spontaneous *adj* خود بخود	**squash** *v* کچلنا
spooky *adj* آسیب زدہ	**squeak** *v* چیخنا
spool *n* پھرکی	**squeaky** *adj* چلابٹ والا
spoon *n* چمچ	**squeamish** *adj* زیادہ محتاط

S

squeeze v نچوڑنا	stamp v زمین پر پائوں مارنا
squeeze in v دبائو ڈالنا	stamp n مہر
squeeze up v استحصال	stamp out v جڑ سے اکھاڑنا
squid n قیر ماہی	stampede n بھگدڑ
squirrel n گلہری	stand iv کھڑے ہونا
stab n چبھن	stand n اقامت
stability n قیام پذیری	stand for v علامت ہونا
stable adj مستحکم	stand out v باہر کو نل آنا
stable n اصطبل	stand up v سیدھا کھڑے ہونا
stack v انبار یا ڈھیر لگانا	standard n معیار
stack n ٹال	standardize v معیاری بنانا
staff n عصا	standing n مقام
stage n مرحلہ؛ درجہ	standpoint n نقطہء نظر
stage n سٹیج	standstill adj بے حرکت
stage v ڈرامہ بنانا	staple n قلابہ
stagger v لڑکھڑانا	stapler n جکڑ بند
staggering adj لڑکھڑاتا ہوا	star n ستارہ
stagnant adj بے حرکت	starch n نشاستہ
stagnation n جمود	starchy adj کلف دار
stain v دھبہ لگنا	stare v گھورنا
stain n دھبہ	stark adj محض
stair n سیڑھی	start v شروع کرنا
staircase n سیڑھیاں	start n آغاز
stairs n سیڑھیاں	startle v چونکا دینا
stake n کھونٹی؛ کِلا	startled adj حیرت زدہ
stake v دائو پر لگانا	starvation n فاقہ
stale adj باسی	starve v فاقے کرنا
stalemate n تعطل	state n حالت؛ کیفیت
stalk v پیچھے چلنا	state v بیان کرنا
stall n تھان	statement n بیان
stall v سٹال لگانا	station n قیام
stammer v ہکلانا	stationary adj ساکن

S

stationery *n* سامانِ تحریر	**sternly** *adv* کرختگی سے
statistic *n* شماریات کا جزو	**stew** *n* سٹُو
statue *n* مجسمہ	**stewardess** *n* داروغہ عورت
status *n* مقام؛ رتبہ	**stick** *n* چھڑی
statute *n* قانون	**stick** *iv* چبھونا
staunch *adj* پکا وفادار	**stick around** *v* انتظار کرنا
stay *v* ٹھہرنا	**stick to** *v* لگے رہنا
stay *n* قیام	**sticker** *n* چسپاں ہو جانیوال
steady *adj* جما ہوا؛ مستحکم	**sticky** *adj* چمٹنے والا
steak *n* گوشت کا قتلا	**stiff** *adj* کرخت
steal *iv* چرانا	**stiffen** *v* اکڑانا
steam *n* بھاپ	**stiffness** *n* سختی
steel *n* فولاد	**stifle** *v* دم گھٹنا
steep *adj* ڈھلوان	**stifling** *adj* دم گھوٹ
stem *n* تنا	**still** *adj* ساکن
stem *v* مطلب ہونا	**still** *adv* ابھی تک
stench *n* سڑاند	**stimulant** *n* محرک
step *n* قدم؛ چال	**stimulate** *v* تحریک دینا
step down *v* کم ہونا	**stimulus** *n* مہیج
step out *v* متروک ہو جانا	**sting** *iv* ڈنک مارنا
step up *v* بڑھانا	**sting** *n* ڈنک؛ دکھن
stepbrother *n* سوتیلا بھائی	**stinging** *adj* کاٹنے والا
step-by-step *adv* درجہ بہ درجہ	**stingy** *adj* نہایت کجوس
stepdaughter *n* سوتیلی بیٹی	**stink** *iv* بدبو خارج کرنا
stepfather *n* سوتیلا باپ	**stink** *n* قابلِ نفرت بدبو
stepladder *n* گھوڑی	**stinking** *adj* بدبو دار
stepmother *n* سوتیلی ماں	**stir** *v* ملانا؛ حل کرنا
stepsister *n* سوتیلی بہن	**stir up** *v* ملانا
stepson *n* سوتیلا بیٹا	**stitch** *v* ٹانکنا
sterile *adj* بَنجَر	**stitch** *n* ٹانکا
stern *n* دنبال	**stock** *v* ذخیرہ کرنا
stern *adj* کرخت	**stock** *n* ذخیرہ؛ آلات

S

stocking n موزہ	strawberry n سٹرابری
stockpile n انبار یا ڈھیر لگانا	stray adj بھٹکا ہوا
stockroom n گودام	stray v آوارہ گردی کرنا
stomach n معدہ	stream n ندی؛ چشمہ
stone n پتھر	street n گلی
stone v پتھر مارنا	streetcar n ٹرام
stool بے بازو تپائی	streetlight n سڑک پر لگی بتی
stop v روکنا	strength n طاقت
stop n ٹھہراؤ	strengthen v طاقتور بنانا
stop by مختصر دورہ کرنا	strenuous adj مستعد
stop over v وقفہ کرنا	stress n دباؤ؛ شدت
storage n ذخیرہ خانہ	stressful adj تاکیدی
store v ذخیرہ کرنا	stretch n وسعت
store n دوکان	stretch v پھیلانا
stork n سارس	stretcher n سٹریچر
storm n طوفان	strict adj سخت
stormy adj طوفانی	strife n لمبا قدم
story n کھانی	strike n چوٹ
stove n چولھا	strike iv ٹکرانا؛ چوٹ لگانا
straight adj سیدھا	striking adj زور دار
straighten out پکا کرنا	string n ڈوری؛ رسی
strain v زور لگانا	stringent adj مجبور کن
strain n دباؤ	strip n کترن
strained adj کھنچا ہوا	strip v چھین لینا
strainer n چھلنی	stripe n دھاری
strait n آبنائے	striped adj دھاری دار
strange adj عجیب	strive iv کوشش کرنا
stranger n اجنبی	stroke n ضرب؛ دھکا
strangle v گھوٹنا	stroll v مٹر گشت کرنا
strap n پٹی	strong adj مضبوط
strategy n حکمتِ عملی	structure n ڈھانچہ
straw n تنکا	struggle v جدوجہد کرنا

S

struggle *n* جدوجہد	**subsidy** *n* اعانت
stub *n* درخت کا ٹھنٹھہ	**subsist** *v* موجود پونا
stubborn *adj* ضدی	**substance** *n* وجود
student *n* طالب علم	**substandard** *adj* معیار سے کم
study *v* مطالعہ	**substitute** *v* بطور متبادل لگانا
stuff *n* مواد؛ مادہ	**substitute** *n* متبادل چیز
stuff *v* ٹھوسنا	**subtitle** *n* ضمنی عنوان
stuffing *n* بھرائی	**subtle** *adj* دقیق
stuffy *adj* حبس وال	**subtract** *v* تفریق کرنا
stumble *v* ٹھوکر کھا جانا	**subtraction** *n* تفریق
stun *v* حیرت زدہ کرنا	**suburb** *n* مضافات
stunning *adj* حیرت انگیز	**subway** *n* زمین دوز برقی ریل
stupendous *adj* حیران کن	**succeed** *v* کامیاب ہونا
stupid *adj* بے وقوف	**success** *n* کامیابی
stupidity *n* بے وقوفی	**successful** *adj* کامیاب
sturdy *adj* مضبوط	**successor** *n* جا نشین
stutter *v* ہکلانا	**succulent** *adj* رسدار
style *n* انداز	**succumb** *v* مغلوب ہو جانا
subdue *v* زیر کر لینا	**such** *adj* ایسا
subdued *adj* مغلوب	**suck** *v* چوسنا
subject *v* تابع بنانا	**sucker** *adj* چوسنے والا
subject *n* موضوع؛ رعایا	**sudden** *adj* اچانک
sublime *adj* ارفع	**suddenly** *adv* اچانک طور سے
submerge *v* غرقآب کرنا	**sue** *v* حق کے مقدمہ کرنا
submissive *adj* اطاعت شعار	**suffer** *v* مبتلا ہونا
submit *v* کچھ پیش کرنا	**suffer from** *v* بیماری
subpoena *n* پروانہء حاضری	**suffering** *n* مصیبت
subscribe *v* چندہ دینا	**sufficient** *adj* کافی
subscription *n* چندہ	**suffocate** *v* گلاگھونٹنا
subsequent *adj* متاخر	**sugar** *n* چینی
subsidiary *adj* معانت سے متعلق	**suggest** *v* تجویز کرنا
subsidize *v* ارزاں مہیا کرنا	**suggestion** *n* تجویز

S

suggestive adj مجوز	**supervision** n نگرانی
suicide n خودکشی	**supper** n شام کا کھانا
suit n جوڑا	**supple** adj لچک دار
suitable adj موزوں	**supplier** n مہیا کرنے والا
suitcase n کپڑوں والا صندوق	**supplies** n لوازمات
sullen adj روکھا	**supply** v رسد
sulphur n گندھک	**support** v سہارا دینا
sum n کل مقدار	**supporter** n حامی
sum up v ماحصل نکالنا	**suppose** v فرض کرنا
summarize v اختصار کرنا	**supposing** c بشرطیکہ
summary n خلاصہ	**supposition** n مفروضہ
summer n موسمِ گرما	**suppress** v دبانا
summit n چوٹی	**supremacy** n بالا دستی
sumptuous adj گراں قیمت	**supreme** adj بالادست
sun n سورج	**surcharge** n اضافی محصول
sunburn n دھوپ جلن	**sure** adj یقینی
Sunday n اتوار	**surely** adv یقینی طور پر
sundown n غروبِ آفتاب	**surface** n سطح
sunglasses n دھوپ چشمہ	**surge** n تموج
sunken adj دھنسا ہوا	**surgeon** n جراح
sunny adj روشن	**surname** n نام کا ثانوی جزو
sunrise n طلوعِ آفتاب	**surpass** v آگے نکل جانا
sunset n غروبِ آفتاب	**surplus** n فاضل رقم یا چیز
superb adj شان دا	**surprise** v حیران کر دینا
superfluous adj فالتو	**surprise** n حیرت
superior adj برتر	**surrender** v تسلیم کر لینا
superiority n برتری	**surrender** n دست برداری
supermarket n بڑی بازار	**surround** v گھیرا ڈالنا
superpower n بڑی طاقت	**surroundings** n گردونواح
supersede v ہٹا کرجگہ لینا	**surveillance** n نگرانی
superstition n توہم	**survey** n معائنہ
supervise v نگرانی کرنا	**survival** n بقا

S

survive v زندہ بچ رہنا	**swell** iv سوج جانا
survivor n باقی ماندہ	**swelling** n سوجن
susceptible adj اثرپذیر	**swift** adj تیز رو
suspect v شبہ کرنا	**swim** iv تیرنا
suspect n مشتبہ شخص	**swimmer** n تیراک
suspend v معطل کر دینا	**swimming** n تیراکی
suspenders n پتلون کے تسمے	**swindle** v فریب دینا
suspense n شش و پنج	**swindle** n فریب
suspension n تعطل	**swindler** n ٹھگ
suspicion n شبہ	**swing** iv جھلانا
suspicious adj مشکوک	**swing** n جھولا؛ خمدار رستہ
sustain v سہارنا	**Swiss** adj سوئٹزرلینڈ کا
sustenance n معاش	**switch** v پٹائی کرنا
swallow v نگلنا	**switch** n سوئچ
swamp n دلدل	**switch off** v قریب
swan n راج ہنس	**switch on** v کھولنا
swap v تبادلہ کرنا	**Switzerland** n سوئٹزرلینڈ
swap n تبادلہ	**swivel** v چول چھلا
swarm n کیڑوں کا لشکر	**swollen** adj سوجا ہوا
sway v جھولنا	**sword** n تلوار
swear iv قسم کھانا	**syllable** n ہجا
sweat n پسینہ	**symbol** n علامت
sweat v پسینہ آنا	**symbolic** adj علامتی
sweater n سویٹر	**symmetry** n تناسب
Sweden n سویڈن	**sympathize** v ہمدردی کرنا
Sweedish adj سویڈنی	**sympathy** n ہمدردی
sweep iv جھاڑو دینا	**symphony** n سمفونی
sweet adj میٹھا	**symptom** n علامت
sweeten v میٹھا کرنا	**synagogue** n صومعہ
sweetheart n محبوبہ	**synchronize** v ہم وقت ہونا
sweetness n مٹھاس	**synonym** n مترادف
sweets n مٹھائیاں	**synthesis** n ترکیب

S

syphilis n آتشک

syringe n پچکاری

syrup n شربت

system n نظام

systematic adj نظام کا حامل

T

table n میز

tablecloth n میزپوش

tablespoon n کھانے کا چمچ

tablet n گولی

tack n کوکا؛ میخ

tackle v نمٹنا

tact n تدبیر

tactful adj با تدبیر

tactical adj تدبیرائی

tactics n فنِ تدبیرات

tag n دھجی

tail n دم

tail v ٹانکنا

tailor n درزی

tainted adj داغدار

take iv لینا

take apart v تباہ کر دینا

take away v ساتھ لے جانا

take in v آنے دینا

take off v اتارنا

take out v نچوڑنا

take over v غلبہ پا لینا

tale n کہانی

talent n فطانت

talk v باتیں کرنا

talkative adj باتونی

tall adj لمبا

tame v سدھانا

tangent n مماسی

tangerine n طنجوی نارنگی

tangible adj محسوس باللمس

tangle n الجھنا؛ الجھانا

tank n حوض؛ تالاب

tantrum n غضب

tap n ٹونٹی

tap into v بے دھڑک کودنا

tape n فیتہ؛ ٹیپ

tape recorder n ٹیپ ریکارڈر

tapestry n پھلکاری

tar n تارکول

tarantula n ٹارنٹو کی مکڑی

tardy adv دیر سے آنیوالا

target n ہدف

tariff n نرخ

tarnish v داغدار کرنا

tart n ترش ذائقہ

tartar n تلچھٹ

task n کام؛ مہم

taste v ذائقہ چکھنا

taste n ذائقہ؛ ذوق

tasteful adj خوش ذائقہ

tasteless adj بے ذائقہ

S
T

tasty *adj* مزیدار	**temperature** *n* درجہ حرارت
tavern *n* مے کدہ	**tempest** *n* طوفان
tax *n* ٹیکس	**temple** *n* مندر
tea *n* چائے	**temporary** *adj* عارضی
teach *iv* پڑھانا	**tempt** *v* تحریص دینا
teacher *n* استاذ	**temptation** *n* تحریص
team *n* ٹیم	**tempting** *adj* لبھانے والا
teapot *n* چائے دانی	**ten** *adj* دس
tear *iv* آنسو بہانا؛ پھاڑنا	**tenacity** *n* ہٹ دھرمی
tear *n* آنسو	**tenant** *n* کرایہ دار
tearful *adj* اشکباری	**tendency** *n* میلان
tease *v* چھیڑنا	**tender** *adj* نازک؛ گداز
teaspoon *n* چائے کا چمچ	**tenderness** *n* ملائمت؛ نازکی
technical *adj* تکنیکی	**tennis** *n* ٹینس
technicality *n* تکنیکیت	**tenor** *n* روش؛ ڈھب
technician *n* تکنیک کار	**tense** *adj* تنا ہوا
technique *n* تکنیک	**tension** *n* تنائو؛ کھنچائو
technology *n* ٹکنالوجی	**tent** *n* خیمہ
tedious *adj* اجیرن	**tentacle** *n* شاخک
tedium *n* تھکاوٹ	**tentative** *adj* عارضی
teenager *n* نوخیز	**tenth** *n* دسواں
teeth *n* دانت	**tenuous** *adj* پتلا؛ نازک
telegram *n* تار	**tepid** *adj* نیم گرم
telepathy *n* خیال رسانی	**term** *n* مدت؛ معیاد
telephone *n* ٹیلی فون	**terminate** *v* ختم کرنا
telescope *n* دور بین	**terminology** *n* اصطلاحیات
televise *v* دور نمائی کرنا	**termite** *n* دیمک
television *n* ٹیلی وژن	**terms** *n* شرائط
tell *iv* بتانا	**terrace** *n* چبوترا
teller *n* بتانے والا	**terrain** *n* قطعہ زمین
telling *adj* موءثر؛ کارگر	**terrestrial** *adj* ارضی
temper *n* ذہنی اطمنان	**terrible** *adj* خوفناک

terrific adj نہایت عمدہ	**there** adv وہاں
terrify v خوفزدہ کرنا	**therefore** adv اس لیے
terrifying adj ڈرانے والا	**thermometer** n تپش پیما
territory n علاقہ	**thermostat** n تھرمو سٹیٹ
terror n دہشت	**these** adj (جمع) یہ
terrorism n دہشت گردی	**thesis** n مقالہ
terrorist n دہشت گرد	**they** pro وہ لوگ
terrorize v دہشت زدہ کرنا	**thick** adj موٹا
terse adj عمدہ اور جامع	**thicken** v موٹا بنانا
test v آزمائش کرنا	**thickness** n موٹائی
test n آزمائش	**thief** n چور
testament n انجیل	**thigh** n ران
testify v گواہی دینا	**thin** adj پتلا؛ باریک
testimony n حلفی شہادت	**thing** n چیز؛ شے
text n متن	**think** iv سوچنا
textbook n نصابی کتاب	**thinly** adv باریکی سے
texture n بناوٹ؛ بافت	**third** adj تیسرا
thank v شکریہ ادا کرنا	**thirst** v پیاس
thankful adj ممنون	**thirsty** adj پیاسا
thanks n شکریہ	**thirteen** adj تیرہ
that adj وہ	**thirty** adj تیس
thaw v پگھلنا؛ گھلنا	**this** adj (واحد) یہ
thaw n پگھلاہٹ	**thorn** n کانٹا
theater n تھیٹر	**thorny** adj کانٹے دار
theft n چوری	**thorough** adj مکمل
theme n موضوع؛ مطلب	**those** adj (جمع) وہ
themselves pro وہ آپ (جمع)	**though** c اگرچہ؛ گرچہ
then adv تب؛ پھر	**thought** n سوچ
theologian n دینی عالم	**thoughtful** adj متفکر
theology n الہیات	**thousand** adj ہزار
theory n نظریہ	**thread** n دھاگہ
therapy n معالجہ؛ علاج	**threat** n دھمکی

T

threaten v دھمکی دینا	tidy adj صاف ستھرا
three adj تین	tie v باندھنا؛ جوڑنا
thresh v غلے کو گابنا	tie n نکٹائی
threshold n دہلیز	tiger n شیر
thrifty adj کفایت شعار	tight adj چست
thrill v جوش پیدا کرنا	tighten v کس دینا
thrill n جوش	tile n کھپر
thrive v فروغ پانا	till adv تاوقتیکہ
throat n گلہ	till v کاشتکاری کرنا
throb n دھڑکن	tilt v جھکانا
throb v دھڑکنا؛ پھڑکنا	timber n لکڑی؛ کاٹھ
thrombosis n خون بستگی	time n وقت؛ دور
throne n تختِ شاہی	timeless adj ابدی؛ لازماں
throng n مجمع؛ ہجوم	timely adj بر وقت
through pre آرپار	timetable n اوقات نامہ
throw iv پھینکنا	timid adj ڈرپوک
throw away v ترک کرنا	timidity n ڈرپوکی
throw up v قے آنا	tin n ٹین کا ڈبہ
thug n ٹھگ؛ بدمعاش	tiny adj چھوٹا؛ حقیر
thumb n انگوٹھا	tip n نوک
thumbtack n چپٹی کیل	tired adj تھکا ہوا
thunder n گھن گرج	tiredness n تھکن
thunderbolt n بجلی کا کڑکا	tireless adj ان تھک
thunderstorm n طوفانِ برق و باد	tiresome adj تھکا دینے والا
Thursday n جمعرات	tissue n ریشہ؛ بافت
thus adv اس طرح	title n عنوان؛ موضوع
thwart v آڑا ترچھا گزارنا	to pre تک؛ کو
thyroid n کنٹھ	toad n مینڈک
tickle v گدگدانا	toast v جام نوش کرنا
tickle n گدگدی	toast n توس
tidal wave n مدوجزری موج	tobacco n تمباکو
tide n جواربھاٹا	today adv آج

toddler n شیرخوار	**torrent** n تیز دھار
toe n پائوں کی انگلی	**torrid** adj حار
together adv اکٹھے	**torso** n انسانی دھڑ
toil v مشقت کرنا	**tortoise** n کچھوا
toilet n سنگھار	**torture** v تشدد کرنا
token n نشانی	**torture** n تشدد
tolerable adj قابلِ برداشت	**toss** v اچھالنا
tolerance n برداشت	**total** adj کامل
tolerate v برداشت کرنا	**totalitarian** adj ہمہ گیر
toll v جمع کرنا	**totality** n کلیت
tomato n ٹماٹر	**touch** n لمس
tomb n مقبرہ؛ مزار	**touch** v چھونا
tombstone n لوحِ مزار	**touch on** معمولی ذکر کرنا
tomorrow adv کل	**touch up** درستی کرنا
ton n ٹن	**touching** adj متاثر کن
tone n آواز؛ صدا	**tough** adj جفاکش
tongs n چمٹا؛ چمٹی	**toughen** v سخت ہونا
tongue n زبان	**tour** n دورہ
tonic n مقوی	**tourism** n سیاحت
tonight adv آج کی رات	**tourist** n سیرو سیاحت
tonsil n ٹانسل	**tournament** n ٹورنامنٹ
too adv بھی	**tow** v کھینچن
tool n آلہ	**tow truck** n کھینچ گاڑی
tooth n دانت	**towards** pre کی طرف
toothache n دانت درد	**towel** n تولیہ
toothpick n خلال	**tower** n برج
top n چوٹی	**towering** adj بہت اونچا
topic n موضوع	**town** n شہر؛ قصبہ
topple v شکست دینا	**town hall** n ٹائون ہال
torch n مشعل	**toxic** adj زہریلا
torment v اذیت دینا	**toxin** n ٹاکسن
torment n اذیت	**toy** n کھلونا

T

trace v	سراغ
track n	راستہ
track v	کھوج لگانا
traction n	کشش
tractor n	ٹریکٹر
trade n	تجارت
trade v	تجارت کرنا
trademark n	مارکہ
trader n	تاجر
tradition n	روایت
traffic n	ٹریفک
tragedy n	المیہ
tragic adj	المناک
trail v	کھینچنا
trail n	پگڈنڈی
trailer n	تھیلا؛ ٹریلر
train n	ریل گاڑی
train v	تربیت کرنا
trainee n	زیرِ تربیت شخص
trainer n	تربیت کرنیوالا
training n	تربیت
trait n	خصلت
traitor n	غدار
trajectory n	خطِ حرکت
tram n	ٹرام گاڑی
trample v	روندنا
trance n	وجد
tranquility n	سکون
transaction n	سودا
transcend v	بڑھ جانا
transcribe v	نقل کرنا
transfer v	منتقل کرنا

transfer n	انتقال
transform v	ہیئت بدلنا
transformation n	آواگون
transient adj	مستعل
transit n	گزر
transition n	عبور
translate v	ترجمہ کرنا
translator n	مترجم
transmit v	منتقل کرنا
transparent adj	شفاف
transport v	ڈھونا
trap n	پھندہ
trash n	ردی
trash can n	ردی کی ٹوکری
traumatize v	زخم پہنچانا
travel v	سفر کرنا
traveler n	مسافر
tray n	طشت
treacherous adj	دغاباز
treachery n	غداری
tread iv	چلنا
treason n	غداری
treasure n	خزانہ
treasurer n	خزانچی
treat v	سلوک کرنا
treat n	ضیافت؛ سلوک
treatment n	معالجہ؛ برتاؤ
treaty n	معاہدہ
tree n	درخت
tremble v	کانپنا
tremendous adj	بہت بڑا
tremor n	لرزش

T

trench n کھائی	**trousers** n پاجامہ
trend n میلان	**trout** n ٹرائوٹ
trendy adj جھکائو	**truce** n عارضی صلح
trespass v تجاوز کرنا	**truck** n چھکڑا
trial n آزمائش؛ جانچ	**trucker** n ٹرک والا
triangle n مثلث	**trumped-up** adj گھڑی ہوئی
tribe n قبیلہ	**trumpet** n نقیری
tribulation n مصیبت	**trunk** n سونڈ
tribunal n ٹریبیونل	**trust** v اعتبار کرنا
tribute n نذر	**trust** n اعتبار
trick v چالیں چلنا	**truth** n سچ
trick n کرتب؛ دائو	**truthful** adj سچا
trickle v رسنا	**try** v آزمانا
tricky adj چالباز	**tub** n ٹب
trigger v بندوق چلا دینا	**tuberculosis** n تپ دق
trigger n لبلبی	**Tuesday** n منگل
trim v تراشنا	**tuition** n ٹیوشن
trimmings n درستی	**tulip** n گلِ لالہ
trip n پھیرا؛ سیر	**tumble** v گرپڑنا
trip v دورہ کرنا	**tummy** n پیٹ
triple adj تگنا	**tumor** n ٹیومر
tripod n تپائی	**tumult** n بلوا
triumph n فتح	**tumultuous** adj مضطرب
triumphant adj فتحیاب	**tune** n تان
trivial adj غیر اہم	**tune** v سُر ملانا
trivialize v بے قدر بنانا	**tune up** v نظر ثانی کرنا
trolley n ٹرالی	**tunic** n پیراہن
troop n دستہ	**tunnel** n سرنگ
trophy n ٹرافی	**turbine** n ٹربائن
trouble n پریشانی	**turbulence** n ہیجان
trouble v تکلیف میں ہونا	**turf** n دوب تختہ
troublesome adj تکلیف دہ	**Turk** adj تُرک

Turkey *n* ترکی

turmoil *n* کھلبلی

turn *n* موڑ

turn *v* مڑنا

turn back *v* موڑنا

turn down *v* رد کر دینا

turn in *v* گھسنانا

turn off *v* نل بند کرنا

turn on *v* شروع کرنا

turn out *v* نکال دینا

turn over *v* الٹنا پلٹنا

turn up *v* تہ کرنا

turret *n* مینار

turtle *n* کچھوا

tusk *n* ہاتھی دانت

tutor *n* ٹیوٹر

tweezers *n* موچنا

twelfth *adj* بارہواں

twelve *adj* بارہ

twentieth *adj* بیسواں

twenty *adj* بیس

twice *adv* دو بار

twilight *n* دھندلکا

twin *n* جڑواں

twinkle *v* ٹمٹمانا

twist *v* مروڑنا

twist *n* بل؛ چکر

twisted *adj* مڑا ہوا

twister *n* گردباد

two *adj* دو

tycoon *n* بہت بڑا تاجر

type *n* مثل؛ نمونہ؛ ٹانپ

type *v* ٹائپ کرنا

typical *adj* مخصوص

tyranny *n* جبر

tyrant *n* جابر

U

ugliness *n* بد صورتی

ugly *adj* بد صورت

ulcer *n* ناسور

ultimate *adj* قطعی

ultimatum *n* التی میٹم

ultrasound *n* الٹراسائونڈ

umbrella *n* چھتری

umpire *n* امپائر

unable *adj* ناقابل

unanimity *n* اتفاقِ رائے

unarmed *adj* غیر مسلح

unassuming *adj* سیدھا سادہ

unattached *adj* غیر منسلک

unavoidable *adj* ناگزیر

unaware *adj* بے خبر

unbearable *adj* ناقابلِ برداشت

unbeatable *adj* ناقابلِ شکست

unbelievable *adj* ناقابلِ یقین

unbiased *adj* بے تعصب

unbroken *adj* سالم

unbutton *v* بٹن کھولنا

uncertain *adj* غیر یقینی	**uneducated** *adj* ان پڑھ
uncle *n* ماموں	**unemployed** *adj* بے روزگار؛ بے کار
uncomfortable *adj* بے آرام	**unemployment** *n* بے کاری
uncommon *adj* نادر	**unending** *adj* نہ ختم ہونے والا
unconscious *adj* بے ہوش	**unequal** *adj* غیر مساوی
uncover *v* ننگا کرنا	**unequivocal** *adj* غیر مبہم
undecided *adj* غیر طے شدہ	**uneven** *adj* نابموار
undeniable *adj* ناقابل تردید	**uneventful** *adj* سپاٹ
under *pre* نیچے	**unexpected** *adj* غیر متوقع
undercover *adj* بھیدی	**unfailing** *adj* یقینی
underdog *n* مغلوب	**unfair** *adj* نا واجب
undergo *v* جھیلنا	**unfairly** *adv* بے انصافی سے
underground *adj* زیر زمین	**unfairness** *n* بے انصافی
underline *v* خط کشیدہ کرنا	**unfaithful** *adj* بے وفا
underlying *adj* اساسی	**unfamiliar** *adj* غیر مانوس
undermine *v* سرنگ بنانا	**unfasten** *v* کھولنا
underneath *pre* نیچے	**unfavorable** *adj* نامساعد
understand *v* سمجھنا	**unfit** *adj* ناقابل
understanding *n* سمجھ	**unfold** *v* کھولنا
undertake *v* بیڑا اٹھانا	**unforeseen** *adj* غیر متوقع
underwear *n* زیر جامہ	**unforgettable** *adj* ناقابلِ فراموش
underwrite *v* ضمانت دینا	**unfounded** *adj* بے بنیاد
undeserved *adj* ناحق	**unfriendly** *adj* بے مروت
undesirable *adj* ناپسندیدہ	**unfurnished** *adj* غیر آراستہ
undisputed *adj* مسلّم	**ungrateful** *adj* ناشکرگزار
undo *v* کالعدم کرنا	**unhappiness** *n* بد بختی
undoubtedly *adv* بلاشبہ	**unhappy** *adj* ناخوش
undress *v* لباس اتارنا	**unharmed** *adj* بے چوٹ
undue *adj* ناحق؛ ناواجب	**unhealthy** *adj* غیر صحتمند
unearth *v* کھودنا	**unheard-of** *adj* نا شنیدہ
uneasiness *n* بے چینی	**unhurt** *adj* بے چوٹ
uneasy *adj* بے چین	**unification** *n* وحدت

U

uniform n بموار	**unpopular** adj غیر مقبول
uniformity n یکسانیت	**unpredictable** adj ناقابل پیش گوئی
unify v ایک کرنا	**unprofitable** adj غیر نفع بخش
unilateral adj یک طرفہ	**unprotected** adj غیر محفوظ
union n اتحاد	**unravel** v سلجھانا
unique adj یکتا	**unreal** adj غیر حقیقی
unit n اکائی	**unreasonable** adj ناروا
unite v متحد کرنا	**unrelated** adj غیر متعلقہ
unity n اتحاد	**unreliable** adj ناقابل بھروسہ
universal adj آفاقی	**unrest** n تشویش
universe n کائنات	**unsafe** adj غیر محفوظ
university n یونیورسٹی	**unselfish** adj بے غرض
unjust adj غیر منصفانہ	**unspeakable** adj نا گفتہ بہ
unjustified adj ناانصافی پر مبنی	**unstable** adj ناپائدار
unknown adj مانوس	**unsteady** adj متزلزل
unlawful adj غیر قانونی	**unsuccessful** adj ناکامیاب
unleash v زنجیر کھول دین	**unsuitable** adj نامناسب
unless c تاوقتیکہ	**unthinkable** adj ناقابلِ تصور
unlike adj مختلف	**untie** v کھولنا
unlikely adj خلافِ قیاس	**until** pre حتٰی کہ
unlimited adj لا محدود	**untimely** adj بے وقت
unload v ہلکا کرنا	**untouchable** adj اچھوت
unlock v تالا کھولنا	**untrue** adj جھوٹا
unlucky adj بد قسمت	**unusual** adj انوکھا
unmarried adj غیر شادی شدہ	**unveil** v پردہ اٹھانا
unmask v نقاب اتارنا	**unwillingly** adv نارضامندی سے
unmistakable adj بے چوک	**unwind** v بل کھولنا
unnecessary adj غیر ضروری	**unwise** adj بے عقل
unoccupied adj غیر آباد	**upbringing** n پرورش
unpack v بنڈل سے نکالنا	**upcoming** adj آمدہ
unpleasant adj ناخوشگوار	**update** v تازہ ترین بنانا
unplug v ڈاٹ اتارنا	**upgrade** v درجہ بڑھانا

U

upheaval _n_ انتشار	usefulness _n_ افادیت
uphill _adv_ مشکل	useless _adj_ بے کار
uphold _v_ اٹھائے رکھنا	user _n_ صارف
upholstery _n_ گدیاں وغیرہ	usher _n_ حاجب
upkeep _n_ نگہداشت	usual _adj_ معمول کا
upon _pre_ اوپر	usurp _v_ دبا لینا
upper _adj_ بالائی	utensil _n_ برتن
upright _adj_ عمودی	uterus _n_ بچہ دانی
uprising _n_ بغاوت	utilize _v_ فائدہ اٹھانا
uproar _n_ ہنگامہ	utmost _adj_ حتی المقدور
uproot _v_ چننا	utter _v_ آواز نکالنا
upset _v_ اداس	
upside-down _adv_ درہم برہم	
upstairs _adv_ بالائی منزل	
uptight _adj_ پریشان حال	
up-to-date _adj_ تازہ ترین	
upturn _n_ الٹا دینا	
upwards _adv_ اوپر کی جانب	
urban _adj_ شہری	vacancy _n_ خالی جگہ
urge _n_ ترغیب	vacant _adj_ خالی
urge _v_ دھکیلنا	vacate _v_ خالی کرنا
urgency _n_ تقاضا	vacation _n_ تعطیل
urgent _adj_ فوری	vaccinate _v_ ٹیکا لگانا
urinate _v_ پیشاب کرنا	vaccine _n_ ویکسین
urine _n_ پیشاب	vacillate _v_ لڑکھڑانا
urn _n_ پھول دان	vagrant _n_ خانہ بدوش
us _pro_ ہمیں	vague _adj_ مبہم
usage _n_ استعمال	vain _adj_ کھوکھلا
use _v_ ملازم رکھنا	vainly _adv_ گھمنڈ سے
use _n_ استعمال	valiant _adj_ بہادر
used to _adj_ عادی	valid _adj_ درست
useful _adj_ مفید	validate _v_ جواز بنانا

validity *n* جواز	velvet *n* مخمل
valley *n* وادی	venerate *v* تعظیم دینا
valuable *adj* قابلِ قدر	vengeance *n* مکافات
value *n* قدر	venison *n* ہرن کا گوشت
valve *n* صمام؛ والو	venom *n* زہر
vampire *n* چمگادڑ	vent *n* نکاس
van *n* گاڑی	ventilate *v* تازہ ہوا آنے دینا
vandal *n* دانستہ غارت گر	ventilation *n* ہواداری
vandalism *n* غارت گری	venture *v* جرات کرنا
vandalize *v* غارت کرنا	venture *n* جوکھم
vanguard *n* ہراول دستہ	verb *n* فعل
vanish *v* غائب ہونا	verbally *adv* زبانی طور پر
vanity *n* خودنمائی	verbatim *adv* لفظ بہ لفظ
vanquish *v* پسپا کرنا	verdict *n* فیصلہ
vaporize *v* بخارات بنانا	verge *n* کنارہ
variable *adj* متغیرہ	verification *n* تصدیق
varied *adj* مختلف	verify *v* تصدیق کرنا
variety *n* تنوع	versatile *adj* ہمہ گیر
various *adj* متعدد	verse *n* شعر
varnish *v* وارنش لگا	versed *adj* ماہر
varnish *n* وارنش	version *n* نسخہ
vary *v* بدل دینا	versus *pre* بالمقابل
vase *n* گلدان	vertebra *n* مہرہ
vast *adj* کشادہ	very *adv* بہت
veal *n* بچھڑا	vessel *n* ظرف
vegetable *v* سبزی	vest *n* صدری
vegetarian *v* سبزی خور	vestige *n* نشان
vegetation *n* سبزہ	veteran *n* آزمودہ کار
vehicle *n* گاڑی	veterinarian *n* بیطار
veil *n* پردہ	veto *v* ویٹو
vein *n* رگ	viaduct *n* پل
velocity *n* رفتار	vibrant *adj* مرتعش

vibrate v جھولنا	**virility** n مردانہ پن
vibration n ارتعاش	**virtually** adv فی الواقع
vice n برائی	**virtue** n نیکی
vicinity n پڑوس	**virtuous** adj صالح
vicious adj فاسق	**virulent** adj مہلک
victim n شکار	**virus** n وائرس
victimize v پھانسنا	**visibility** n ظہور
victor n فاتح شخص	**visible** adj مرئی
victorious adj فاتح	**vision** n خیالی صورت
victory n فتح	**visit** n دورہ
view n نظارہ	**visit** v دورہ کرنا
view v دیکھنا	**visitor** n ملاقاتی
viewpoint n موءقف	**visual** adj بصری
vigil n محتاط	**visualize** v تخیل میں لانا
village n گاؤں	**vital** adj حیات بخش
villager n دیہاتی	**vitality** n جان؛ روح
villain n ولن	**vitamin** n وٹامن
vindicate v منوا لینا	**vivacious** adj بشاش
vindictive adj کینہ پرور	**vivid** adj واضح
vine n بیل	**vocabulary** n ذخیرہء الفاظ
vinegar n سرکہ	**vocation** n پیشہ
vineyard n انگور کا باغ	**vogue** n رواج
violate v خلل ڈالنا	**voice** n آواز
violence n تشدد	**void** adj کالعدم؛ باطل
violent adj پر تشدد	**volatile** adj طیران پذیر
violet n بنفشہ	**volcano** n آتش فشاں
violin n وائلن	**volleyball** n والی بال
violinist n وائلن نواز	**voltage** n وولٹیج
viper n ناگ	**volume** n حجم؛ ضخامت
virgin n کنواری	**volunteer** n رضا کار
virginity n کنوارہ پن	**vomit** v الٹی کرنا
virile adj مردانہ	**vomit** n الٹی

V

vote ووٹ ڈالنا v	walk سیر n
vote ووٹ n	walkout ہڑتال کرنا n
vouch for توثیق کرنا v	wall دیوار n
voucher شاہد n	wallet بٹوہ n
vow عہد کرنا v	walnut اخروٹ n
vowel حرفِ علت n	walrus والرس n
voyage بحری سفر n	waltz جوڑا رقص n
vulgar عامیانہ adj	wander اِدھر اُدھر پھرنا v
vulgarity بیہودگی n	wanderer آوارہ گرد n
vulnerable زد پذیر adj	wane گھٹنا؛ کم ہونا v
vulture گدھ n	want چاہنا؛ محتاج ہونا v
	war جنگ n
	warden پاسبان n
	wardrobe کپڑوں کی الماری n
	warehouse گودام n
	warfare جنگ و جدل n

wafer ایک کاغذی بسکٹ n	warm گرم adj
wag جنبش کرنا v	warm up گرم ہونا v
wage اجرت n	warmth تپش n
wagon ویگن n	warn خبردار کرنا v
wail غم میں چلّانا v	warning انتباہ n
wail ماتم n	warp موڑنا؛ بل دینا v
waist کمر n	warped مڑا ہوا adj
wait انتظار کرنا v	warrant اجازت دینا v
waiter بیرا n	warrant وارنٹ؛ اختیار n
waiting خدمت n	warranty اقرار n
waitress ملازمہ n	warrior جنگ جو n
waive چھوڑ دینا v	warship جنگی بحری جہاز n
wake up جاگنا iv	wart مسّا n
walk چلنا v	wary چوکس adj
	wash دھونا v
	wasp بھڑ n

V
W

waste v	ضائع کرنا
waste n	کوڑا؛ ردی
waste basket n	ردی کی ٹوکری
wasteful adj	فضول خرچ
watch n	گھڑی
watch v	دیکھنا
watch out v	ہوشیار
watchful adj	چوکنّا
watchmaker n	گھڑی ساز
water n	پانی
water v	پانی دینا
water down v	بہکانا
waterfall n	آبشار
watermelon n	تربوز
waterproof adj	پانی روک
watershed n	پن دھارا
watertight adj	پن روک
watery adj	سیال
watt n	واٹ
wave n	موج
waver v	ڈگمگانا
wavy adj	لہردار
wax n	موم
way n	راستہ؛ طریقہ
way in n	داخلے کا رستہ
way out n	خروج کا رستہ
we pro	ہم
weak adj	کمزور
weaken v	کمزور بنانا
weakness n	کمزوری
wealth n	دولت
wealthy adj	دولت مند

weapon n	ہتھیار
wear n	لباس؛ پوشاک
wear iv	پہننا؛ زیب تن کرنا
wear out v	گھس جانا
weary adj	تھکا ہوا
weather n	موسم
weave iv	گوندھنا
web n	جالا؛ بافت
web site n	ویب سائٹ
wed iv	بیاہ کرنا
wedding n	شادی
wedge n	کھونٹا؛ بھانا
Wednesday n	بدھ
weed n	گھاس پھونس
weed v	چھانٹنا
week n	ہفتہ
weekend n	اختتام ہفتہ
weekly adv	ہفتہ وار
weep iv	رونا؛ چلّانا
weigh v	وزن کرنا
weight n	وزن
weird adj	پراسرار
welcome v	خیر مقدم کرنا
welcome n	خوش آمدید
weld v	جوڑنا
welder n	ویلڈ کرنے والا
welfare n	بہبود
well n	کنواں
well-known adj	معروف
well-to-do adj	خوشحال
west n	مغرب
western adj	مغربی

W

wet *adj* گیلا	**whiten** *v* سفید کرنا
whale *n* وہیل مچھلی	**whittle** *v* کاٹنا؛ کترنا
wharf *n* گھاٹ	**who** *pro* کون
what *adj* کیا	**whoever** *pro* جو بھی
whatever *adj* جو کچھ بھی	**whole** *adj* سالم
wheat *n* گندم	**wholehearted** *adj* تہ دل سے
wheel *n* پہیہ	**wholesale** *n* تھوک فروشی
wheelbarrow *n* ہاتھ ریڑھی	**wholesome** *adj* صحت بخش
wheelchair *n* وہیل چیئر	**whom** *pro* کسے
wheeze *v* خرخر کرنا	**why** *adv* کیوں
when *adv* کب	**wicked** *adj* بد؛ فاسق
whenever *adv* جب کبھی	**wickedness** *n* برائی
where *adv* کہاں	**wide** *adj* چوڑا؛ کشادہ
whereabouts *n* ٹھکانا	**widely** *adv* دور دور تک
whereas *c* جبکہ	**widen** *v* چوڑا کرنا
whereupon *c* جس پر	**widespread** *adj* پھیلا ہوا
wherever *c* کہاں سے	**widow** *n* بیوہ
whether *c* آیا کہ	**widower** *n* رنڈوا
which *adj* کون سا	**width** *n* عرض؛ چورائی
while *c* جب تک کہ	**wield** *v* استعال کرنا
whim *n* وہم؛ خیال	**wife** *n* بیوی
whine *v* کراہنا	**wig** *n* وگ
whip *v* اچھلنا؛ کودنا	**wiggle** *v* جنبش دینا
whip *n* کوڑا	**wild** *adj* جنگلی
whirl *v* گھوم جانا	**wild boar** *n* جنگلی سور
whirlpool *n* بھنور؛ گرداب	**wilderness** *n* بیابان
whiskers *n* لمبی قلمیں	**wildlife** *n* جنگلی حیات
whisper *v* سرگوشی کرنا	**will** *n* مرضی
whisper *n* سرگوشی	**willfully** *adv* دیدہ دانستہ
whistle *v* سیٹی بجانا	**willing** *adj* رضامند
whistle *n* سیٹی	**willingly** *adv* رضامندی سے
white *adj* سفید	**willingness** *n* رضامندی

willow *n* بید کا درخت	withdrawal *n* واپس لینے کا عمل
wily *adj* عیّار	wither *v* مرجھانا
wimp *adj* ایک عورت یا لڑکی	withhold *iv* روک لینا
win *iv* جیتنا	within *pre* اندر
win back دوبارہ حاصل کرنا	without *pre* باہر
wind *n* ہوا	withstand *v* مقابلہ کرنا
wind *iv* گھمانا	witness *n* گواہ
wind up *v* گھڑی کو چابی دینا	witty *adj* ذہین
winding *adj* خم دار	wives *n* بیویاں
windmill *n* پون چکی	wizard *n* ساحر
window *n* کھڑکی	wobble *v* لڑکھڑانا
windpipe *n* سانس نالی	woes *n* غم و الم
windshield *n* ونڈ شیلڈ	wolf *n* بھیڑیا
windy *adj* تیز ہوا کی زد میں	woman *n* عورت (واحد)
wine *n* شراب	womb *n* رحم
wing *n* پر؛ پنکھ	women *n* عورت (جمع)
wink *v* آنکھ مارنا	wonder *v* حیران ہونا
winner *n* فاتح	wonderful *adj* حیرت انگیز
winter *n* سرما	wood *n* لکڑی
wipe *v* صاف کرنا	wooden *adj* چوبی
wipe out *v* حذف کرنا	wool *n* اون؛ پشم
wire *n* تار؛ تار برقی	word *n* لفظ
wireless *adj* لاسلکی	wording *n* اسلوب
wisdom *n* دانائی	work *n* کام
wise *adj* عقلمند	work *v* کام کرنا
wish *v* خواہش کرنا	work out *v* حل کرنا
wish *n* خواہش	workable *adj* قابلِ عمل
wit *n* ذہانت	workbook *n* مشقی کتاب
witch *n* جادو گرنی	worker *n* کارکن
witchcraft *n* جادوگری	workshop *n* کارخانہ
with *pre* ساتھ	world *n* دنیا
withdraw واپس لے لینا	worldly *adj* دنیا دار

worldwide *adj* عالمگیر
worm *n* کینچوا
worn-out *adj* پھٹا ہوا
worrisome *adj* پریشان کن
worry *v* پریشان ہونا
worry *n* پریشانی
worse *adj* بد تر
worsen *v* بد تر کرنا
worship *n* عبادت
worst *adj* بد ترین
worth *adj* صمام؛ والو
worthless *adj* بے وقعت
worthwhile *adj* کارآمد؛ با مصرف
worthy *adj* عمدہ؛ لائق
would-be *adj* متمنی
wound *n* گھائو
wound *v* زخمی کرنا
woven *adj* بُنا ہوا
wrap *v* لپیٹنا
wrap up *v* مکمل کرنا
wrapping *n* لفافہ
wrath *n* قہر؛ غصہ
wreath *n* مالا؛ ہار
wreck *v* تباہ کرنا
wreckage *n* شکستگی
wrench *n* اینٹھن؛ مروڑ
wrestle *v* کشتی کرنا
wrestler *n* پہلوان
wrestling *n* کشتی
wretched *adj* غمگین
wring *iv* دبانا
wrinkle *v* شکن پڑنا

wrinkle *n* جھری
wrist *n* کلائی
write *iv* لکھنا
write down *v* لکھ لینا
writer *n* مصنف
writhe *v* تلملانا
writing *n* تحریر
written *adj* لکھا ہوا
wrong *adj* غلط

X-mass *n* کرسمس
X-ray *n* ایکس رے

Y

yacht n کشتی

yam n میٹھا آلو

yard n گز؛ احاطہ

yarn n ڈوری

yawn n جمائی

yawn v جمائی لینا

year n سال

yearly adv سالانہ

yearn v شدید خواہش ہونا

yeast n خمیر

yell v چلّانا؛ نعرہ لگانا

yellow adj پیلا

yes adv ہاں

yesterday adv گزشتہ کل

yet c ابھی

yield v دینا؛ پھل دینا

yield n پیداوار؛ فائدہ

yoke n جوت

yolk n انڈے کی زردی

you pro آپ

young adj جوان

youngster n نوجوان

your adj آپ کا

yours pro آپ کا

yourself pro آپ خود

youth n جوانی

youthful adj نو جوان

Z

zap v دفعتاً برباد کر دینا

zeal n سرگرمی

zealous adj سرگرم

zebra n زیبرا

zero n صفر

zest n لطف

zinc n زنک

zip code n پوسٹ کوڈ

zipper n زِپ

zone n حلقہ

zoo n چڑیا گھر

zoology n حیوانیات

Y
Z

Urdu-English

Bilingual Dictionaries, Inc.

Abbreviations

a - article - آرٹیکل

adj - adjective - اسم صفت

adv - adverb - متعلقِ فعل

c - conjunction - حرف عطف

e - exclamation - ندائیہ/استعجابیہ

n - noun - اسم

pre - preposition - حرف ربط/حرف جار

pro - pronoun - اسم ضمیر

v - verb - فعل

آنتش گیر	explosive *adj*
آتشک	syphilis *n*
آتشین اسلحہ	firearm *n*
آٹا	flour *n*
آٹھ	eight *adj*
آٹھواں	eighth *adj*
آج	today *adv*
آج کی رات	tonight *adv*
آجر	employer *n*
آجکل	nowadays *adv*
آخر	end *n*
آخر کار	eventually *adv*
آخری	conclusive *adj*
آداب	greetings *n*
آداب کرنا	greet *v*
آدم خور	cannibal *n*
آدم کھوج	manhunt *n*
آدمی	cove *n*
آدھا	half *adj*
آدھا حصہ	half *n*
آدھا کرنا	halve *v*
آراستگی	garnish *n*
آراستہ کرنا	garnish *v*
آرام	relief, rest *n*
آرام دہ	restful *adj*
آرام کرنا	rest *v*
آرپار	through *pre*
آرزو ۔ تمنا	ambition *n*
آرزو کرنا	long for *v*

آ

آ ملنا	come over *v*
آب بند پھاٹک	floodgate *n*
آب درہ	canyon *n*
آب و ہوا	climate *n*
آب و ہوا راس آنا	acclimatize *v*
آباد کرنا	populate *v*
آبادکار	settler *n*
آبادی	population *n*
آباو اجداد	ancestor *n*
آبائی شہر	hometown *n*
آبراہ ۔ نالی	aqueduct *n*
آبشار	waterfall *n*
آبلہ	cyst *n*
آبنائے	strait *n*
آبی	aquatic *adj*
آبی غذا	seafood *n*
آبیاری	irrigation *n*
آبیاری کرنا	irrigate *v*
آپ	you *pro*
آپ خود	yourself *pro*
آپ کا	your *adj*
آپریشن	operation *n*
آتش بازی	fireworks *n*
آتش پذیر	flammable *adj*
آتش زن	arsonist *n*
آتش زنی	arson *n*
آتش فشاں	volcano *n*

آرزومند lustful *adj*	آغازِ کار debut *n*
آرک ۔ قَوس arc *n*	آغاز کرنا initiate *v*
آرکسٹرا orchestra *n*	آغاز ہونا begin *v*
آرگن organ *n*	آفاقی universal *adj*
آرگن بجانیوالا organist *n*	آفت calamity *n*
آری saw *n*	آفرین applause *n*
آری سے کاٹنا saw *v*	آقا lord *n*
آڑ coverup *n*	آکاش بیل parasite *n*
آڑا oblique *adj*	آکٹوپس octopus *n*
آڑا ترچھا sideways *adv*	آکسیجن oxygen *n*
آڑاترچھا گزارنا thwart *v*	آگ fire *n*
آڑو peach *n*	آگ بجھانا extinguish *v*
آزاد free *adj*	آگ بجھانے والا fireman *n*
آزاد کرانا liberate *v*	آگ دکھانا ignite *v*
آزاد کرنا extricate *v*	آگ لگانا fire *v*
آزادی freedom *n*	آگاہ aware *adj*
آزادی دلانا emancipate *v*	آگاہ ہونا notice *v*
آزمانا try *v*	آگاہی awareness *n*
آزمائش trial, test *n*	آگے ahead *pre*
آزمائش کرنا test *v*	آگے آنا come forward *v*
آزموده کار veteran *n*	آگے بڑھنا go ahead *v*
آسان easy *adj*	آگے جانا proceed *v*
آسانی سے easily *adv*	آگے کو forward *adv*
آستین sleeve *n*	آگے کو جھکنا bow *v*
آسمان sky *n*	آگے نکل جانا surpass *v*
آسمانی heavenly *adj*	آل descendant *n*
آسیب زده spooky *adj*	آلات stock *n*
آشنا familiar *adj*	آلاتِ جنگ armor *n*
آغاز opening *n*	آلہ device, tool *n*

elevator n آلہ ارتفاع	take in v آنے دینا
camera n آلہ تصویر کشی	sigh n آہ
potato n آلو	sigh v آہ بھرنا
plum, prune n آلو بخارہ	slowly adv آہستگی سے
contamination n آلودگی	slow adj آہستہ
contaminate v آلودہ کرنا	slow down v آہستہ ہو جانا
infect v آلودہ ہونا	rhythm n آہنگ
set about v آمادہ کرنا	castaway n آوارہ
blend n آمتزاج	bum n آوارہ گرد
arrival n آمد	stray v آوارہ گردی کرنا
Advent n آمد یا وَرُود	sound, voice n آواز
revenue n آمدنی	sound v آواز پیدا کرنا
coming adj آمدہ	ring v آواز پیدا ہونا
dictator n آمر	utter v آواز نکالنا
dictatorial adj آمرانہ	transformation n آواگون
authoritarian adj آمریَت پَسَند	whether c آیا کہ
dictatorship n آمریَت	item, article n آیٹم
omelette n آملیٹ	iodine n آیوڈین
mixture n آمیزہ	Irish adj آئرلنیڈ کا
come v آنا	Ireland n آئرلینڈ
colon, gut n آنت	ice cream n آئس کریم
hernia n آنت ترنا	mirror n آئینہ
tear n آنسو	
rip apart v آنسو بہانا	
hook n آنکڑا	
eye n آنکھ	
blink v آنکھ جھپکنا	
wink v آنکھ مارنا	
blindfold v آنکھیں بند کرنا	

۱

اتالیق coach n	اب now adv
اتالیقی coaching n	ابالنا boil, simmer v
اتحاد union, unity n	ابتدا origin n
اترنا descend v	ابتدا کرنا commence v
اتصال conjunction n	ابتداء beginning n
اتفاق chance n	ابتدائی preliminary adj
اتفاقی رائے consensus n	ابتدائ طور پر primarily adv
اتفاقی casual adj	ابتدائی initial adj
اتفاقی طور پر incidentally adv	ابتدائی طور پر initially adv
اتھاہ bottomless adj	ابتدائی قدم initiative n
اتھلا shallow adj	ابتدائی ہدایات briefing n
اتوار Sunday n	نیات‌ابتدا basics n
اٹابونا infested adj	ابتر chaotic adj
اٹکل پچو randomly adv	ابتری chaos n
اٹل inflexible adj	ابدی timeless adj
اٹلی Italy n	ابدیت eternity n
اٹلی کا Italian adj	ابر آلود cloudy adj
اٹھاره eighteen adj	ابرو eyebrow n
اٹھانا elevate v	ابلاغ communication n
اٹھائے رکھنا uphold v	ابہام obscurity n
اٹھنا rise v	ابھار bulge n
اثاثہ asset n	ابھرا ہوا burly adj
اثاثے assets n	ابھی yet c
اثباتِ جرم conviction n	ابھی تک still adv
اثباتی demonstrative adj	اپاہج invalid n
اثر effect, impact n	اپنا ذاتی own v
اثر انداز ہونا affect v	اتارنا take off v
اثرانداز ہونا impact v	
اثرپذیر susceptible adj	

monopoly *n* اجاره داری	اچھی صحت *n* fitness
desolate *adj* اجاڑ	احاطہ *n* enclosure
permission *n* اجازت	احاطہ بند کرنا *v* incarcerate
allow, permit *v* اجازت دینا	احتجاج *n* protest
brush up *v* اجالنا	احتجاج کرنا *v* protest
assembly *n* اجتماع	احتراز کرنا *v* shun
avoidance *n* اِجتَناب	احتساب *n* censorship
brusque *adj* اجڈ	احتمال *n* eventuality
reward *n* اجر	احتیاط *n* precaution
reward *v* اجر دینا	احساس *n* feeling
issue *n* اجرا	احساسِ اضطراب *n* scruples
wage *n* اجرت	احساس ہونا *v* realize
session *n* اجلاس	احساسات *n* feelings
parsley *n* اجمود	احسان کرنا *v* oblige
stranger *n* اجنبی	احمق *n* idiot
celery *n* اجوائن	احیا کرنا *v* revive
tedious *adj* اجیرن	اخبار *n* newspaper
sudden *adj* اچانک	اخباری دکان *n* newsstand
suddenly *adv* اچانک طور سے	اختتام *n* ending
come across *v* اچانک ملنا	اختتام کرنا *v* finish
grab *v* اچک لینا	اختتامِ ہفتہ *n* weekend
pick *v* اچکنا	اختراع پسندی *n* ingenuity
amazement *n* اچنبھا ۔ حیرانی	اختصار *n* abbreviation
good *adj* اچھا	اختصار کرنا *v* abbreviate
toss *v* اچھالنا	اختلاف *n* controversy
goodness *n* اچھائی	اختلافی *adj* controversial
bounce *n* اچھل کود	اِختیار نامَہ *n* authorization
jump, skip *v* اچھلنا	اختیار *n* authority
untouchable *adj* اچھوت	اختیار دینا *v* charter

optional adj اختیاری	borrow v ادهار لینا
assume v اَخَذ کَرنا	wander v اِدهر اُدهر پهرنا
derive v اخذکرنا	agonizing adj اذِیَت خیز
expulsion n اخراج	torment n اذیت
bleeding n اخراجِ خون	torment v اذیت دینا
expenditure n اخراجات	hurtful adj اذیت رساں
walnut n اخروٹ	distressing adj اذیت ناک
sincerity n اخلاص	intend v ارادہ ہونا
ethical adj اخلاقی	deliberate adj ارادی
moral n اخلاقی سبق	vibration n ارتعاش
morality n اخلاقیات	evolution n ارتقا
fraternity n اخوت	commit v ارتکاب کرنا
institution n ادارہ	concentration n ارتکاز
sad adj اداس	about adv ارد گرد
sadden v اداس کرنا	inexpensive adj ارزاں
sadness n اداسی	subsidize v ارزاں مہیا کرنا
actor n اداکار	dispatch v ارسال کرنا
actress n اداکارہ	globe n ارض نما کرہ
payment n ادائے قرض	terrestrial adj ارضی
literature n ادب	landscape n ارضی منظر
decorum n ادب آداب	geology n ارضیات
hindsight n ادراک	purple adj ارغوانی
receptive adj ادراک پذیر	sublime adj ارفع
discern v ادراک کرنا	fly v اڑنا
ginger n ادرک	afresh adv از سر نو
alternate v اَدَل بَدَل کَرنا	disillusion n ازالہء التباس
below adv ادنیٰ	conjugal adj ازدواجی
debt n ادهار	marital adj ازدواجی
lend v ادهار دینا	jokingly adv ازراہِ مذاق

anew *adv* ازسر	metaphor *n* استعاره
serpent *n* اژدها	استعال کرنا *v* wield
her *adj* اس (لڑکی) کا	recourse *n* استعانت
his *adj* اس (مرد) کا	proficiency *n* استعداد
meanwhile *adv* اس اثنا میں	resignation *n* استعفیٰ
meantime *adv* اس دوران	resign *v* استعفیٰ دینا
thus *adv* اس طرح	colonization *n* استعمار
his *pro* اس کا	use *n* استعمال
therefore *adv* اس لیے	consumer *n* استعمال کرنا
since *c* اس وقت سے	reception *n* استقبال
hers *pro* اس(عورت)کا	receptionist *n* استقبالی افسر
essential *adj* اساسی	consistent *adj* استوار
teacher *n* استاذ	consistency *n* استواری
exemption *n* استثنا	sponge *n* اسفنج
exception *n* استثناء	abortion *n* اسقاطِ حمل
exceptional *adj* استثنائی	miscarry *v* اسقاط حمل ہونا
assimilation *n* اِستحالہ	Islamic *adj* اسلامی
exploitation *n* استحصال	armaments *n* اسلَحَہ
extortion *n* استحصال با لجبر	wording *n* اسلوب
prerogative *n* استحقاق کامل	noun *n* اسم
request *v* استدعا کرنا	gerund *n* اسمِ مصدر
reasoning *n* استدلال	diarrhea *n* اسہال
rational *adj* استدلالی	eighty *adj* اسی
lining *n* استر	like *pre* اسی انداز میں
razor *n* استرا	likewise *adv* اسی طرح
repose *n* استراحت	clue, hint *n* اشاره
iron *v* استری کرنا	beckon *v* اشارَہ دینا
referendum *n* استصواب	insinuate *v* اشاره دینا
afford *v* استطاعت رکهنا	inkling *n* اشاره‌ء خفیف

coverage *n* اشاعت	docile *adj* اصیل
communion *n* اشتراک	addition *n* اضافہ
communist *adj* اشتراک پسند	additional *adj* اضافہ شدہ
socialist *adj* اشتراکی	redouble *v* اضافہ کرنا
socialism *n* اشتراکیت	adjective *n* اضافی
provocation *n* اشتعال	reinforcements *n* اضافی دستے
infuriate *v* اشتعال دلانا	surcharge *n* اضافی محصول
irritating *adj* اشتعل انگیز	commotion *n* اضطراب
appetizer *n* اِشتہا آور	impulsive *adj* اضطراری
poster *n* اشتہار	docility *n* اطاعت پسندی
advertising *n* اِشتہار بازی	obedient *adj* اطاعت شعار
advertise *v* اشتہار دینا	obedience *n* اطاعت شعاری
eagerness *n* اشتیاق	inform *v* اطلاع دینا
aristocrat *n* اشراف	newsletter *n* اطلاع نامہ
aristocracy *n* اشرافیہ	apply *v* اطلاق کرنا
academic *adj* اشرافی	gratify *v* اطمنان بخشنا
radiator *n* اشعاع کنندہ	content *v* اطمنان دینا
tearful *adj* اشکباری	expression *n* اظہار
foodstuff *n* اشیائے خوردنی	express *v* اظہار کرنا
insistence *n* اصرار	repetition *n* اعادہ
insist *v* اصرار کرنا	subsidy *n* اعانت
stable *n* اصطبل	lean on, trust *v* اعتبار
terminology *n* اصطلاحیات	trust *v* اعتبار کرنا
originally *adv* اصل میں	moderation *n* اعتدال
reform *n* اصلاح	moderate *adj* اعتدال پسند
reform *v* اصلاح کرنا	objection *n* اعتراض
genuine, real *adj* اصلی	object *v* اعتراض کرنا
principle *n* اصول	confession *n* اعتراف
axiom *n* اصول مُتعارفہ	confess *v* اعتراف کرنا

confessor *n* اعتراف کرنیوالا	افسوس کرنا *v* deplore
confessional *n* اعترافی	افسوس ناک *adj* deplorable
confidence *n* اعتماد	افشا کرنا *v* divulge
distrust *v* اعتماد نہ کرنا	افشاء کرنا *v* disclose
complimentary *adj* اعزازی	افق *n* horizon
decimal *adj* اعشاری	افقی *adj* horizontal
grand *adj* اعظم	افواہ *n* rumor
declaration *n* اعلان	افوہ *n* hearsay
announce *v* اعلان کرنا	افیون *n* opium
announcer *n* اعلانچی	اقامت *n* stand
publicly *adv* اعلانیہ طور پر	اقتباس *n* quotation
de luxe *adj* اعلٰی	اقتدارِ اعلٰی *n* sovereignty
kidnapping *n* اغوا	اقرار *n* warranty
kidnapper *n* اغوا کار	اقرار کرنا *v* agree
abduct *v* اغوا کرنا	اقرار نامہ *n* agreement
usefulness *n* افادیت	اقلیت *n* minority
inauguration *n* افتتاح	اکا *n* ace
inaugurate *v* افتتاح کرنا	اکا دکا *adj* sporadic
people *n* افراد	اکائی *n* unit
manpower *n* افرادی قوت	اکتاہٹ *n* boredom
inflation *n* افراطِ زر	اکتاہٹ بھرا *adj* monotonous
development *n* افزائش	اکتایا ہوا *adj* bored
fiction *n* افسانہ	اکتوبر *n* October
bureaucrat *n* افسر	اکٹھ *n* assembly
bureaucracy *n* افسر شاہی	اکٹھا کرنا *v* gather
depression *n* افسردگی	اکٹھے *adv* together
dejected *adj* افسردہ	اکٹھے رہنا *v* coexist
depress *v* افسردہ کرنا	اکثر *adv* often
depressing *adj* افسردہ کن	اکثریت *n* majority

stiffen v اکڑانا	confusion n الجھاؤ
cramp n اکڑن	entangle v الجھانا
provoke v اکسانا	confusing adj الجھانے والا
incitement n اکساہٹ	involved v الجھاہوا
arena n اکھاڑا	tangle n الجھنا
sole adj اکیل	atheism n الحاد
single adj اکیلا	affiliation n الحاق
alone adj اکیلا ۔ تنہا	affiliate v الحاق کَرنا
premonition n اگاہی	allergy n الَرجی ۔ خارِش
if c اگر	blame, charge n الزام
although c اگرچہ	slur v الزام تراشی کرنا
August n اگست	blame v الزام دینا
forthcoming adj اگلا	incriminate v الزام لگانا
forefront n اگلا حصہ	asunder adv اَلَگ ۔ جُدا
grow v اگنا	secluded adj الگ تھلگ
bonfire n الاؤ	lay off v الگ کرنا
beseech v التجا کرنا	cabinet n الماری
request n التجاء	tragic adj المناک
postpone v التوا کرنا	tragedy n المیہ
upturn n الٹا دینا	theology n الٰہیات
backfire v الٹا نتیجہ نکالنا	owl n الو
reversal n الٹائو	dupe v الو بنانا
ultrasound n الٹراسائونڈ	farewell n الوداع
capsize v الٹنا	divinity n الوہیت
turn over v الٹنا پلٹنا	umpire n امپائر
vomit n الٹی	examination n امتحان
vomit v الٹی کرنا	distinction n امتیاز
countdown n الٹی گنتی	distinguish v امتیاز کرنا
ultimatum n الٹی میٹم	distinctive adj امتیازی

امداد aid n	انتشار dispersal n
امریکی American adj	انتظار کرنا wait v
امریکہ کا ایک گدھ buzzard n	اِنتَظام کَرنا administer v
امکان contingency n	انتظامی executive n
امن peace n	انتقال transfer n
امورِ خانہ داری housework n	انتقام reprisal n
امومت maternity n	انتہا پسند extremist adj
امیرُ البَحَر admiral n	انتہائی highly adv
امید hope n	انتہائی اہم grave adj
امیدوار candidate n	اِنتِہائی دِلکَش adorable adj
امیدواری candidacy n	انتہائی ظلم outrage n
امیر chancellor n	انٹرپرنیور entrepreneur n
امیرزادہ nobleman n	انٹرویو interview n
ان پڑھ uneducated adj	انجام conclusion n
ان تھک tireless adj	انجام دینا accomplish v
اناج meal, cereal n	انجن engine n
انار pomegranate n	انجیر fig n
انانیت egoism n	انجیل gospel n
انانیت پسند egoist n	انجینئر engineer n
انبار dump n	انچ inch n
انبار لگا دینا huddle v	انحراف aberration n
انبار لَگانا agglomerate v	انحصار dependence n
انبار یا ڈھیر لگانا stockpile n	انحصار کرنا rely on v
انتباہ caution n	انحطاط deterioration n
انتخاب choice n	انحطاط ہونا deteriorate v
انتخاب کرنا opt for v	انداز mode, style n
انتڑی intestine n	انداز ترتیب setup n
انتساب dedication n	اندازِ زندگی lifestyle n
انتساب کرنا dedicate v	اندازہ estimation n

estimate v اندازه لگانا	justice n انصاف
in, within pre اندر	just adj انصاف پر مبنی
come in v اندر آنا	fairness n انصاف پسندی
let in v اندر آنے دینا	merger n انضمام
inside pre اندر کی طرف	prize, award n انعام
registration n اندراج	gratuity n انعامیہ
indoor adv اندرانِ خانہ	menopause n انقطاعِ حیض
inland adj اندراونِ ملک	radical adj انقلاب پسند
downtown n اندرونِ شہر	refusal n انکار
inland adv اندرونِ ملک کا	deny v انکار کرنا
inside, inner adj اندرونی	condescend v انکسار کرنا
blind adj اندھا	revelation n انکشاف
blindness n اندھا پن	revealing adj انکشاف کرنیوالا
blindly adv اندھا دھند	embers n انگارے
darkness n اندھیرہ	English adj انگریزی
jeopardize v اندیشہ	finger n انگلی
serious adj اندیشہ ناک	fingerprint n انگلی کا نشان
egg n انڈہ	England n انگلینڈ
yolk n انڈے کی زردی	thumb n انگوٹھا
outpouring n انڈیلنا	grape n انگور
human being n انسان	vineyard n انگور کا باغ
orangutan n انسان نما بندر	grapevine n انگوری بیل
human adj انسانی	pinpoint v انگی اٹھانا
torso n انسانی دھڑ	fireplace n انگیٹھی
encyclopedia n انسائیکلوپیڈیا	pineapple n اناس
distraction n انشارِ توجہ	digestion n انہضام
rupture n انشقاق	unusual adj انوکھا
insurance n انشورنس	gimmick n انوکھا دائو
insure v انشورنس کروانا	eccentric adj انوکھاہ

anemia *n* انیمیا	olympics *n* اولمپک کھیل
anemic *adj* انیمیا کا مَریض	اولہ *n* hail
nineteen *adj* انیس	hail *v* اولے پڑنا
affirmative *adj* اِجاب	foremost *adj* اولین
competent *adj* اہل	oven, wool *n* اون
inmate *n* اہل خانہ	camel *n* اونٹ
official *adj* اہلکار دفتری	high, loud *adj* اونچا
merit *n* اہلیت	height *n* اونچائی
qualify *v* اہلیت پر پورا اترنا	ounce *n* اونس
significant *adj* اہم	doze, nap *n* اونگھ
significance *n* اہمیت	snooze *v* اونگھنا
above, upon *pre* اوپر	apron *n* ایپرن ۔ تہ بند
overlap *v* اوپر چڑھنا	an *a* ایک
go up *v* اوپر چڑھنا	align *v* ایک خَط میں لانا
upwards *adv* اوپر کی جانب	invention *n* ایجاد
opera *n* اوپیرا	invent *v* ایجاد کرنا
culminate *v* اوج پر ہونا	edition *n* ایڈیشن
otter *n* اود بلائو	affliction *n* ایذا
beaver *n* اودبلا	spur *v* ایڑ
odyssey *n* اوڈیسی	spur *n* ایڑ
and *c* اور	heel *n* ایڑی
overcoat *n* اورکوٹ	such *adj* ایسا
resuscitate *v* اوسان بحال کرنا	Easter *n* ایسٹر
average *n* اوسط	a *a* ایک
timetable *n* اوقات نامہ	one *adj* ایک
okay *adv* اوکے	peck *n* ایک پیمانہ
principal *adj* اول	sidestep *v* ایک جانب ہو جانا
prime *adj* اول درجے کی	each other *adj* ایک دوسرے کو
offspring *n* اولاد	reel *n* ایک رقص

ایک شخص single n	ب
ایک طرف aside adv	
ایک طرف کر دینا put aside v	با تدبیر tactful adj
ایک عورت یا لڑکی wimp adj	با سہولت convenient adj
ایک کاغذی بسکٹ wafer n	باادب respectful adj
ایک کرنا unify v	باب chapter n
ایک مرتبہ once c	بابت concerning pre
ایک یا دوسرا either adj	باتونی talkative adj
ایکا ایکی abruptly adv	باتیں کرنا talk v
ایکس رے X-ray n	باخبر conscious adj
ایلم elm n	بادام almond n
ایلومنم aluminum n	بادبان sail n
ایمان faith n	بادبانی کشتی sailboat n
ایماندار believer n	بادشاہ king n
اینٹ brick n	بادل cloud n
اینٹھ لینا extort v	بادل چھانا overcast adj
اینٹھن wrench n	باربکیُو barbecue n
ایندھن fuel n	بارش rain n
ایوانِ بلدیہ city hall n	بارش ہونا rain v
انیر فون earphones n	بارہ twelve adj
	بارہواں twelfth adj
	بارود gunpowder n
	بارود خانہ arsenal n
	باریش bearded adj
	باری shift n
	باری بدلنا shift v
	باریک see-through adj
	باریک بین precise adj
	باریکی سے thinly adv

barrier *n* باڑ	bair *n* بال hair
prevent *v* باز رکھنا	بال دار *adj* hairy
desist *v* باز رہنا	بالا خانہ *n* attic
bazaar *n* بازار	بالا دستی *n* supremacy
inquisition *n* بازپرس	بالادست *adj* supreme
arm *n* بازو	بالاراده *adv* purposely
armchair *n* بازو دار کُرسی	بالائی *adj* upper
play *n* بازی لگانا	بالائی اتارنا *v* skim
recovery *n* بازیابی	بالائی منزل *adv* upstairs
basketball *n* باسکِٹ بال	بالآخر *adv* lastly
stale *adj* باسی	بالغ *n* adult
methodical *adj* باضابطہ	بالغ ہونا *v* grow up
falsehood *n* باطل	بالکل *adv* quite
disprove *v* باطل ثابت کرنا	بالکل نیا *adj* brand-new
invalidate *v* باطل کرنا	بالکنی *n* balcony
entertaining *adj* باعث تفریح	بالمقابل *pre* versus
disgraceful *adj* باعثِ ذلت	بالواسطہ *adj* indirect
garden *n* باغ	بام *n* balm
revolt *v* باغی ہونا	بامروت *adj* gentle
regularity *n* باقاعدگی	بامعنی *adj* meaningful
regularly *adv* باقاعدگی سے	بانٹ *n* dispensation
regulate *v* باقاعده بنانا	بانجھ *adj* infertile
duly *adv* باقاعده طور پر	باندھنا *v* bind, tie
remain *v* باقی بچ جانا	بانس *n* bamboo
remaining *adj* باقی کا	بانسری *n* clarinet
survivor *n* باقی مانده	بانہہ *v* arm
remainder *n* باقیات	بانی *n* founder
frugal *adj* باکفایت	باہر *adv* out, without
economize *v* باکفیت بنانا	باہر چلے جانا *v* get out

outsider _n_ باہر کا	discharge _v_ بجا لانا
stand out _v_ باہر کو نل آنا	بَجانا _v_ bang
outward _adj_ باہر کی جانب	budget _n_ بجٹ
pull out _v_ باہر نکالنا	barge _n_ بجرا
mutually _adv_ باہمی طور پر	electricity _n_ بجلی
nevertheless _adv_ باوجود اس کے	electrify _v_ بجلی فراہم کرنا
persuade _v_ باور کرنا	thunderbolt _n_ بجلی کا کڑکا
cook _n_ باورچی	put out _v_ بجھا دینا
kitchen _n_ باورچی خانہ	blow _v_ بجھانا
bison _n_ بائسن	blow out _v_ بجھنانا
rabies _n_ بائولاپن	brat _n_ بچ
bowels _n_ بائولز	elude _v_ بچ نکلنا
bypass _n_ بائی پاس	spare _v_ بچا کر رکھ لینا
bubble gum ببل گم	put away _v_ بچا کر رکھنا
christen _v_ بپتسمہ دینا	save _v_ بچانا
idol _n_ بت	childhood _n_ بچپن
pagan _adj_ بت پرست	savings _n_ بچت
idolatry _n_ بت پرستی	childish _adj_ بچگانہ
tell _v_ بتانا	child _n_ بچہ
teller _n_ بتانے والا	uterus _n_ بچہ دانی
gradual _adj_ بتدریج	calf, veal _n_ بچھڑا
evolve _v_ بتدریج تیار کرنا	scorpion _n_ بچھو
dentures _n_ بتیسی	middleman _n_ بچولیا
button _n_ بٹن	children _n_ بچے
unbutton _v_ بٹن کھولنا	restore _v_ بحال کرنا
intertwine _v_ بٹنا	restoration _n_ بحالی
purse _n_ بٹوا	debate _n_ بحث
wallet _n_ بٹوہ	debate _v_ بحث کرنا
quail _n_ بٹیر	crisis _n_ بحران

بحری marine *adj*	بداخلاق کرنا deprave *adj*
بحری بگلا seagull *n*	بداخلاقی immorality *n*
بحری بیڑا fleet *n*	بدبو خارج کرنا stink *v*
بحری سفر voyage *n*	بدبو دار stinking *adj*
بحری گشت کرنا cruise *v*	بدتمیز شخص rowdy *adj*
بحریہ navy *n*	بدتمیزی کرنا misbehave *v*
بخار fever *n*	بدحواس frantic *adj*
بخار زدہ feverish *adj*	بدخواہ malevolent *adj*
بخارات بن جانا evaporate *v*	بددعا دینا curse *v*
بخارات بنانا vaporize *v*	بددیانتی racketeering *n*
بخرا share *n*	بدذائقہ repugnant *adj*
بخش دینا spare *v*	بدرجہ اتم exceedingly *adv*
بخوبی properly *adv*	بدرقہ escort *n*
بد evil *adj*	بدسلوکی mistreatment *n*
بد اخلاقی depravity *n*	بدسلوکی کرنا mistreat *v*
بد انتظامی کرنا mismanage *v*	بدشکل بنانا disfigure *v*
بَد بَختی adversity *n*	بدشگونی والا ominous *adj*
بد تر worse *adj*	بدعت heresy *n*
بد تر کرنا worsen *v*	بدعتی heretic *adj*
بد ترین worst *adj*	بدعنوان corrupt *adj*
بد دیانت dishonest *adj*	بدعنوانی corruption *n*
بد دیانتی dishonesty *n*	بدقماش rascal *n*
بد زبان abusive *adj*	بدکار dissolute *adj*
بد شکلی deformity *n*	بدل دینا vary *v*
بد صورت ugly *adj*	بدل کا کام کرنا replace *v*
بد صورتی ugliness *n*	بَدلا لینا avenge *v*
بد قسمت unlucky *adj*	بدلنا change, mutate *v*
بد قسمتی misfortune *n*	بدلنے والا adapter *n*
بد نظمی disorder *n*	بدلہ revenge *n*

recourse v بدلہ حاصل کرنا	overthrow n بربادی
revenge v بدلہ لینا	demeanor n برتاؤ
cranky adj بدمزاج	superior adj برتر
drunkenness n بدمستی	superiority n برتری
notorious adj بدنام	utensil n برتن
defame v بدنام کرنا	dishwasher n برتن دھونے والا
scandal n بدنامی کا واقعہ	tower n برج
indigestion n بدہضمی	impromptu adv برجستہ
Wednesday n بدھ	harpoon n برچھی
goof n بدھو	against pre بَرخِلاف
exotic adj بدیسی	tolerance n برداشت
continent n بر اعظم	tolerate v برداشت کرنا
timely adj بر وقت	rainy adj برساتی
manhandle v برا سلوک کرنا	anniversary n بَرسی
equal adj برابر	brush n برش
fifty-fifty adv برابر برابر	brush v برش کرنا
reproach v برابھلا کہنا	British adj برطانوی
brother-in-law n برادرِ نسبتی	Britain n برطانیہ
fraternal adj برادرانہ	dismiss v برطرف کرنا
brotherhood n برادری	removal n برطرفی
mainland n براعظم	adverse adj بر عکس
continental adj براعظمی	ice, snow n برف
brand n برانڈ	snowfall n برف باری
brandy n برانڈی	ice skate v برف جوتے
direct adj براہِ راست	icebox n برف دان
for pre برائے	iceberg n برف کا تودہ
wickedness n برائی	snowflake n برف کا گالا
export v برآمد کرنا	blizzard n برفابی طوفان
corridor n برآمدہ	icy adj برفانی

snow v	برفباری ہونا
avalanche n	بَرفشار
maintain v	برقرار رکھنا
lasting adj	برقرار رہنے والا
electric adj	برقی
fuse n	برقی فیوز
burger n	برگر
opportune adj	برمحل
brunch n	برنچ
irate adj	بربم
chagrin n	برہمی
brochure n	بروشر
bronchitis n	برونکائٹس
amputation n	بُریدگی
badly adv	بُری طرح
bra n	بریسئیر
briefcase n	بریف کیس
brake n	بریک
brake v	بریک لگانا
brigade n	بریگیڈ
main, major adj	بڑا
pontiff n	بڑا پادری
medallion n	بڑا تمغا
leopard n	بڑا چیتا
enlarge v	بڑا کرنا
cathedral n	بڑا گرجا
bishop n	بڑا لاٹھ پادری
metropolis n	بڑا یا اہم شہر
dormitory n	بڑا شبستان

mumble v	بڑبڑانا
bite n	بُڑکا
transcend v	بڑھ جانا
overstate v	بڑھا کر کہنا
old age n	بڑھاپا
increase v	بڑھانا
increasing adj	بڑھتا ہوا
advance v	بڑھنا
capital letter n	بڑے حروف
carol n	بڑے دن کا گیت
supermarket n	بڑی بازار
superpower n	بڑی طاقت
relay v	بز نشر کرنا
coward n	بزدل
cowardly adv	بزدلانہ
cowardice n	بزدلی
buzzer n	بَزر
elderly adj	بزرگ
predecessor n	بزرگ مورث
bus n	بس
bed n	بِستَر
deathbed n	بستر مرگ
bedding n	بسترا
sheets n	بستری چادر
bag n	بَستَہ
biscuit n	بِسکٹ
vivacious adj	بشاش
euphoria n	بشاشت
providing that c	بشرطیکہ

humanities *n* بشری علوم	come apart *v* بکھر جانا
inclusive *adv* بشمول	disseminate *v* بکھیرنا
sight *n* بصارت	crappy *adj* بکواس
visual *adj* بصری	distortion *n* بگاڑ
otherwise *adv* بصورتِ دیگر	aggravate *v* بگاڑنا
duck *n* بطخ	degenerate *adj* بگڑا ہوا
substitute *v* بطور متبادل لگانا	degenerate *v* بگڑنا
apparently *adv* بَظاہر	cyclone *n* بگولا
belated *adj* بعد از وقت	bill *n* بل
later *adj* بعد کا	unwind *v* بل کھولنا
afterwards *adv* بَعد میں	bat *n* بَلا
later *adv* بعد میں	sleeveless *adj* بلا آستین
paradox *n* بعیدالعقل بات	nonstop *adv* بلا توقف
rebellion *n* بغاوت	frankly *adv* بلا جھجھک
revolting *adj* بغاوت پر آمادہ	solely *adv* بلا شرکتِ غیرے
animosity *n* بُغض ۔ کینہ	regardless *adv* بلا لحاظ
armpit *n* بغل	undoubtedly *adv* بلاشبہ
hug *v* بغل گیر ہونا	block *n* بلاک
embrace *n* بغل گیری	call *v* بلانا
embrace *v* بغلگیر ہونا	call *n* بلاوا
lateral *adj* بغلی	bulb *n* بلب
look over *v* بغور جائزہ لینا	nightingale *n* بلبل
survival *n* بقا	bubble *n* بلبلہ
balance *v* بقایا	regarding *pre* بلحاظ
remnant *n* بقیہ	lofty *adj* بلند
sold-out *adj* بکا ہوا	loudly *adv* بلند آواز سے
frequent *adj* بکثرت ہونیوالا	heighten *v* بلند تر کرنا
goat *n* بکری	hoist *v* بلند کرنا
buckle *n* بکسوا	paramount *adj* بلند مرتبہ

ب

بلند ہموار میدان plateau *n*	بند کرنا shut *v*
بلندی raise *n*	بند گوبھی cabbage *n*
بلوا tumult *n*	بندا earring *n*
بلور crystal *n*	بندر monkey *n*
بلوط acorn *n*	بندرگاہ harbor *n*
بلوغت puberty *n*	بندش pact *n*
بلوہ riot *n*	بندھن bond *n*
بلوہ کرنا riot *v*	بندوبست management *n*
بلی cat *n*	بندوبست کرنا improvise *v*
بلی کا بچہ kitten *n*	بندوق gun *n*
بلیغ concise *adj*	بندوق چلا دینا trigger *v*
بم bomb *n*	بندوق کا دہانہ muzzle *n*
بم برسانا bomb *v*	بندوق کی نال barrel *n*
بم پھٹنا detonate *v*	بندوقچی gunman *n*
بمباری bombing *n*	بنڈل سے نکالنا unpack *v*
بمشکل hardly *adv*	بنفشہ violet *n*
بن bun *n*	بُننا knit *v*
بن مانس ape *n*	بُنیاد basis *n*
بُنا ہوا woven *adj*	بنی نوع انسان humankind *n*
بنانا fabricate *v*	بنیاد base *n*
بنانے والا maker *n*	بنیاد سے متعلق grassroots *adj*
بناوٹ fabric, texture *n*	بنیادی fundamental *adj*
بناوٹی sham *n*	بنیادی پتھر cornerstone *n*
بنائو سنگھار کرنا spruce up *v*	بنیادی خاکہ blueprint *n*
بَنجَر barren, arid *adj*	بَہ آواز بُلَند aloud *adv*
بند closed *adj*	بہادر brave *adj*
بند رستہ dead end *n*	بہادری bravery *n*
بند رکھانا contain *v*	بہادری سے bravely *adv*
بند کر دینا cordon off *v*	بہار spring *n*

ب

valiant *adj* بهاردر	delude *v* بہکانا
shed *v* بہانا	sister *n* بہن
pretense *n* بہانہ	flow *v* بہنا
pretend *v* بہانہ کرنا	drift *v* بہہ جانا
welfare *n* بہبود	daughter-in-law *n* بہو
very *adv* بہت	ledger *n* بہی
momentous *adj* بہت اہم	sister-in-law *n* بھابھی
towering *adj* بہت اونچا	steam *n* بھاپ
tremendous *adj* بہت بڑا	ebb *v* بھاٹا
tycoon *n* بہت بڑا تاجر	heavy *adj* بھاری
skinny *adj* بہت دبلا	run away *v* بھاگ جانا
overcrowded *adj* بہت زیادہ بھرا ہوا	flee *v* بھاگ کھڑا ہونا
guzzle *v* بہت زیادہ پینا	chase away *v* بھاگ نکلنا
abundant *adj* بہت سا	runner *n* بھاگنے والا
marvelous *adj* بہت عجیب	size up *v* بھانپ جانا
lurid *adj* بہت نمایاں	comedian *n* بھانڈ
fabulous *adj* بہت ہی خوب	brother *n* بھائی
abundance *n* بہتات	nephew *n* بھتیجا
slander *n* بہتان	niece *n* بھتیجی
better *adj* بہتر	stray *adj* بھٹکا ہوا
outdo *v* بہتر کام کرنا	nipple *n* بھٹنی
best *adj* بہترین	furnace *n* بھٹی
improvement *n* بہتری	chant *n* بھجن
anyhow *pro* بَہَر صُورَت	clumsy *adj* بھدہ
deaf *adj* بہرہ	clumsiness *n* بھدہ پن
deafness *n* بہرہ پن	pad *v* بھر دینا
deafen *v* بہرہ کر دینا	full *adj* بھرا ہوا
simulate *v* بہروپ بھرنا	filling *n* بھرائی
paradise *n* بہشت	fragile *adj* بھربھرا

ب

بھرتی	recruitment _n_	بھونکنا	bark _v_
بھرتی کرنا	enlist _v_	بھوننا	broil, roast _v_
بھرنا	fill _v_	بھوننے والا	broiler _n_
بھروسا	assurance _n_	بھی	too _adv_
بھڑ	wasp _n_	بھی ۔ مزید	also _adv_
بھڑک	flare _n_	بھیانک	formidable _adj_
بھڑک پڑنا	blaze _v_	بھیجنا	send _v_
بھڑک دار	flashy _adj_	بھیجنے والا	sender _n_
بھڑکانا	set off _v_	بھیدی	undercover _adj_
بھڑکنا	burst _v_	بھیڑ	lamb, sheep _n_
بھڑکیلا	flamboyant _adj_	بھیڑیا	wolf _n_
بھڑنا	bump _n_	بھیس	disguise _n_
بھک سے اڑنا	blow up _v_	بھیس بدلنا	disguise _v_
بھکاری	beggar _n_	بھیک مانگنا	beg, exhort _v_
بھگدڑ	stampede _n_	بھینچنا	clinch _v_
بھگونا	immerse _v_	بھینس	buffalo _n_
بھگی	carriage _n_	بو	odor _n_
بھنا ہوا گوشت	roast _n_	بو دار	smelly _adj_
بھنبھنانا	hum, buzz _v_	بوائلر	boiler _n_
بھنگی	janitor _n_	بوتل	bottle _n_
بھنھناہٹ	buzz _n_	بوتلوں میں بھرنا	bottle _v_
بھنور	whirlpool _n_	بوتھ	booth _n_
بھوت	ghost _n_	بَوَجَہ	because of _pre_
بھوترا	beetle _n_	بوجھ	burden _n_
بھورا	brown _adj_	بوجھل	cumbersome _adj_
بھوک	hunger _n_	بوجھل پن	heaviness _n_
بھوکا	hungry _adj_	بورژوا	bourgeois _adj_
بھول بھلیّاں	labyrinth _n_	بوڑھا	senile _adj_
بھول جانا	forget _v_	بوسہ	kiss _n_

ب
بیہ

بوسہ لینا	kiss v
بوسیدہ	rotten adj
بولنا	speak v
بولی	bid n
بولی دینا	bid v
بونا	dwarf n
بوندا باندی	drizzle n
بوندا باندی ہونا	drizzle v
بونس	bonus n

بیہ

بیچ میں	amid pre
بیدار	awake adj
بیدار ہونا	arouse v
بیراج	barrage n
بیس بال	baseball n
بیکٹیریا	bacteria n
بینچ	bench, pew n
بیابان	wilderness n
بیامبر	messenger n
بیان	description n
بیان کرنا	describe v
بیانیہ	descriptive adj
بیاہ	matrimony n

بیاہ کرنا	wed iv
بیٹا	son n
بیٹری بھرنا	recharge v
بیٹھا ہوا	seated adj
بیٹھنا	sit iv
بیٹھنے کا انداز	sitting n
بیٹھنے کی جگہ	seat n
بیٹی	daughter n
بیج	grain, seed n
بیج	n
بیجدار	seedy adj
بیچ میں	between pre
بیچ میں پڑنا	intercede v
بیچنا	sell iv
بیچنے والا	salesman n
بیخ کنی کرنا	eradicate v
بید	cane n
بید کا درخت	willow n
بَیر	malignancy n
بیرا	waiter n
بیرمی نظام	leverage n
بیرون خانہ	outdoors adv
بیرونی	exterior adj
بیرونی	outdoor adv
بیرونی سطح	outside adv
بیرونی مریض	outpatient n
بیڑا اٹھانا	undertake v
بیڑی	raft n
بیزار	indisposed adj

بیزار کر دینے والا sickening *adj*	بے
بیس twenty *adj*	
بیساکھی crutch *n*	بے اتھاہ boundless *adj*
بیسواں twentieth *adj*	بے اخلاصی insincerity *n*
بیش قدر invaluable *adj*	بے ادبی disrespect *n*
بیضہ دانی ovary *n*	بے استعداد inept *adj*
بیضوی oval *adj*	بے اطمنان grouchy *adj*
بیضیہ protein *n*	بے اعتمادی distrust *n*
بیطار veterinarian *n*	بے انتہا immense *adj*
بیکری bakery *n*	بے انتہا گہرا abysmal *adj*
بیگار کا سپاہی conscript *n*	بے انصافی unfairness *n*
بیل bull, ox *n*	بے انصافی سے unfairly *adv*
بیلجئیم Belgium *n*	بے اولاد childless *adj*
بیلجئیم کا Belgian *adj*	بے آرام restless *adj*
بیلچ shovel *n*	بے آرامی discomfort *n*
بیمار ill, sick *adj*	بے بازو تپائی stool *n*
بیماری disease *n*	بے باکی boldness *n*
بینائی eyesight *n*	بے بس helpless *adj*
بیہودگی vulgarity *n*	بے بنیاد unfounded *adj*
بیہودہ grotesque *adj*	بے بیج seedless *adj*
بیوہ widow *n*	بے پرواہ careless *adj*
بیوی wife *n*	بے پرواہی carelessness *n*
بیویاں wives *n*	بے تار cordless *adj*
	بے ترتیب messy *adj*
	بے تعصب unbiased *adj*
	بے تکلف intimate *adj*
	بے تکلفی frankness *n*
	بے جان lifeless *adj*
	بے جھجھک forthright *adj*

بے جوڑ	seamless *adj*	بے صبر	impatient *adj*
بے چوٹ	unharmed *adj*	بے صبری	impatience *n*
بے چوک	unmistakable *adj*	بے ضرر	harmless *adj*
بے چین	uneasy *adj*	بے عزتی	disgrace *n*
بے چینی	uneasiness *n*	بے عقل	unwise *adj*
بے حد خفا کرنا	exasperate *v*	بے عیب	flawless *adj*
بے حرکت	stagnant *adj*	بے غرض	unselfish *adj*
بے حرکت بنانا	immobilize *v*	بے فکرا	carefree *adj*
بے حرمتی	blasphemy *n*	بے قاعدہ	irregular *adj*
بے حرمتی کرنا	sacrilege *n*	بے قدر بنانا	trivialize *v*
بے حس	heartless *adj*	بے قدر کرنا	debase *v*
بے حس کر دینا	deaden *v*	بے قصور	blameless *adj*
بے حسی	apathy *n*	بے کار	jobless *adj*
بے حَکُومتی	anarchy *n*	بے کاری	unemployment *n*
بے خبر	unaware *adj*	بے لچک	firm *adj*
بے خطا	foolproof *adj*	بے لطف	insipid *adj*
بے خطا ٹھہرانا	exonerate *v*	بے محل	discordant *adj*
بے خوابی	insomnia *n*	بے مروت	unfriendly *adj*
بے دھڑک	desperate *adj*	بے مصرف	futile *adj*
بے دھڑک کودنا	tap into *v*	بے معنی	pointless *adj*
بے ڈَھب	awkward *adj*	بے مَقصَد	aimless *adj*
بے ذائقہ	tasteless *adj*	بے نامی	anonymity *n*
بے رحم	ruthless *adj*	بے نتیجہ رہنا	fall through *v*
بے روزگار	unemployed *adj*	بے نشان	spotless *adj*
بے ریڑھ	spineless *adj*	بے ہوش	unconscious *adj*
بے سبب	groundless *adj*	بے ہوش ہونا	faint *v*
بے شرم	shameless *adj*	بے وفا	unfaithful *adj*
بے شَکلا	amorphous *adj*	بے وفائی	infidelity *n*
بے شمار	numerous *adj*	بے وقت	untimely *adj*

worthless *adj* بے وقعت	پار کرنا *v* cross
stupid *adj* بے وقوف	پارسا *adj* devout
stupidity *n* بے وقوفی	پارسل *n* package
indecisive *adj* بے استقلالی	پارسل ڈاک *n* parcel post
grudgingly *adv* بے دلی سے	پارکرنا *n* crossing
homeless *adj* بے گھر	پارگی *n* disintegration
obnoxious *adj* بے ہودہ	پارہ *n* mercury
fool *v* بے وقوف بنانا	پارہ پارہ کرنا *v* disintegrate
	پاسبان *n* warden
	پاش پاش کر دینا *v* shatter
پ	پاک دامن *adj* chaste
	پاک صاف کرنا *v* purify
foot *n* پاءوں	پاکدامنی *n* modesty
committed *adj* پابند	پاکیزگی *n* purity
abide by *v* پابند رہنا	پاگل *n* madman
law-abiding *adj* پابندِ قانون	پاگل بنانا *v* madden
obligate *v* پابند کرنا	پالتو جانور *n* pet
obligation *n* پابندی	پالنا پوسنا *v* nurture, rear
sanction *v* پابندی لگانا	پامال *adj* beaten
apostolic *adj* پاپائی	پانا *v* find
span *n* پاٹ	پانچ *adj* five
span *v* پاٹنا	پانچ فٹ کا پیمانہ *v* pace
trousers *n* پاجامہ	پانچواں *adj* fifth
pastor, priest *n* پادری	پانی *n* water
pastoral *adj* پادری سے متعلق	پانی اڑانا *v* dehydrate
diocese *n* پادری کا حلقہ	پانی پر *adv* afloat
parish *n* پادری کا علاقہ	پانی دینا *v* water
	پانی روک *adj* waterproof
	پانی کا ریلا بہانا *v* flush

pipeline n پائپ لائن	pajamas n پجامہ
feet n پانوں	fifty adj پچاس
toe n پانوں کی انگلی	syringe n پچکاری
eyelid n پیوٹا	regret v پچھتانا
leaf n پتا	repentance n پچھتاوا
shellfish n پترا مچھلی	former adj پچھلا
tenuous adj پتلا	backyard n پچھلا احاطہ/صحن
dilute v پتلا کرنا	backwards adv پچھلی جانِب
suspenders n پتلون کے تسمے	rear n پچھواڑا
puppet n پتلی	mosaic n پچی کاری
kite n پتنگ	maturity n پختگی
stone n پتھر	ingrained adj پختہ
stone v پتھر مارنا	fatherly adj پدرانہ
reef n پتھریلا ساحل	paternity n پدری رشتہ
concrete n پتھریلامسالہ	on pre پر
helm, rudder n پتوار	at pre پر - کے - سے
blade n پتّا	effective adj پر اثر
lessor n پتّا دہندہ	mysterious adj پر اسرار
firecracker n پتاخہ	confident adj پر اعتماد
switch v پٹائی کرنا	optimistic adj پر امید
rail n پٹڑی	hearty adj پر تپاک
derail v پٹڑی سے اترنا	violent adj پر تشدد
lease n پٹہ	end up v پر خاتمہ ہونا
lease v پٹہ پر لینا	hazardous adj پر خطر
sirloin n پٹھ کا گوشت	resolute adj پر عزم
muscle n پٹھہ	energetic adj پر قوت
strap, leash n پٹی	enjoyable adj پر لطف
priestess n پجارن	blissful adj پُر مسرت
priesthood n پجاری کا عہدہ	weird adj پراسرار

deranged *adj*	پراگنده	پروانهء حاضری *n* subpoena
peaceful *adj*	پرامن	پرواہ ہون *v* care about
hopeful *adj*	پرامید	پرورش *n* upbringing
hopefully *adv*	پرامید طور پر	پرورش کرنا *v* bring up
outdated *adj*	پرانا	پروقار *adj* majestic
old-fashioned *adj*	پرانے انداز کا	پَرے *adv* away, off
crust *n*	پرت	پرے ہٹا دینا *v* repulse
permanent *adj*	پرثبات	پری *n* fairy
exciting *adj*	پرجوش	پریشان حال *adj* uptight
ovation *n*	پرجوش استقبال	پریشان کرنا *v* embarrass
shadow *n*	پرچھائی	پریشان کن *adj* worrisome
glutton *n*	پرخور شخص	پریشان ہونا *v* worry
curtain, drape *n*	پرده	پریشانی *n* trouble, worry
unveil *v*	پرده اٹھانا	پڑتال *n* check
blindfold *n*	پرده یا پٹی	پڑتال کرنا *v* check
fan *n*	پرستار	پڑھا لکھا *adj* literate
composed *adj*	پرسکون	پڑھانا *v* teach
devious *adj*	پرفریب	پڑھائی *n* reading
compass *n*	پرکار	پڑھنا *v* read, recite
compact *v*	پرکار بنانا	پڑھنے والا *n* browser
charming *adj*	پرکشش	پڑوس *n* vicinity
funny *adj*	پرمذاق	پژمرده *adj* downcast
humorous *adj*	پرمزاح	پَس انبار *n* backlog
joyful *adj*	پرمسرت	پَس زَنی *n* backlash
bird *n*	پرنده	پس مانده *adj* backward
crowded *adj*	پربجوم	پس منظر *n* background
flight *n*	پرواز	پسپا کرنا *v* vanquish
moth *n*	پروانہ	پسپا ہونا *v* retreat
passport *n*	پروانہ راه داری	پسپائی *n* retreat

pistol n پستول	پکڑنا v seize, grasp
rib n پسلی	پکڑنے کا عمل n seizure
downtrodden adj پسماندہ	ripen v پکنا
liking n پسند	trail n پگڈنڈی
like v پسند کرنا	fusion n پگھاٶ
likable adj پسندیدہ	defrost v پگھلانا
flea n پسو	thaw n پگھلاہٹ
relent v پسیج جانا	melt, thaw v پگھلنا
perspiration n پسینہ	bridge n پل
sweat v پسینہ آنا	puppy n پلا
perspire v پسینہ نکلنا	plaster v پلاستر لگانا
back n پشت	plastic n پلاسٹک بنانا
patron n پشت پناہ	revert v پلٹ آنا
backing n پشت پناہی	plaster n پلستر
backpack n پشتی تھیلا	eyelash n پلک
fleece n پشم	bedspread n پَلَنگ پوش
remorseful adj پشیمان	pump n پمپ
prediction n پشین گوہی	watershed n پن دھارا
predict v پشین گوہی کرنا	watertight adj پن روک
resolve v پکا ارادہ کرنا	refuge n پناہ
straighten out v پکا کرنا	shelter v پناہ دینا
ripe adj پکا ہوا	shelter n پناہ گاہ
staunch adj پکا وفادار	refugee n پناہ گزین
call, calling n پکار	cage n پنجرہ
exclaim v پکار اٹھنا	claw, paw n پنجہ
cry out v پکارنا	fifteen adj پندرہ
cook v پکانا	chandelier n پنساریا
grasp n پکڑ	pension n پنشن
overtake v پکڑ لینا	fan n پنکھا

بنگھوڑا	cradle *n*	پھاوڑا	spade *n*
پنیر	cheese *n*	پھپھوندی	mildew *n*
پہاڑ	mountain *n*	پھپھوندی لگا	moldy *adj*
پہاڑ کی چوٹی	peak *n*	پھٹ پڑنا	erupt *v*
پہاڑی	hill, mount *n*	پھٹ پڑنے کا عمل	eruption *n*
پہاڑی بنگلہ	chalet *n*	پھٹا پرانا	ragged *adj*
پہاڑی کوا	raven *n*	پھٹا ہوا	worn-out *adj*
پہچان	recognition *n*	پھٹکارنا	damn *v*
پہچان کا لفظ	password *n*	پھٹنا	rupture *v*
پہچاننا	recognize *v*	پھدکنا	hop *v*
پہلا	first *adj*	پھر جینا	relive *v*
پہلا نمونہ	prototype *n*	پھر سے بھر دینا	replenish *v*
پہلو	aspect, facet *n*	پھُرتیلا	agile *adj*
پہلوان	wrestler *n*	پھرتے رہنا	prowl *v*
پہلے	before *pre*	پھرکی	reel, spool *n*
پہلے سے اندازہ	anticipate *v*	پھڑپھڑانا	flutter *v*
پہلے متنبہ کرنا	forewarn *v*	پھسلانا	coax, lure *v*
پہلے ہی	beforehand *adv*	پھسلانے والا	persuasive *adj*
پہلے ہی سے	already *adv*	پھسلنا	slip, slide *v*
پہنچانا	convey *v*	پھسلنی	slippery *adj*
پہنچنا	reach *v*	پھل	fruit *n*
پَہُنچنا ۔ آنا	arrive *v*	پھل کا چھلکا	hull *n*
پہننا	wear *v*	پھلکاری	tapestry *n*
پہیلی	puzzle, riddle *n*	پھندا	snare *n*
پہیہ	wheel *n*	پھندہ	trap *n*
پھاٹک	gate *n*	پھنس جانا	jam *n*
پھاڑنا	rip *v*	پھوار ڈالنا	spray *v*
پھانسنا	victimize *v*	پھوٹک	brittle *adj*
پھانک	chip *n*	پھوٹنا	sprout *v*

پھول	flower *n*
پھول جانا	bloat *v*
پھول دان	urn *n*
پھول کی پتی	petal *n*
پھولا ہوا	bloated *adj*
پھولوں کو کھلنا	blossom *v*
پھولوں کی خاک	pollen *n*
پھونک	puff *n*
پھیپھڑا	lung *n*
پھیرا	detour, trip *n*
پھیکا	faded *adj*
پھیکا پڑنا	fade *v*
پھیلا ہوا	widespread *adj*
پھیلانا	spread, expand *v*
پھیلائو	expansion *n*
پھیلنا پھولنا	prosper *v*
پھینکنا	throw, hurl *v*
پوتا	grandchild *n*
پوترا	diaper *n*
پوچھنا	ask *v*
پودا	plant *n*
پودینہ	mint *n*
پورا کرنا	fulfill *v*
پوری	sack *n*
پوست	poppy *n*
پوسٹ کارڈ	postcard *n*
پوسٹ کوڈ	zip code *n*
پوشاک	clothing *n*
پوشیدگی	privacy *n*

پوشیدہ	clandestine *adj*
پول کھولنا	debunk *v*
پولیس	police *n*
پولیس کا سپاہی	policeman *n*
پولینڈ	Poland *n*
پولینڈ کا باشندہ	Polish *adj*
پون چکی	windmill *n*
پیٹ	belly *n*
پیش نامَہ	agenda *n*
پیشگی	advance *n*
پیادہ فوج	infantry *n*
پیار	love *n*
پیار سے	dearly *adv*
پیار کرنا	love *v*
پیارا	lovely, dear *adj*
پیاز	onion *n*
پیاس	thirst *v*
پیاس بجھانا	quench *v*
پیاسا	thirsty *adj*
پیالہ	mug, pail *n*
پیالی	cup, bowl *n*
پیام دینا	herald *n*
پیانوا	piano *n*
پیپ	pus *n*
پیپ پڑنا	fester *v*
پیپا	container *n*
پیپا،حقہ	pipe *n*
پیٹ	tummy *n*
پیٹنا	maul *v*

پ

پیٹھا pumpkin n	پیش کرنا present, offer v
پیچ screw n	پیش گوئی کرنا foretell v
پیچ کس screwdriver n	پیش لفظ foreword n
پیچ لگانا screw v	پیش منظر foreground n
پیچھے after, behind pre	پیشاب urine n
پیچھے چلنا follow, stalk v	پیشاب کرنا urinate v
پیچھے رہ جانا fall behind v	پیشانی forehead n
پیچیدگی complication n	پیشتر درج کرنا prefix n
پیچیدہ intricate adj	پیشکش offer n
پیچیدہ بنانا complicate v	پیشگوئی کرنا forecast v
پیدا کرنا generate v	پیشگی مشاہدہ preview n
پیدا کرنے والا productive adj	پیشن گوئی prophecy n
پیدا ہونا be born v	پیشہ occupation n
پیداوار product n	پیشہ کے متعلق professional adj
پیداواری/نتیجہ production n	پیشہ profession n
پیدائش birth n	پیشوا precursor n
پیدائشی innate adj	پیغام message n
پیدل چلنا march v	پیلا yellow adj
پیدل سفر march n	پیمانہ ruler n
پیر Monday n	پیمائش measurement n
پیراہن tunic n	پیمائش کرنا measure v
پیروکار follower n	پیندا bottom n
پیسنا crush, grind v	پینے کے قابل drinkable adj
پیش آنا behave v	پینے والا drinker n
پیش بندی anticipation n	پیوستگی cohesion n
پیش بندی کرنا premeditate v	پیوند graft n
پیش بینی کرنا foresee v	پیوند لگانا graft, patch v
پیش دست foreman n	
پیش عملی کرنا overdo v	

ت

تا کنا peep v	تازه ترین بنانا update v
تاباں luminous adj	تازه دم کرنے والا refreshing adj
تابع بنانا subject v	تازه ہوا آنے دینا ventilate v
تابوت casket, coffin n	تازیانہ lash n
تأثر behavior n	تاش کا پتا card n
تاثیر effectiveness n	تاکید emphasis n
تاج crown n	تاکید سے particularly adv
تاج پاشی کرنا crown v	تاکید کرنا emphasize v
تاج پوشی coronation n	تاکیدی stressful adj
تاجر merchant n	تالا lock n
تاخیر delay n	تالا کھولنا unlock v
تاخیر کرنا delay v	تالا لگا lock v
تار cable n	تالو palate n
تار برقی wire n	تالی بَجانا applaud v
تارک وطن immigrant n	تالیف composition n
تارکول tar n	تالیف کرنا compile v
تاریخ history n	تان tune n
تاریخ ڈالنا date v	تانبا copper n
تاریک dark, somber adj	تاہم however c
تاریک بنانا darken v	تاوان indemnity n
تاریکی gloom n	تاوان دینا ransom v
تازگی freshness n	تاوقتیکہ till adv
تازگی بخشنا refresh v	تائید collaboration n
تازہ fresh adj	تائید کرنا collaborate v
تازہ بنانا freshen v	تائید کندہ collaborator n
تازہ تر latter adj	تب then adv
تازہ ترین latest adj	تب سے اب تک since then adv
	تبادل کرنا interchange v
	تبادلہ barter, swap v

communicate v تبادلہ خیال	curiosity n تجسس
exchange v تبادلہ کرنا	proposal n تجویز
doomed adj تباہ شدہ	suggest v تجویز کرنا
dismount v تباہ کر دینا	writing n تحریر
exterminate v تباہ کر ڈالنا	enticement n تحریص
destroy, wreck v تباہ کرنا	tempt v تحریص دینا
devastating adj تباہ کن	inspiration n تحریک
destroyer n تباہ کنندہ	motivate v تحریک دینا
crash v تباہ ہو جانا	appreciation n تحسین
devastation n تباہی	acclaim v تحسین
alter v تبدیل کرنا	commend v تحسین کرنا
replacement n تبدیلی	conservation n تحفظ
relic n تبرک	gift n تحفہ
preceding adj تبلیغ	disdain n تحقیر
tuberculosis n تپ دق	inquiry n تحقیق
tripod n تپائی	research v تحقیق کرنا
warmth n تپش	inquest n تحقیقات
thermometer n تپش پیما	dissolution n تحلیل
butterfly n تتلی	dissolve v تحلیل ہونا
trade n تجارت	custody n تحویل
trade v تجارت کرنا	throne n تختِ شاہی
commercial adj تجارتی	board n تختہ
boom n تجارتی تیزی	blackboard n تختہ سیاہ
trespass v تجاوز کرنا	board v تختہ لگانا
renewal n تجدید	springboard n تختہء جست
renovate v تجدید کرنا	cut back v تخفیف
experience n تجربہ	disarmament n تخفیفِ اسلحہ
analyze v تجزیہ کَرنا	devaluation n تخفیفِ قدرِ زر
analysis n تجزیہ	rebate n تخفیف کرنا

ت

تخفیف کرنا reduce v	ترغیب آمیز enticing adj
تخلیق creation n	ترغیب دینا induce v
تخلیق کرنا create v	ترقی headway n
تخلیق نو reproduction n	ترقی دینا promote v
تخلیقی creative adj	ترقی کرنے والا progressive adj
تخمینہ appraisal n	تُرک Turk adj
تخیل کی تخلیق fantasy n	ترک کر دینا discard v
تخیل میں لانا visualize v	ترک کرنا throw away v
تدبیر tact n	تَرک کوشش back down v
تدبیر کرنا devise, plan v	ترکِ وطن immigration n
تدبیرائی tactical adj	ترکِ وطن کرنا immigrate v
تدفین burial n	ترکہ legacy n
تذبذب میں پڑنا confuse v	ترکھان carpenter n
تذلیل کرنا insult v	ترکھان کا پیشہ carpentry n
تراشن trim v	ترکی Turkey n
تراشنا prune v	ترکیب synthesis n
تربوز watermelon n	ترکیب پکوان recipe n
تربیت training n	ترکیب دینا compose v
تربیت کرنا coach, train v	ترکیبی جزو component n
تربیت کرنیوالا trainer n	ترمیم amendment n
ترتیب shift n	ترمیم کرنا۔ amend v
ترجمہ کرنا translate v	تَرنا buoy n
ترجیح preference n	ترنگ heyday n
ترجیح دینا priority n	تریاق antidote n
ترچھا ٹائپ italics adj	تسدید deterrence n
تردید کرنا contradict v	تسکین دہ gratifying adj
ترسیلِ زر remittance n	تسکین کرنا indulge v
ترش ذائقہ tart n	تسلسل continuity n
ترغیب incentive n	تسلی satisfaction n

ت

تسلی بخش satisfactory adj	تصور کرنا imagine v
تسلی دینا console v	تصویر portrait n
تسلیم کر لینا surrender v	تصویر کھینچنا portray v
تسلیم کرنا acknowledge v	تصویر کی مانند picturesque adj
تسمہ lace n	تصویر کینچھنا picture v
تشخیص کا عمَل assessment n	تصویری خاکہ silhouette n
تشخیص diagnosis n	تضاد discrepancy n
تشخیص کرنا diagnose v	تضحیک mockery n
تشدد violence n	تطہیر کرنا sanctify v
تشدد کرنا torture v	تعارف introduction n
تشریح interpretation n	تعاقب chase n
تشریح الاعضا anatomy n	تعاقب کرنا pursue v
تشریح کرنا interpret v	تعاون cooperation n
تشکر gratitude n	تعاون کرنا cooperate v
تشکیل دینا constitute v	تعاون کرنیوالا cooperative adj
تشنج spasm n	تعاونی coefficient n
تشنج پیدا کرنا convulse v	تعبیر ہونا denote v
تشہیر publicity n	تعداد number n
تشویش unrest n	تعداد بڑھانا multiply v
تصادم clash n	تعدد frequency n
تصادم ہونا clash v	تعریف definition n
تصحیح correction n	تعریف کرنا define v
تَصدیق کَرنا authenticate v	تعریفی complimentary adj
تصدیق ratification n	تعزیت condolences n
تصدیق کرنا verify, ratify v	تعصب prejudice n
تصرف میں لانا exploit v	تعطل deadlock adj
تصفیہ clarification n	تعطیل vacation n
تصلیب crucifixion n	تعظیم دینا venerate v
تصور concept n	تعلق link n

ت

refer to *v* تعلق ہونا	meditation *n* تفکر
learning *n* تعلم	assignment *n* تفویض
educate *v* تعلیم دینا	comparative *adj* تقابلی
educational *adj* تعلیمی	claim *n* تقاضا
scholarship *n* تعلیمی وظیفہ	demand *v* تقاضا کرنا
construction *n* تعمیر	holiness *n* تقدس
build *v* تعمیر کرنا	seniority *n* تقدم
rebuild *v* تعمیر نو کرنا	destiny *n* تقدیر
constructive *adj* تعمیری	consecration *n* تقدیس
compliance *n* تعمیلِ حکم	appoint *v* تَقَرَّر کَرنا
carry out *v* تعمیل کرنا	appointment *n* تقرری
generalize *v* تعمیم کرنا	approximate *adj* تَقریباً
orientation *n* تعین رخ	ceremony *n* تقریب
nutrition *n* تغذیہ	almost *adv* تقریباً
immutable *adj* تغیر نا پذیر	speech *n* تقریر
disparity *n* تفاوت	allot *v* تَقسیم کَرنا
investigation *n* تفتیش	distribution *n* تقسیم
probe *v* تفتیش کرنا	divide, split *v* تقسیم کرنا
schism *n* تفرقہ	almanac *n* تَقویم ۔ جَنتری
amusing *adj* تَفریحی	to *pre* تک
amusement *n* تفریح	recurrence *n* تکرار
recreate *v* تفریح کرنا	reverence *n* تکریم
excursion *n* تفریحی سفر	glorify *v* تکریم دینا
subtraction *n* تفریق	annoying *adj* تَکلیف دہ
subtract *v* تفریق کرنا	pang *n* تکلیف
detail *n* تفصیل	troublesome *adj* تکلیف دہ
detail *v* تفصیل بتانا	perturb *v* تکلیف دینا
recount *n* تفصیل بیان کرنا	trouble *v* تکلیف میں ہونا
in depth *adv* تفصیل سے	complement *n* تکملہ

تکمیل fulfillment _n_	**تلملانا** writhe _v_
تکنیک technique _n_	**تلنا** fry _v_
تکنیک کار technician _n_	**تلنے کا برتن** frying pan _n_
تکنیکی technical _adj_	**تلوار** sword _n_
تکنیکیت technicality _n_	**تلوار بازی** fencing _n_
تکہ بوٹی chop _n_	**تماشائی** spectator _n_
تکیہ pillow _n_	**تمام ـ سب** all _adj_
تکیہ کا غلاف pillowcase _n_	**تمباکو** tobacco _n_
تکیہ کلام catchword _n_	**تمتما اٹھنا** blush _v_
تکیہ لگانا bolster _v_	**تَمثیلی اِستَدلال** analogy _n_
تگ و دو کرنا exert _v_	**تمسخر** ridicule _n_
تگنا triple _adj_	**تمسخر اُڑانا** mock _v_
تِل mole _n_	**تمغا** medal _n_
تَلا sole _n_	**تموج** surge _n_
تلا ہوا fried _adj_	**تمیز** discrimination _n_
تلاش search _n_	**تمیز کرنا** discriminate _v_
تلاش کرنا find out _v_	**تنا** stem _n_
تلافی expiation _n_	**تنا ہوا** tense _adj_
تلافی کر لینا get over _v_	**تناسب** symmetry _n_
تَلافی کَرنا atone, expiate _v_	**تناہی** havoc _n_
تلبیس camouflage _n_	**تنائو** tension _n_
تلبیس کرنا camouflage _v_	**تنخواہ** pay, salary _n_
تلچھٹ residue _n_	**تند** impetuous _adj_
تلخ ذائقہ poignant _adj_	**تند ہوا** gust _n_
تلخہ rye _n_	**تندخو** fierce _adj_
تلخی rancor _n_	**تندرست کرنا** cure _v_
تلخی پیدا کرنا embitter _v_	**تندی** rigor _n_
تَلخی سے bitterly _adv_	**تنزلی کرنا** demote _v_
تلف کرنا dispose _v_	**تنسیخ** cancellation _n_

installation _n_	تنصیب	quiver _v_	تھرتھرانا
install _v_	تنصیب کرنا	thermostat _n_	تھرمو سٹیٹ
organization _n_	تنظیم	exhausting _adj_	تھکا دینے والا
criticism _n_	تنقید	tired _adj_	تھکا ہوا
criticize _v_	تنقید کرنا	tedium _n_	تھکاوٹ
critical _adj_	تنقیدی	fatigue _n_	تھکن
straw _n_	تنکا	muzzle _n_	تھوتھنی
narrow _adj_	تنگ	slightly _adv_	تھوڑا سا
bottleneck _n_	تنگ راستہ	span _n_	تھوڑا سا عرصہ
loophole _n_	تنگ سوراخ	wholesale _n_	تھوک فروشی
pinch _v_	تنگ کرنا	spit _v_	تھوکنا
lonely _adv_	تنہا	theater _n_	تھیٹر
isolate _v_	تنہا کردینا	equilibrium _n_	توازن
segregation _n_	تنہاسازی	recant _v_	توبہ کرنا
isolation _n_	تنہائی	cannon _n_	توپ
diversity _n_	تنوع	bombshell _n_	توپ کا گولا
hypnosis _n_	تنویم	gunshot _n_	توپ گولا
mesmerize _v_	تنویم کرنا	artillery _n_	توپخانہ
basement _n_	تہ خانہ	endorsement _n_	توثیق
civilization _n_	تہذیب	endorse _v_	توثیق کرنا
calumny _n_	تہمت	attention _n_	تَوَجُہ
coat, layer _n_	تہہ	cater to _v_	توجہ دینا
cellar _n_	تہہ خانہ	noteworthy _adj_	توجہ کے قابل
wholehearted _adj_	تہہ دل سے	notice _v_	توجہ میں لانا
turn up _v_	تہہ کرنا	parcel _n_	تودہ گٹھری
hold _v_	تھامنا	abolish _v_	توڑ دینا
stall _n_	تھان	break open _v_	توڑ کر کھولنا
plummet _v_	تھاہ لینے کا لنگر	counteract _v_	توڑ کرنا
slap _v_	تھپڑ مارنا	smash _v_	توڑپھڑ دینا

توڑنا مروڑنا distort v	تیز رفتاری سے speedily adv
توڑنے کا عمل breach n	تیز رو swift adj
توس toast n	تیز روشنی floodlight n
توسیع enlargement n	تیز کرنا sharpen v
توقع expectation n	تیز ہوا کی زد میں windy adj
توقع رکھنا expect v	تیزاب acid n
توقف postponement n	تیزابیت acidity n
توقیر esteem v	تیس thirty adj
تولنا scale v	تیسرا third adj
تولیہ towel n	تیل oil n
توندل obese adj	تیل دینا lubricate v
توہم superstition n	تیمارداری کرنا nurse v
توہین libel n	تین three adj
توہین آمیز derogatory adj	تیندوا panther n
توہین کرنا disgrace v	تیوری چڑھانا frown v
تِیر arrow n	تیوہاری festive adj
تیار ready adj	
تیار کرنا brace for v	
تیاری readiness n	
تیتر pheasant n	
تیراک swimmer n	
تیراکی swimming n	
تیرنا float, swim v	
تیرہ thirteen adj	
تیز brisk, fast adj	
تیز تر کرنا quicken v	
تیز دھار torrent n	
تیز دھار والا edgy adj	
تیز رفتار speedy adj	

ٹ

ٹارنٹو کی مکڑی tarantula n
ٹاکسن toxin n
ٹال stack n
ٹال دینا fend v
ٹال مٹول evasion n
ٹالنا put off v
ٹانسل tonsil n

ٹانکا	stitch *n*
ٹانکا لگانا	solder *v*
ٹانکنا	stitch *v*
ٹانگ	leg *n*
ٹائپ کرنا	type *v*
ٹاؤن ہال	town hall *n*
ٹائی	necktie *n*
ٹب	tub *n*
ٹپکانا	instil *v*
ٹٹو	nag *v*
ٹخنہ	ankle *n*
ٹڈی	locust *n*
ٹرافی	trophy *n*
ٹرالی	trolley *n*
ٹرام	streetcar *n*
ٹرام گاڑی	tram *n*
ٹرائوٹ	trout *n*
ٹربائن	turbine *n*
ٹرک والا	trucker *n*
ٹریبیونل	tribunal *n*
ٹریفک	traffic *n*
ٹریکٹر	tractor *n*
ٹکانا	lay *v*
ٹکر روک	bumper *n*
ٹکراؤ	crash *n*
ٹکرانا	crash, strike *v*
ٹکرائو	collision *n*
ٹکرنا	collide *v*
ٹکڑا	slice, piece *n*

ٹکڑے ٹکڑے کرنا	splinter *v*
ٹکڑے کرنا	scrap *v*
ٹکنالوجی	technology *n*
ٹماٹر	tomato *n*
ٹمٹمانا	twinkle *v*
ٹن	ton *n*
ٹہلنا	pace *n*
ٹہنی	bough *n*
ٹھوڑا	counter *n*
ٹھکانا	whereabouts *n*
ٹھگ	hoodlum *n*
ٹھگنا	defraud *v*
ٹھنڈا	frigid, cool *adj*
ٹھنڈا کرنا	chill, cool *v*
ٹھنڈک	coolness *n*
ٹھنڈک بخش	cooling *adj*
ٹھہرائو	stop *n*
ٹھہرنا	stay *v*
ٹھوڑی	chin *n*
ٹھوس	solid *adj*
ٹھوس بنانا	consolidate *v*
ٹھوسنا	stuff *v*
ٹھوکر کھا جانا	stumble *v*
ٹھوکر مارنا	kick *v*
ٹھیک ٹھیک	exact *adj*
ٹھیک ہے	alright *adv*
ٹھیلا	trailer, cart *n*
ٹوپی	hat, cap *n*
ٹوٹ	break *n*

ث

ثابت شدہ proven *adj*
ثابت قدم consistent *adj*
ثابت قدم رہنا persist *v*
ثابت قدمی persistence *n*
ثالث mediator *n*
ثالث بَننا arbitrate *v*
ثالثی arbitration *n*
ثانوی secondary *adj*
ثانوی معنی دینا connote *v*
ثبات constancy *n*
ثبوت proof *n*
ثبوت دینا prove *v*
ثمردار fruity *adj*
ثنا praise *n*

ج

جا نشین successor *n*
جابر despot *n*
جابرانہ despotic *adj*
جاپان Japan *n*
جاپانی Japanese *adj*
جادو magic *n*
جادو گرنی witch *n*

ٹوٹ پھوٹ split *n*
ٹوٹا پھوٹا dilapidated *adj*
ٹوٹا ہوا broken *adj*
ٹوٹنا break, sever *v*
ٹورنامنٹ tournament *n*
ٹوکری basket *n*
ٹولہ gang *n*
ٹونٹی faucet, tap *n*
ٹیڑھا کَرنا bend *v*
ٹیپ ریکارڈر tape recorder *n*
ٹیڑھا crook *n*
ٹیکا injection *n*
ٹیکا لگانا inject *v*
ٹیکس tax *n*
ٹیکسی cab *n*
ٹیلی فون telephone *n*
ٹیلی فون کا آلہ phone *n*
ٹیلی وژن television *n*
ٹیم team *n*
ٹین کا ڈبہ tin *n*
ٹینس tennis *n*
ٹینس کا چھکا racket *n*
ٹیوٹر tutor *n*
ٹیوشن tuition *n*
ٹیومر tumor *n*

magician n جادوگر	diligence n جانفشانی
sorcery n جادوگری	briefs n جانگھیا
magical adj جادوئی	know v جاننا
absorbent adj جاذب	animal n • جانور
aggressive adj جارحانہ	let go v جانے دینا
aggression n جارحیت	ignorant adj جاہل
aggressor n جارحیت پسند	ignorance n جاہلیت
continuous adj جاری	lawful adj جائز
continue v جاری رکھنا	review n جائزہ
spy n جاسوس	review v جائزہ لینا
espionage n جاسوسی	hideaway n جائےپناہ جگہ
eavesdrop v جاسوسی کرنا	estate n جائیداد
awake v جاگنا	while c جب تک کہ
mesh, net n جال	whenever adv جب کبھی
gauze n جالی	constraint n جبر
screen v جالی لگانا	compelling adj جبری
chalice n جام	jaw n جبڑا
academy n جامعہ	whereas c جبکہ
bathrobe n جامہ غُسَل	instinct n جبلت
devotion n جان نثاری	cassock, robe n جبہ
vitality n جان	batch n جتھا
rescue v جان بچانا	aloof adj جُدا
animate v جان ڈالنا	apart adv جدا ۔ الگ
diligent adj جان فشان	insulate v جدا کرنا
go v جانا	contentious adj جدال پسن
behalf (on) adv جانب سے	innovation n جدت
scrutiny n جانچ	conservative adj جدت کا مخالف
appraise v جانچنا	struggle n جدوجہد
hardy adj جانفشاں	battle v جدوجہد کرنا

جدول schedule v	جزیرہ island n
جدید modern adj	جزیرہ نما peninsula n
جدید بنانا modernize v	جس پر whereupon c
جذب کرنا absorb v	جسارت audacity n
جذبات کا مظاہرہ scene n	جسامت bulk n
جذباتی emotional adj	جست کاری کرنا galvanize v
جذبہ emotion n	جست لگانا spring v
جذر ebb v	جسم body n
جراب sock n	جسم کل عضو پتہ pancreas n
جرات courage n	جسمانی bodily adj
جرات کرنا dare v	جسمانی طور پر physically adv
جرات مند courageous adj	جسمانی معائنہ check up n
جراح surgeon n	جسمیہ corpuscle n
جراحی کرنا operate v	جسیم massive adj
جرثومہ germ n	جعل سازی forgery n
جرسی jersey n	جعل سازی کرنا forge v
جرم crime n	جعلی fake adj
جرمانہ fine n	جعلی روپ دینا fake v
جرمانہ کرنا fine v	جغرافیہ geography n
جرمن German adj	جفاکش tough adj
جرمنی Germany n	جکڑ بند stapler n
جریان خون hemorrhage n	جگ jug n
جڑ root n	جگانا rouse v
جڑسے اکھاڑنا stamp out v	جگر liver n
جڑواں twin n	جگہ place n
جڑی بوٹی herb n	جل اچھل cataclysm n
جز ingredient n	جل پری mermaid n
جزوی partial adj	جلا وطن کرنا banish v
جزوی طور پر partially adv	جلا وطنی banishment n

جلانا scald v	جمعہ Friday n
جلاوطن کرنا exile v	جملہ sentence v
جلاوطنی exile n	جملہ متعرضہ parenthesis n
جلد skin n	جمنازیم gymnasium n
جلدبازی کرنا rash v	جمہوری democratic adj
جلدی early adv	جمہوریت democracy n
جلدی سے quickly adv	جمہوریہ republic n
جلدی کرنا hasten v	جمود stagnation n
جلن burn n	جنازہ funeral n
جلنا burn v	جنبش دینا wiggle v
جَلنے کا اِحساس ardent adj	جنبش کرنا wag v
جلوس procession n	جنت heaven n
جمِ غفیر legion n	جنتری calendar n
جما رہنا adhere v	جنریٹر generator n
جما ہوا steady adj	جنس sex n
جماعت class n	جنسی کشش sexuality n
جماعت بندی کرنا classify v	جنگ war n
جَمالیاتی artistic adj	جنگ جو fighter n
جمالیاتی aesthetic adj	جنگ و جدل warfare n
جمانا implant v	جنگاری spark n
جماوٹ coagulation n	جنگجو militant adj
جمائی yawn n	جنگل forest, jungle n
جمائی لینا yawn v	جنگلا fence n
جمع plural n	جنگلہ handrail n
جمع کرنا accumulate v	جنگلی savage adj
جمع کرنے والا collector n	جنگلی بلا lynx n
جمع کروانا deposit n	جنگلی پن savagery n
جمع ہونا convene v	جنگلی حیات wildlife n
جمعرات Thursday n	جنگلی سور wild boar n

ج

warship n جنگی بحری جهاز	bush, shrub n جهاڑی
battleship n جنگی جَهاز	fringe n جهالر
procreate v جننا	rake n جهانپنا
south n جنوب	freckle n جهائی
southerner n جنوب کا باسی	jerk n جهٹکا
southeast n جنوب مشرق	jerk v جهٹکے دینا
southern adj جنوبی	cluster n جهرمٹ
January n جنوری	cluster v جهرمٹ بنانا
craziness n جنون	chute n جهرنا
crazy adj جنونی	groove, slot n جهری
embryo n جنین	skirmish n جهڑپ
ship n جهاز	rebuff v جهڑکنا
aboard adv جهاز پر	rebuff n جهڑکی
disembark v جهاز سے اترنا	pour v جهڑنا
prow n جهاز کا اگلا حصہ	curve v جهکا ہونا
pilot n جهاز کا رہنما	tilt v جهکانا
airfare n جهاز کا کرایہ	leaning n جهکائو
berth n جهاز کا کمرا	gale n جهکڑ
navigation n جهازرانی	lean v جهُکنا
navigate v جهازرانی کرنا	brawl n جهگڑا
shipyard n جهازگاہ	quarrelsome adj جهگڑالو
shipment n جهازی سامان	swing v جهلانا
barbarism n جَهالَت	scorch v جهلسانا
inasmuch as c جهاں تک	glimpse n جهلک
hell n جهنم	glimpse v جهلک دکهانا
plutonium n جهنمی	glimmer n جهلمل کرنا
dowry n جهیز	membrane n جهلی
broom n جهاڑو	flag n جهنڈا
sweep v جهاڑو دینا	lie n جهوٹ

جھوٹ بولنا	lie v
جھوٹ موٹ بننا	feign v
جھوٹا	untrue adj
جھوٹی تعبیر کرنا	misinterpret v
جھولا	swing n
جھولن کھٹولا	hammock n
جھولنا	dangle, sway v
جھیل	lake n
جھیلنا	undergo v
جھینگا	lobster, shrimp n
جھینگا مچھلی	prawn n
جَو	barley n
جو بھی	whoever pro
جو کچھ بھی	whatever adj
جوا کھیلنا	gamble v
جواب	answer, reply v
جواب دہی	liability n
جواب دہی کرنا	account for v
جواب دینا	answer, reply n
جوابی رائے	feedback n
جواربھاٹا	tide n
جواز	validity n
جواز بنانا	validate v
جوان	grown-up n
جوانمردانہ	heroic adj
جوانی	youth n
جوب مغرب	southwest n
جوت	yoke n
جوتا	footwear n

جوتوں کی دوکان	shoestore n
جوتے کا تسمہ	shoelace n
جوتے کی پالش	shoepolish n
جوڑ	connection n
جوڑ بنانا	match v
جوڑ کی سوزش	arthritis n
جوڑا	couple, pair n
جوڑا رقص	waltz n
جوڑنا	adjoin, link v
جوڑنے والا	riveting adj
جوز دار	nutty adj
جوش	excitement n
جوش آنا	boil over v
جوش پیدا کرنا	thrill v
جوش دلانا	excite v
جوش دینا	stir v
جوش و خروش	enthusiasm n
جوکھم	venture n
جولائی	July n
جوں	louse n
جوں (جمع)	lice n
جون	June n
جونک	leech n
جونئیر	junior adj
جوہر	jewel, gem n
جوہرِ قہوہ	caffeine n
جوہری	jeweler n
جوہری ۔ ذَراتی	atomic adj
جوہڑ	pond n

جیسا as adv	چاره bait n
جی چرانا shirk v	چاروں طرف around pre
جیب pocket n	چاک chalk n
جیب تراش pickpocket n	چاکلیٹ chocolate n
جیتنا win v	چال ruse n
جیک پاٹ jackpot n	چال چلن conduct n
جیکٹ jacket n	چالاک clever adj
جیل jail n	چالباز crooked adj
جیل بھیجنا jail v	چالیس forty adj
جیل خانہ prison n	چالیں چلنا trick v
جیلر jailer n	چانٹا slap n
جین gene n	چاند moon n
جینز jeans n	چاندی silver n
جینی genetic adj	چاندی چڑھا ہوا silverplated adj
جیوری jury n	چاندی کے برتن silverware n
جیومیٹری geometry n	چاہنا aspire, want v
جئی کا کھانا oatmeal n	چاہیے must v
	چاول rice n
	چائے tea n
	چائے دانی teapot n
	چائے کا چمچ teaspoon n
چ	چپ dent n
	چپ پڑنا dent v
	چبانا chew v
چابک scourge n	چبھن stab, sting n
چابی key n	چبھنا prick v
چاپلوسی adulation n	چبھونا prod, stick v
چاٹنا lick v	چبوترا terrace n
چار four adj	چبوتره platform n
چارٹ chart n	

ج
چ

چپاتی loaf, cake n	چرنا graze v
چپٹا flat adj	چڑچڑا fussy adj
چپٹی کیل thumbtack n	چڑچڑا آدمی grumpy adj
چپٹی کھپچی splint n	چڑھنا climb v
چِپَڑنا anoint v	چڑھاوا offering n
چپکانے والے adhesive adj	چڑھائی hike n
چپکتی چیز مَلنا smear v	چڑھنا mount v
چپو oar n	چڑیا sparrow n
چپو چلانا paddle v	چڑیا گھر zoo n
چٹ label n	چسپاں ہو جانیوال sticker n
چٹ کر جانا eat away v	چست smart adj
چٹان rock n	چُست ۔ تَوانا athletic adj
چٹانی کھاڑی fjord n	چسکا propensity n
چٹائی mat n	چسکی sip n
چٹخارہ smack n	چسکی لینا sip v
چٹخنی latch n	چشم پوش ہونا connive v
چٹکی nip, pinch n	چشمہ fountain n
چٹنی sauce n	چغہ cloak n
چچی aunt n	چقندر beet n
چڈّا groin n	چکر cycle n
چرا لے جانا snitch v	چکر کاٹنا circle v
چراغاں lighting n	چکر لگانا frequent v
چراگاہ meadow n	چَکرا دینا baffle v
چرانا steal v	چکمہ hoax n
چربی دار fatty adj	چکنا balmy adj
چرٹیوں پر چڑھنا climbing n	چِکنا کرنا grease v
چرخی pulley n	چکنا مواد smear n
چرمرانا creak v	چکنائو lubrication n
چرمراہٹ creak n	چکنائی fat n

چکنی سطح polish n	چندھیا جانا dazzle v
چکی mill n	چندھیا دینا glare n
چلّانا yell, shout v	چننا pluck, uproot v
چلّاہٹ والا squeaky adj	چہرہ face n
چلتا زینہ escalator n	چہرہ مہرہ figure n
چلنا walk v	چہل قدمی promenade n
چمپین champion n	چھا مارنا raid v
چمٹا tongs n	چھاپا raid n
چمٹنا cling v	چھاپا مار raider n
چمٹنے والا sticky adj	چھاپنے کا ہنر printing n
چمچ spoon n	چھاپنے والا printer n
چمچ بھر spoonful n	چھاپہ خانہ،ضرورت press n
چمڑا leather n	چھاپہ مار guerrilla n
چمک brightness n	چھاتی chest, breast n
چمک دمک gloss n	چھال bark n
چمک والا brilliant adj	چھالا blister n
چمکانا brighten v	چھان بین probing n
چمکدار shiny adj	چھانٹنا weed v
چمکنا glow, shine v	چھاننا filter, sift v
چمکیلا کرنا polish v	چھائونی garrison n
چمگادڑ vampire n	چھپاکی rash n
چمنی chimney n	چھپانا conceal v
چنا gram n	چھپنا print v
چنابا munch v	چھت ceiling, roof n
چنانچہ hence adv	چھتر سپاہی paratrooper n
چنت ڈالنا pleat n	چھتری umbrella n
چند few adj	چھتہ hive n
چندہ subscription n	چھٹا sixth adj
چندہ دینا subscribe v	چھٹکارہ پانا rid of v

postman n	چھٹی رساں	hamlet n	چھوٹا گاءوں
holiday n	چھٹی کا دن	cubicle n	چھوٹامکعب کمرہ
mole n	چھچھوندر	chore n	چھوٹاموٹا کام
sparse adj	چھدرا	dart n	چھوٹی برچھی
bayonet n	چھرا	ripple n	چھوٹی سی موج
knife n	چھری	handbook n	چھوٹی کتاب
cutlery n	چھری کانٹے	forsake v	چھوڑ دینا
redeem v	چھڑا لینا	absolve v	چھوڑنا
disentangle v	چھڑانا	pass away v	چھوڑ جانا
sprinkle v	چھڑکنا	waive, quit v	چھوڑ دینا
stick n	چھڑی	touch v	چھونا
truck n	چھکڑا	bore v	چھیدنا
bruise v	چھل جانا	tease v	چھیڑنا
curl n	چھلا	obliterate v	چھیل دینا
curl v	چھلا بنانا	strip v	چھین لینا
jump, leap n	چھلانگ	splash v	چھینٹے اڑانا
leap v	چھلانگ لگانا	sneeze n	چھینک
peel n	چھلکا	sneeze v	چھینکنا
overflow v	چھلکنا	snatch v	چھیننا
crusty adj	چھلکے دار	chisel n	چھینی
peel v	چھلنا	wooden adj	چوبی
filter n	چھلنی	hip n	چوتڑ
six adj	چھ	fourth adj	چوتھا
remission n	چھوٹ	quarter n	چوتھا حصہ
short, small adj	چھوٹا	hit, strike n	چوٹ
deacon n	چھوٹا پادری	summit, top n	چوٹی
bit n	چھوٹا سا ٹکڑا	fourteen adj	چودہ
speck n	چھوٹا سا دھبہ	thief n	چور
shorten v	چھوٹا کرنا	crumb n	چورا

چورا چورا کرنا crumble v	چیخنا scream v
چوراہا crossroads n	چیخنے کا عمل shouting n
چوری theft n	چیرا cut n
چوڑ broad adj	چیرنا hack v
چوڑا wide adj	چیز thing n
چوڑا کرنا broaden v	چیک بک checkbook n
چوڑائی breadth n	چیل کا درخت pine n
چوزہ chick n	چینی sugar n
چوسنا suck v	
چوسنے والا sucker adj	
چوغہ gown n	
چوکس alert n	
چوکنّا watchful adj	ح
چوکھٹا frame n	
چوکی desk n	حاجب usher n
چول hinge n	حاجی pilgrim n
چول چھلا swivel v	حادثہ accident n
چولھا stove n	حار torrid adj
چونا پتھر limestone n	حاسد jealous adj
چونچ beak n	حاشیہ margin n
چونکا دینا startle v	حاصل کردہ نمبر score n
چونکا دینے والا mind-boggling adj	حاصل کرنا achieve, get v
چونکہ as c	حاضر present adj
چوہا mouse, rat n	حاضر کرنا produce v
چوہے (جمع) mice n	حاضر ہونا attend v
چیونٹی ant n	حاضری attendance n
چیتھڑا rag n	حافظہ memory n
چیچک smallpox n	حاکم president n
چیخ scream, shout n	حاکم کا علاقہ presidency n

حال ہی میں lately *adv*	حرارت heat *n*
حالات circumstance *n*	حرارہ calorie *n*
حالات ۔ مقابل antecedents *n*	حراست detention *n*
حالت position *n*	حرامی bastard *n*
حالیہ recent *adj*	حرص frailty *n*
حامِل bearer *n*	حرف اضافت preposition *n*
حاملہ pregnant *adj*	حرفِ صحیح consonant *n*
حامی supporter *n*	حرفِ علت vowel *n*
حائل ہونا intervene *v*	حرکت movement *n*
حبس والا stuffy *adj*	حرکت کرنا move *v*
حتمی final *adj*	حرم sanctuary *n*
حتمی بیان ۔ الزام allegation *n*	حرمت sanctity *n*
حتمی طور پر کہنا pronounce *v*	حروفِ تہجی alphabet *n*
حتمی وقت deadline *n*	حَریص avaricious *adj*
حتی المقدور utmost *adj*	حَریف adversary *n*
حتٰی کہ until *pre*	حریص insatiable *adj*
حتٰی کہ اگر even if *c*	حس sense *n*
حج pilgrimage *n*	حساب کتاب account *n*
حَجَام barber *n*	حساب کرنا compute *v*
حجامت haircut *n*	حساب کرنیوالا computer *n*
حجرہ cabin *n*	حساب لکھنے والا accountant *n*
حجم volume *n*	حساس sensitive *adj*
حد limit, range *n*	حسب الحکم according to *pre*
حد سے گزر جانا exceed *v*	حسب قاعدہ normal *adj*
حدِ فاصل borderline *adj*	حَسب و نَسَب ancestry *n*
حدود میں رکھنا confine *v*	حسد jealousy *n*
حذف omission *n*	حسد کرنا envy *v*
حذف کرنا eliminate *v*	حسن elegance *n*
حَذفی علامَت apostrophe *n*	حسین elegant *adj*

ح

حشر resurrection *n*	حکم دیتے رہنا boss around *v*
حشیش hashish *n*	حکم دینا decree *v*
حصاربندی کرنا fortify *v*	حکم عدولی defiance *n*
حصہ portion, share *n*	حکم ماننا comply *v*
حصہ داری participation *n*	حکمتِ عملی strategy *n*
حصہ ڈالنا contribute *v*	حکمران ruler *n*
حصہ ڈالنے والا contributor *n*	حکمرانی کرنا dominate *v*
حصہ لینا participate *v*	حکومت government *n*
حصول attainment *n*	حکومت کرنا govern *v*
حصے بخرے کرنا part *v*	حکیم doctor *n*
حصے دار shareholder *n*	حل پذیر soluble *adj*
حفاظت safety *n*	حل کر لینا figure out *v*
حق right *n*	حل کرنا solve *v*
حَق جَتانا affirm *v*	حل ناپذیر insoluble *adj*
حق داخلہ entree *n*	حلف oath *n*
حق کھو دینا forfeit *v*	حلفی شہادت testimony *n*
حق کے مقدمہ کرنا sue *v*	حلقہ circle, ring *n*
حق ملکیت royalty *n*	حلقہ بنانا encircle *v*
حقارت affront *n*	حلقے میں لینا encompass *v*
حقارت آمیز scornful *adj*	حلوہ pudding *n*
حقارت برتنا snub *v*	حلیف allied *adj*
حقدار ہونا own *adj*	حلیمی gentleness *n*
حقیر meager *adj*	حلیہ countenance *n*
حقیقت fact *n*	حماقت folly *n*
حقیقت پسند down-to-earth *adj*	حمایت کرنا patronize *v*
حقیقتاً really *adv*	حمد hymn *n*
حقیقی actual *adj*	حمل pregnancy *n*
حکم decree, order *n*	حمل گرانا abort *v*
حکمِ الہٰی commandment *n*	حملہ assault *n*

ح

attacker *n*	حملہ آور
invade *v*	حملہ آور ہونا
assault, mug *v*	حملہ کرنا
embalm *v*	حنوط کرنا
reference *n*	حوالہ
quote *v*	حوالہ دینا
hand over *v*	حوالے کرنا
encourage *v*	حوصلہ بڑھانا
daunting *adj*	حوصلہ شکن
discouragement *n*	حوصلہ شکنی
ambitious *adj*	حوصلہ مند
cistern *n*	حوض
edifice *n*	حویلی
biological *adj*	حَیاتیاتی
astounding *adj*	حیرَت انگیز
beast *n*	حیوان
bestial *adj*	حیوانی
vital *adj*	حیات بخش
surprise *v*	حیران کر دینا
stupendous *adj*	حیران کن
wonder *v*	حیران ہونا
surprise *n*	حیرت
astonishing *adj*	حیرت انگیز
startled *adj*	حیرت زدہ
stun *v*	حیرت زدہ کرنا
menstruation *n*	حیض
zoology *n*	حیوانیات

خ

closure *n*	خاتمہ
lady *n*	خاتون
hostess *n*	خاتون میزبان
porcupine *n*	خارپشت
extraneous *adj*	خارج از
outcast *adj*	خارج شدہ
quotient *n*	خارج قسمت
pump *v*	خارج کرنا
emanate *v*	خارج ہونا
external *adj*	خارجی
special *adj*	خاص
mannerism *n*	خاص ڈھب
oriented *adj*	خاص رخ پرمتیعن
especially *adv*	خاص طور پر
mission *n*	خاص مقصد
sizable *adj*	خاصا بڑا
characteristic *adj*	خاصیت
entertain *v*	خاطرمدارت کرنا
humble *adj*	خاکسار
grayish *adj*	خاکستری سا
profile, sketch *n*	خاکہ
sketch *v*	خاکہ بنانا
outline *v*	خاکہ بیان کرنا
pure *adj*	خالص
creator *n*	خالق
empty *adj*	خالی
emptiness *n*	خالی پن

divine *adj*	خدائی
service *n*	خدمت
serve *v*	خدمت کرنا
attendant *n*	خِدمَت گار
feature *n*	خدوخال
bad *adj*	خراب
break down *v*	خراب ہوجانا
snore *v*	خراٹے لینا
leakage *n*	خراج
bruise *n*	خراش
melon *n*	خربوزہ
cantaloupe *n*	خربوزہ نما پھل
consumption *n*	خرچ
spend *v*	خرچ کرنا
spending *n*	خرچہ
wheeze *v*	خرخر کرنا
snore *n*	خرخراہٹ
raccoon *n*	خرسک
hare, rabbit *n*	خرگوش
exit *n*	خروج کا رستہ
buyer *n*	خریدار
purchase *n*	خریداری
shop *v*	خریداری کرنا
buy *v*	خریدنا
autumn *n*	خزاں
cashier *n*	خزانچی
treasure *n*	خزانہ
deficit *n*	خسارہ
crisp *adj*	خستہ

vacancy *n*	خالی جگہ
empty, vacate *v*	خالی کرنا
coarse *adj*	خام
calm, serene *adj*	خاموش
silence *v*	خاموش کرانا
quietness *n*	خاموشی
shortcoming *n*	خامی
family *n*	خاندان
feud *n*	خاندانی رقابت
butler *n*	خانساماں
abbey *n*	خانقاہ
domestic *adj*	خانگی
vagrant *n*	خانہ بدوش
seclusion *n*	خانہ نشینی
husband *n*	خاوند
spouse *n*	خاوند یا بیوی
information *n*	خبر
reportedly *adv*	خبر کے لحاظ سے
newscast *n*	خبر نامہ
warn *v*	خبردار کرنا
terminate *v*	ختم کرنا
end *v*	ختم کرنا/ہونا
expire *v*	ختم ہو جانا
circumcision *n*	ختنے
circumcise *v*	ختنے کرنا
mule *n*	خچر
God *n*	خدا
piety *n*	خدا ترسی
prophet *n*	خدا کا رسول

خ

خلاصہ summary n	خستہ حال decrepit adj
خلاصہ بیان کرنا v recap	خستہ حالی misery n
خلاصہ کرنا v epitomize	خسرہ measles n
خلاصی rescue n	خشک dried, dry adj
خلاف averse adj	خشک ساز dryer n
خلافِ شان beneath pre	خشک سالی drought n
خلافِ قانون illicit adj	خشک کرنا v dry, parch
خلافِ قیاس unlikely adj	خشکی پر اترنا v land
خلاف معمول abnormal adj	خصاب dye n
خلال toothpick n	خصلت trait n
خلانورد astronaut n	خصوصیت specialty n
خلط ملط mix-up n	خط letter, line n
خلل disturbance n	خط استوا equator n
خلل ڈالنا v disturb	خطِ حرکت trajectory n
خلل ڈالنے والا alarming adj	خطِ ربط hyphen n
خلوتی کمرہ closet n	خط کشیدہ کرنا v underline
خَلیج bay n	خط منحنی curve n
خلیج gulf n	خطاب کرنا v address
خم دار winding adj	خطائی cookie n
خم دینا v flex	خطبہ address n
خمدار رستہ swing n	خطرناک dangerous adj
خمیدہ crooked adj	خطرہ danger n
خمیر ferment n	خطرہ مول لینا v endanger
خمیر اٹھانا v ferment	خطرے کی اطلاع alarm n
خنجر dagger n	خطہ region n
خنزیر hog n	خفا کرنا gripe n
خواب dream n	خفا ہونا v resent
خواب دیکھنا v dream	خفگی resentment n
خواب گاہ bedroom n	خفیہ confidential adj

خ

خواستگار ہونا crave v	خوش قسمت lucky adj
خواہش desire, wish n	خوش کرنا please v
خواہش کرنا desire, wish v	خوش ہونا rejoice v
خوب کھلانا pamper v	خوش وضع graceful adj
خُوبانی apricot n	خوشامد flattery n
خوبرو handsome adj	خوشامد کرنا flatter v
خوبصورت beautiful adj	خوشبو perfume n
خوبصورتی beauty n	خُوشبُو دار aromatic adj
خُود auto n	خوشبودار fragrant adj
خود آئینی autonomous adj	خوشحال well-to-do adj
خود بخود spontaneous adj	خوشخلقی courtesy n
خود پسند conceited adj	خوشگوار cordial adj
خُود توقیری self-esteem n	خوشی happiness n
خُود کار automatic adj	خوشی سے joyfully adv
خُود مُتَحَرک automobile n	خوف fright, fear n
خود مختارانہ arbitrary adj	خوف زدہ fearful adj
خودغرض selfish adj	خوف زدہ کرنا horrify v
خودغرضی selfishness n	خوفزدہ dreaded adj
خودکشی suicide n	خوفزدہ کرنا frighten v
خودنمائی vanity n	خوفناک dreadful adj
خوراک ration n	خوفناک لگنا loom v
خوراک دینا feed v	خول shell n
خوش glad, happy adj	خون blood n
خُوش اِخلاق affable adj	خون بستگی thrombosis n
خوش آمدید welcome n	خون خوار ferocious adj
خوش خلق courteous adj	خون خواری ferocity n
خوش ذائقہ tasteful adj	خون کا پیاسا bloodthirsty adj
خوش شکل good-looking adj	خون نکلنا bleed v
خوش طبع pleasant adj	خونی bloody adj

خ

avenue *n* خَیابان	داد رسی کرنا *v* redress
alms *n* خیرات	دادا *n* grandfather
mall *n* خیابان	دادا دادی *n* grandparents
notion, idea *n* خیال	داداگیر *n* gangster
fancy *adj* خیال آفرینی	دادی *n* grandmother
telepathy *n* خیال رسانی	دار چینی *n* cinnamon
care *v* خیال رکھنا	دارُالامان *n* asylum
ideal *adj* خیالی	داروغہ عورت *n* stewardess
daydream *v* خیالی پلاعو	داڑھی *n* beard
vision *n* خیالی صورت	داڑھی بنانا *v* shave
plunder *v* خیانت کرنا	داستان *n* myth
goodwill *n* خیر سگالی	داغ *n* scar
welcome *v* خیر مقدم کرنا	داغ دوش *n* blemish
blind *v* خیرہ کرنا	داغ لگانا *v* blemish
dazzling *adj* خیرہ کن	داغدار *adj* tainted
tent, camp *n* خیمہ	داغدار کرنا *v* tarnish
camp *v* خیمہ زن ہونا	دافع *adj* repulsive
	دافع بد بو *n* deodorant
	دالان *n* gallery
د	داماد *n* son-in-law
	دانا *adj* prudent
	دانائی *n* prudence
insert *v* داخل کرنا	دانت *n* teeth
log in *v* داخل ہونا	دانت درد *n* toothache
entrance, entry *n* داخلہ	دانت سے کاٹنا *v* bite
way in *n* داخلے کا رستہ	دانستہ *adv* knowingly
inward *adj* داخلی	دانستہ غارت گر *n* vandal
inwards *adv* داخلی طرف	دانہ چگنا *v* peck
	دایاں *adj* right

دایہ	midwife *n*
دائرہ نما	circular *adj*
دائرہٴ نور	spotlight *n*
دائمی	chronic *adj*
دائو پر لگانا	stake *v*
دائو کی رقم	stake *n*
دائیں طرف کو	right *adv*
دب جانا	give in *v*
دبا لینا	usurp *v*
دبانا	quell, suppress *v*
دبانا،مجبور کرنا	press *v*
دباؤ	pressure *n*
وٴ ڈالنادبا	pressure *v*
دبائو	coercion, stress *n*
دبائو ڈالنا	coerce *v*
دبلا	lean *adj*
دبلا پتلا	slender *adj*
دبیز	crass *adj*
دخل اندازی	intervention *n*
دخل دینا	meddle *v*
دخول	infiltration *n*
دَر حَقیقَت	actually *adv*
دراڑ	cleft *n*
دراز	drawer *n*
درانتی	sickle *n*
درآمد	influx *n*
درآمد کاری	importation *n*
درآمد کرنا	import *v*
دربان	porter *n*

دربستہ	built-in *adj*
درج کرنا	file *v*
درجن	dozen *n*
درجہ	class, rank *n*
درجہ بڑھانا	upgrade *v*
درجہ بندی کرنا	rank, rank *v*
درجہ بہ درجہ	step-by-step *adv*
درجہ حرارت	temperature *n*
درجہ کم کرنا	degrade *v*
درحقیقت	indeed *adv*
درخت	tree *n*
درخت کا ٹھنٹھ	stub *n*
درخشاں ہونا	glitter *v*
درخشانی	splendor *n*
درخواست	application *n*
درخواست دینا	apply for *v*
دَرخُواست گُزار	applicant *n*
درد	ache, pain *n*
درد بغیر	painless *adj*
درد سے خلاصی	relieve *v*
دردمند	compassionate *adj*
دردمندی	compassion *n*
درز	crevice, gap *n*
درزن	seamstress *n*
درزی	tailor *n*
درس	lecture *n*
درست	accurate *adj*
درست کرنا	rectify *v*
درستی	accuracy *n*

د

درستی کرنا touch up v	دستی manual adj
دَرُشت austere adj	دستی اسلحہ handgun n
دَرُشتی austerity n	دستی بم grenade n
دَرمِیان among pre	دستی بیگ handbag n
درہم برہم upside-down adv	دستیاب available adj
دروازہ door n	دسمبر December n
دریا river n	دسواں tenth n
دریا کا چوڑا دہانہ estuary n	دشمن enemy, foe n
دریادل charitable adj	دشمن بنانا antagonize v
دریافت discovery n	دشواری hangup n
دریافت کرنا discover v	دعا کرنا bless v
دس ten adj	دعا ماگنا pray v
دست بردار ہونا abdicate v	دعوت نامہ invitation n
دست برداری surrender n	دعویٰ claim n
دست پناہ pincers n	دعویٰ ۔ اصرار assertion n
دست رومال napkin n	دغا fraud n
دستانہ glove n	دغا باز deceitful adj
دستاویز document n	دغاباز fraudulent adj
دستاویز کاری documentation n	دفاع defense n
دستاویزی چیز documentary n	دفاع کرنا defend v
دستبردار ہونا renounce v	دفتر bureau, office n
دستخط signature n	دفع کرنا repel v
دستخط کرنا sign v	دفعتاً برباد کر دینا zap v
دسترس mastery n	دفعدار فوجی corporal n
دستک knock n	دفن کرنا bury v
دستک دینا knock v	دقیانوسی orthodox adj
دستکار craftsman n	دقیق subtle adj
دستہ troop n	دکھ دینا excruciating adj
دستور constitution n	دکھانا indicate v

د

دکھاوا کرنا v	show off	دم دار ستارہ n	comet
دکھنے والا	sore adj	دم گھٹنا v	smother, stifle
دگنا کرنا v	double	دم گھوٹ	stifling adj
دل n	heart	دَم گھونٹنا v	asphyxiate
دل بڑھانا v	hearten	دماغ n	brain
دل بہلانا v	amuse	دماغی	cerebral adj
دل خراش	harrowing adj	دماغی سکون n	composure
دل شکستگی n	melancholy	دمک n	gleam
دل شکستہ	despondent adj	دمکنا v	gleam
دل کش	attractive adj	دمہ n	asthma
دل کی حرکت n	pants	دمہ زدہ	asthmatic adj
دل کی دھڑکن n	heartbeat	دن n	day
دِلاسا n	appeasement	دنبال n	stern
دِلاسا دینا v	appease	دنگل n	duel
دلالی کرنا v	pander	دنیا n	world
دلچسپ	interesting adj	دنیا دار	worldly adj
دلچسپی n	interest	دہانہ آتش فشاں n	crater
دلدل n	quagmire	دہائی n	decade
دِلرُبائی n	allure	دہائی دینا v	conjure up
دلکش	appealing adj	دہرا	double adj
دِلکَشی n	attraction	دہرانا v	repeat
دلہا n	bridegroom	دہرائی n	rehearsal
دلہن n	bride	دہری پڑتال v	double-check
دلہن کی خادمہ n	bridesmaid	دہقان n	farmer
دلیر	bold adj	دہلیز n	threshold
دلیل n	plea	دہندہ n	donor
دلیل دینا v	argue	دھات n	metal
دم n	tail	دھات گر n	smith
دَم پُخت کرنا v	bake	دھاتی	metallic adj

د

دھاتی اشیاء hardware n	دھماکے کا غبار fallout n
دھاتی مرکب alloy n	دھمکانا intimidate v
دھاری stripe n	دھمکی threat n
دھاری دار striped adj	دھمکی دینا threaten v
دھاڑ roar n	دھند fog, mist n
دھاڑنا roar v	دھندلا hazy, blurred adj
دھاگہ thread n	دھندلا کرنا blur v
دھاوا onset n	دھندلکا nightfall n
دھب spot n	دھنس جانا cave in v
دھبہ stain, blot n	دھنسا ہوا sunken adj
دھبہ لگانا smear v	دھواں smoke v
دھبہ لگنا localize, spot v	دھوبی گھر laundry n
دھتکار snub n	دھوپ جلن sunburn n
دھتکارنا scoff v	دھوپ چشمہ sunglasses n
دھجی shred, tag n	دھوپ عینک goggles n
دھڑام سے گرنا slump v	دھوکا deception n
دھڑکن beat, throb n	دھوکا دہی double-cross v
دھڑکنا throb v	دھوکا دینا beguile v
دہشت terror, horror n	دھوکا دینا deceive v
دہشت زدہ کرنا terrorize v	دھوکے باز cheater n
دہشت گرد terrorist n	دھوکے کی جگہ pitfall n
دہشت گردی terrorism n	دھونا wash v
دہشت ناک horrendous adj	دھونی دینا fumigate v
دھکا shove n	دھیان کرنا mind, heed v
دھکا دینا dash v	دھیان نہ دینا overlook v
دھکیل drive v	دھیکیلنا boost v
دھکیلنا urge, push v	دھیما mellow adj
دھماکا blast n	دھیما کرنا mellow v
دھماکا کرنا set off v	دھیما ہونا calm down v

دو two *adj*	دوباره قرضہ دینا refinance *v*
دو بار twice *adv*	دوباره کرنا redo *v*
دو چشمہ binoculars *n*	دوباره مبتلا ہونا relapse *n*
دو زبانی bilingual *adj*	دوباره ملاپ reunion *n*
دو زوجیت bigamy *n*	دوباره منتخب ہونا reelect *v*
دو صوتیہ diphthong *n*	دوباره منظم کرنا reorganize *v*
دو ماہی bimonthly *adj*	دوباره نمودار ہونا reappear *v*
دوا medicine *n*	دوباره ہونا recur *v*
دوا ساز pharmacist *n*	دوپہر afternoon *n*
دوا سازی pharmacy *n*	دودھ milk *n*
دوا یا نشہ لینا drug *v*	دودھ کا جمنا curdle *v*
دواخانہ drugstore *n*	دودھیا milky *adj*
دوب تختہ turf *n*	دور distant, far *adj*
دوبارہ again *adv*	دور افتادہ remote *adj*
دوبارہ ابھرنا resurface *v*	دور اندیشی providence *n*
دوبارہ بجانا/چلانا replay *n*	دور بین telescope *n*
دوبارہ بنانا remake *v*	دور چلے جانا drive away *v*
دوبارہ بھرنا refill, refuel *v*	دور حکومت reign *n*
دوبارہ تعمیر کرنا reconstruct *v*	دور دراز abroad *adv*
دوبارہ جوان کرنا rejuvenate *v*	دور دور تک widely *adv*
دوبارہ چمکانا refurbish *v*	دور نمائی کرنا televise *v*
دوبارہ چھاپنا reprint *v*	دورانیہ duration *n*
دوبارہ حاصل کرنا regain *v*	دورہ visit, tour *n*
دوبارہ حصول retrieval *n*	دورہ کرنا visit, trip *v*
دوبارہ داخلہ reentry *n*	دوڑ race *n*
دوبارہ شامل ہونا rejoin *v*	دوڑ جانا overrun *v*
دوبارہ غور کرنا reconsider *v*	دوڑ لگانا race *v*
دوبارہ قانون سازی reenactment *n*	دوڑدوپ کرنا bustling *adj*
دوبارہ قبضہ resumption *n*	دوڑنا run *v*

د

دوست pal, friend n	دیکھنے والا onlooker n
دوست خاتون girlfriend n	دیمک termite n
دوست لڑکا boyfriend n	دینا give v
دوستانہ outgoing adj	دیندار pious adj
دوستانہ ۔ پرامن amicable adj	دینی عالم theologian n
دوستی friendship n	دیہات country n
دوسرا another adj	دیہاتی countryman n
دوکان shop, store n	دیہاتی علاقہ countryside n
دولت wealth n	دیو giant n
دولت مند wealthy adj	دیوار wall n
دولہا groom n	دیوالیہ bankrupt adj
دونالی بندوق shotgun n	دیوالیہ پن bankruptcy n
دونوں both adj	دیوالیہ ہونا bankrupt v
دوہرا dual adj	دیوان خانہ living room n
دوہری مشکل dilemma n	دیوانگی insanity n
دے مارنا bump n	دیوانگی سے madly adv
دیا سلائی match n	دیوانہ insane adj
دیانت دار honest adj	دیوانہ آدمی lunatic adj
دیانت داری honesty n	دیوقامت colossal adj
دیباچہ preface n	دیوی goddess n
دیدہ دانستہ willfully adv	
دیدہ کش eye-catching adj	
دیر سے آنیوالا tardy adv	
دیرپا durable adj	
دیکھ بھال maintenance n	
دیکھ بھال کرنا look after v	
دیکھن watch v	
دیکھنا see, view, look v	
دیکھنے کا عمل look n	

د

ٹ

ڈاٹ	plug _n_
ڈاٹ اتارنا	unplug _v_
ڈاٹ لگانا	plug _v_
ڈاڑھ	molar _n_
ڈاک	mail _n_
ڈاک کا ڈبہ	mailbox _n_
ڈاک، کھمبا	post _n_
ڈاکخانہ	post office _n_
ڈاکہ	robbery _n_
ڈاکو	robber _n_
ڈاکیا	mailman _n_
ڈالر	dollar _n_
ڈالنا	put _v_
ڈانٹ ڈپٹ	reproach _n_
ڈانٹنا	chide _v_
ڈائریکٹری	directory _n_
ڈائل کی آواز	dial tone _n_
ڈائنامائیٹ	dynamite _n_
ڈائنو سار	dinosaur _n_
ڈباٶ	immersion _n_
ڈبہ	box, can, case _n_
ڈبہ بند	canned _adj_
ڈپلومہ	diploma _n_
ڈر	peril _n_
ڈرا کر بھگا دینا	scare away _v_
ڈرامائی	dramatic _adj_
ڈرامہ بنانا	stage _v_

ڈرانا	scare _v_
ڈرانے والا	terrifying _adj_
ڈرائونا	scary _adj_
ڈرائونا خواب	nightmare _n_
ڈرپ	drip _n_
ڈرپوک	timid _adj_
ڈرپوکی	timidity _n_
ڈریگن	dragon _n_
ڈرئیور	driver _n_
ڈسٹرکٹ	district _n_
ڈکار	burp, belch _n_
ڈکار لینا	belch _v_
ڈکشنری	dictionary _n_
ڈکیتی	piracy _n_
ڈگمگانا	waver _v_
ڈلا	lump _n_
ڈمی	dummy _adj_
ڈنڈے سے پیٹنا	bludgeon _v_
ڈنڈا	rod _n_
ڈنڈہ	club _n_
ڈنڈے سے پیٹنا	club _v_
ڈنک	sting _n_
ڈنک مارنا	sting _v_
ڈنمارک	Denmak _n_
ڈھال	precipice _n_
ڈھالنا	cast _v_
ڈھانپنا	clothe, cover _v_
ڈھانچہ	framework _n_
ڈھکا ہوا	shrouded _adj_

ڈھکنا lid, cap, cover n	ن
ڈھَلا ہُوا baguette n	
ڈھلان hillside n	ذات caste n
ڈھلوان steep adj	ذاتی personal adj
ڈھلوانی وضع کا slanted adj	ذاتی مفاد self-interest n
ڈھوانی sloppy adj	ذائقہ savor, taste v
ڈھول drum n	ذائقہ چکھنا taste v
ڈھونا transport v	ذبح کرنا slaughter v
ڈھیر لَگانا amass v	ذبیحہ slaughter n
ڈھیلا ڈھالا baggy adj	ذخیرہ reservoir n
ڈھیٹ obstinate adj	ذخیرہ خانہ storage n
ڈھیٹ پن obstinacy n	ذخیرہ کرنا store, stock v
ڈھیر heap, pile n	ذخیرہء الفاظ vocabulary n
ڈھیر لگانا heap, pile v	ذرائع means n
ڈھیلا loose, lax adj	ذرہ particle n
ڈھیلا چھوڑنا relax v	ذَرَہ ۔ جوہر atom n
ڈھیلا کرنا loosen v	ذریعہ appliance n
ڈوبنا sink, drown v	ذریعہ اظہار outlet n
ڈوری yarn, cord n	ذکر mention n
ڈول bucket n	ذکر کرنا mention v
ڈولفن dolphin n	ذَلیل کَرنا afflict v
ڈونگی canoe n	ذلیل کرنا humiliate v
ڈیٹابیس database n	ذمرہ category n
ڈیری فارم dairy farm n	ذمہ دار responsible adj
ڈیسک desk n	ذمہ داری responsibility n
ڈیم dam n	ذہانت wit n
ڈینگیں مارنا brag v	ذہن mind n
ڈیوڑھی porch n	ذہنی mental adj
ڈیوک duke n	ذہنی اطمنان temper n

frenzy n ذہنی انتشار	secretly adv رازداری سے
mentally adv ذہنی طور پر	cape n راس کوہ
mentality n ذہنیت	path, route, way n راستہ
intelligent adj ذہین	block v راستہ روکنا
gusto n ذوق	constant adj راسخ
appetite n ذوق ۔ میلان	ration v راشن دینا
auxiliary adj ذیلی	rocket n راکٹ
clause n ذیل جملہ	ash n راکھ
	ashtray n راکھ دان
	melody n راگ
	thigh n ران
ر	intercept v راہ میں لینا
	friar, monk n راہب
	monastic adj راہبانہ
coordinator n رابط	rifle n رائفل
contact n رابطہ	opinion n رائے
contact v رابطہ کرنا	ballot n رائے پَرچی
disconnect v رابطہ منقطع ہونا	remark v رائے دینا
night n رات	comment v رائے زنی کرنا
overnight adv رات رات میں	ligament n رباط
bricklayer n راج	rubber n رِبڑ
swan n راج ہنس	affinity n رَبط یا اِتحاد
conducive adj راجع	report v رپورٹ دینا
comfort n راحت	reporter n رپورٹر
soothe v راحت دینا	status n رتبہ
radar n راڈار	cram v رٹا لگانا
mystery n راز	optimism n رجائیت
confide v راز بتانا	aptitude n رُجحان
secrecy n رازداری	irreversible adj رجعت نا پذیر

court v رجھانا	formalize v رسمی بنانا
resort v رجوع کرنا	formally adv رسمی طور پر
lectern n رِحل	trickle, leak v رسنا
demise n رحلت	rope n رسہ
mercy n رحم	infamous adj رسوا
mastermind v رخ کرنا	demeaning adj رسوا کن
cheek n رخسار	scandalize v رسواکرنا
cheekbone n رخساری ہڈی	discredit v رسوائی
slip n رخنہ	string n رسی
reaction n رِد عمل	receipt n رسید
react v رِد عمل دینا	juicy adj رسیلا
turn down v رد کر دینا	relative n رشتہ دار
overrule v رد کرنا	kinship n رشتہ داری
alteration n ردوبدل تبدیلی	bribe n رشوت
modify v ردوبدل کرنا	bribe v رشوت دینا
trash n ردی	bribery n رشوت ستانی
trash can n ردی کی ٹوکری	corrupt v رشوت لینا
raspberry n رس بھری	observatory n رصد گاہ
sap v رس نکالنا	volunteer n رضا کار
pamphlet n رسالہ	acceptance n رضا مندی
access n رسائی	willing adj رضامند
accessible adj رسائی کے قابل	consent n رضامندی
supply v رسد	willingly adv رضامندی سے
succulent adj رسدار	subject n رعایا
rite n رسم	concession n رعایت
script n رسم الخط	awe n رُعب
christening n رسم بپتسمہ	awesome adj رعب دار
formal adj رسمی	predisposed adj رغبت
formality n رسمی بات	ardor n رغبت ۔ حَرارَت

befriend v رفاقت کرنا	crushing adj رگڑائو
speed n رفتار	rub, scrub v رگڑنا
accelerate v رفتار بڑھانا	rim n رم
speed v رفتار تیز کرنا	decipher v رمز کشائی
elevation n رفعت	runway n رن وے
darn v رفو کرنا	grief n رنج
accomplice n رفیق جرم	grieve v رنج دینا
colleague n رفیقِ کار	widower n رنڈوا
rivalry n رقابت	color n رنگ
area n رَقبہ	painting n رنگ آمیزی
dance n رقص	paint n رنگ روغن
dance v رقص کرنا	paintbrush n رنگ روغن کا برش
ballroom n رَقص گاہ	bleach n رنگ کاٹ
jigsaw n رقصندہ آرا	bleach v رنگ کاٹنا
money n رقم	complexion n رنگت
disburse v رقم تقسیم کرنا	color, dye v رنگنا
defray v رقم چکانا	colorful adj رنگین
reimbursement n رقم کی ادائیگی	crayon n رنگین چاک
refund v رقم واپس کرنا	release v رہا کرنا
rival n رقیب	residence n رہائش
plate n رکابی	dwell v رہائش پذیر ہونا
obstacle n رکاوٹ	lodge v رہائش مہیا کرنا
foil v رکاوٹ ڈالنا	acquittal n رہائی
member n رکن	guide n رہبر
cease, halt v رکنا	conduct v رہبری کرنا
membership n رکنیت	poisonous adj رہبریلا
retain, keep v رکھنا	mortgage n رہن
vein n رگ	pledge v رہن رکھنا
friction n رگڑ	leader n رہنما

ر

رہنما اصول guidelines n	روشَن مینار beacon n
رہنما کتاب guidebook n	روشن ہونا light v
رہنما کتابچہ manual n	روشنی light n
رہنمائی guidance n	روشنی ڈالنا enlighten v
رہنمائی کرنا lead v	روک check, curb n
رواج custom n	روک رکھنا restrain v
رواجی customary adj	روک لگانا clog v
رَواں affluent adj	روک لینا withhold v
روانگی departure n	روکنا detain v
روانہ ہو جانا go away v	روکھا sullen adj
روانہ ہونا depart v	رومال handkerchief n
روانی flow n	رومان romance n
روانی سے fluently adv	رونا weep v
روایت tradition n	رونا دھونا crying n
روبہ صحت convalescent adj	روندنا trample v
روپیہ اکٹھا کرنا pool v	رَوَیَّہ attitude n
روٹھا ہوا moody adj	ریچھ bear n
روٹی bread n	ریڑھ کی ہڈی backbone n
روح soul n	ریاست state n
روحانی spiritual adj	ریاضی math n
روداد report n	ریت sand n
روڑے اٹکانا obstruct v	ریٹائر ہونا retire v
روزنامچہ diary n	ریٹائرمنٹ retirement n
روزی livelihood n	ریڈیو radio n
روس Russia n	ریڑھ کی ہڈی spine n
روسی Russian adj	ریزہ scrap n
روش tenor n	ریستوران restaurant n
روشن bright, sunny adj	ریشم silk n
روشن دان skylight n	ریشہ tissue, fiber n

green bean *n* ریشہ دار لوبیہ	زبان بندی gag *n*
referee *n* ریفری	زبان بندی کرنا muzzle *v*
raffle *n* ریفل	زبانی طور پر orally *adv*
record *n* ریکارڈ	زبردستی گھسنا protrude *v*
recorder *n* ریکارڈ کرنے کا آلہ	زِپ zipper *n*
rector *n* ریکٹر	زِچ کرناکرنا harass *v*
sandpaper *n* ریگ مال	زحمت دہ inconvenient *adj*
rail *n* ریل	زحمت دینا annoy *v*
railroad *n* ریل کی پٹڑی	زخم injury *n*
train *n* ریل گاڑی	زخم پہنچانا traumatize *v*
reindeer *n* رینڈئیر	زخمی کرنا hurt, wound *v*
creep, crawl *v* رینگنا	زد پذیر vulnerable *adj*
reptile *n* رینگنے والا	زر نقد cash *n*
revue *n* ریوو	زَراعتی arable *adj*
	زرافہ giraffe *n*
	زرخیز fertile *adj*
	زرخیز بنانا fertilize *v*
	زرخیزی fertility *n*
	زرد pale *adj*
	زرد بلبل canary *n*
ز	زردی paleness *n*
	زرعی agricultural *adj*
	زرق برق glossy *adj*
dispel *v* زاءل کرنا	زریعہ معاش career *n*
czar *n* زارِ روس	زلزلہ earthquake *n*
rapist *n* زانی	زمانہ era *n*
ascetic *adj* زابدانہ	زمانہء حمل gestation *n*
angle *n* زاویہ	زمانی ترتیب chronology *n*
redundant *adj* زائد	زمرد emerald *n*
overdue *adj* زائد المعیاد	
born *adj* زائیدہ	
language *n* زبان	

ر
ز

زور سے پلٹنا v rebound	زمرہ ملازمان n personnel
زور لگانا v strain	زمہ ڈالنا v incur
زیرک adj astute	زمین n earth, land
زیابیطس n diabetes	زمین پر پاؤں مارنا v stamp
زیابیطسی adj diabetic	زمین دوز برقی ریل n subway
زیادتی n excess	زنا بالجبر n rape
زیادتی وزن adj overweight	زنا بالجبر کرنا v rape
زیادہ adv much	زنا کاری n adultery
زیادہ بھاری ہونا v outweigh	زنجیر n chain
زیادہ پکا ہوا adj overdone	زنجیر کھول دین v unleash
زیادہ تخمینہ لگانا v overestimate	زنجیری آرا n chainsaw
زیادہ تر adv mainly	زندگی n life
زیادہ دام لگانا v overrate	زندہ adj live
زیادہ سے زیادہ adj maximum	زندَہ ۔ جیتا جاگتا alive adj
زیادہ طلب والا adj demanding	زندہ بچ رہن v outlive
زیادہ قیمت لینا v overcharge	زندہ بچ رہنا v survive
زیادہ کام کرنا v outlast	زندہ دل adj hilarious
زیادہ محتاط adj squeamish	زندہ رہنا v live
زیبائش n décor	زنک n zinc
زیبائشی adj ornamental	زنگ n rust
زیبرا n zebra	زنگ آلود adj rusty
زیتون n olive	زنگ لگنا v rust
زیر تجویز adj pending	زبر n poison
زیر تربیت شخص n trainee	زبر ملا دینا v poison
زیرِ تربیت ماہر v intern	زبریلا n poisoning
زیر جامہ n underwear	زوال n decay, fall
زیر زمین adj underground	زوال پذیر ہونا v decline
زیر کر لینا v repress	زودکوب n battery
زیر کرنا adj overbearing	زور دار adj forceful

زیرک shrewd *adj*	ساده لوح naive *adj*
زین saddle *n*	ساده مزاج gullible *adj*
زینہ در doorstep *n*	سادیت سند sadist *n*
زیور ornament *n*	سارا entire *adj*
	سارجنٹ sergeant *n*
	سارس stork *n*
س	سارنگی fiddle *n*
	سازباز complicity *n*
	سازش conspiracy *n*
سابقہ previous *adj*	سازش کرنا intrigue *n*
سات seven *adj*	سازشی intriguing *adj*
ساتھ companionship *n*	سازو سامان baggage *n*
ساتھ ساتھ along *pre*	ساس mother-in-law *n*
ساتھ لے جانا take away *v*	ساسیج sausage *n*
ساتھی companion *n*	ساکن still *adj*
ساتواں seventh *adj*	ساکھ reputation *n*
ساٹھ sixty *adj*	سال year *n*
ساحر wizard *n*	سالانہ annual *adj*
ساحل coast *n*	سالم unbroken *adj*
ساحلِ جھیل lagoon *n*	سالمیت integrity *n*
ساحلِ سَمَندَر beach *n*	سامان merchandise *n*
ساحلی coastal *adj*	سامانِ تحریر stationery *n*
ساحلی خط coastline *n*	سامراجی imperial *adj*
ساخت setup *n*	سامراجیت imperialism *n*
سادگی simplicity *n*	سامع listener *n*
ساده simple *adj*	سامعین audience *n*
ساده بنانا simplify *v*	سامن مچھلی salmon *n*
ساده طور پر simply *adv*	سامنا confrontation *n*
	سامنا کرنا confront *v*

come across v سامنا ہونا	سبقت لے جانا v excel
before adv سامنے	سبکدوشی v relieve
come out v سامنے آنا	سبو تاژ کرنا v sabotage
front n سامنے کا حصہ	سبوتاژی sabotage n
sharpener n سان	سپاٹ uneventful adj
snake n سانپ	سپاہی n cop
mold n سانچہ	سپرد کرنا v entrust
breath n سانس	سپردگی n commitment
breathe v سانس لینا	سپرنگ spring n
windpipe n سانس نالی	سپین n Spain
cyanide n سایاناءڈ	ستار n harp
shade n سایہ	ستارہ n star
shady adj سایہ دار	ستانا v molest
awning n سائبان	ستر seventy adj
siren n سائرن	سترہ seventeen adj
science n سائنس	ستمبر n September
scientist n سائنسدان	ستھرائی سے neatly adv
scientific adj سائنسی	ستون n pillar
bicycle n سائیکل	ستیاناس کرنا v botch
most adj سب سے زیادہ	سٹال لگانا v stall
cause n سبب	سٹرابری n strawberry
cause v سبب بننا	سٹریچر n stretcher
attribute v سبب قرار دینا	سٹیج n stage
green adj سبز	سٹیو n stew
greenhouse n سبز خانہ	سجانا v adorn
vegetation n سبزہ	سجاوٹ facing pre
vegetable v سبزی	سجاوٹی decorative adj
vegetarian v سبزی خور	سجدہ کرنا prostrate adj
lesson n سبق	سچ truth n

س

سچا truthful *adj*	سربراہ chief *n*
سچائی سے plainly *adv*	سربراہ شعبہ dean *n*
سحر charm *n*	سرپٹ دوڑنا gallop *v*
سَحَر زَدَہ ہونا bewitch *v*	سرپرست guardian *n*
سخاوت generosity *n*	سرپرستی patronage *n*
سخت rigid, hard *adj*	سرحد boundary *n*
سخت بنانا harden *v*	سرخ red *adj*
سخت ٹھنڈا ice-cold *adj*	سرخ بنانا redden *v*
سخت ظالمانہ outrageous *adj*	سرخ مرچ chill *n*
سخت غصہ rage *n*	سرخی heading *n*
سخت لکڑی hardwood *n*	سرد bleak, cold *adj*
سخت ہو جانا petrified *adj*	سرداری lordship *n*
سخت ہونا toughen *v*	سردرد headache *n*
سختی severity *n*	سردی coldness *n*
سدھارنا improve *v*	سرزنش rebuke *n*
سدھانا tame *v*	سرزنش کرنا rebuke *v*
سر sir *n*	سرسرانا murmur *v*
سرِ انگشت fingertip *n*	سرسرہٹ murmur *n*
سرِ قلم کرنا decapitate *v*	سرسری پڑھنا browse *v*
سُر ملانا tune *v*	سرسوں mustard *n*
سیرا brink *n*	سرطان cancer *n*
سَرا سیمَہ apprehensive *adj*	سرطانِ خون leukemia *n*
سَرا سیمَہ کَرنا bewilder *v*	سرغنہ ringleader *n*
سراب mirage *n*	سرفراز کرنا exalt *v*
سراغ trace *v*	سرفون headphones *n*
سراغ رساں detective *n*	سرقہ larceny *n*
سرامک ceramic *n*	سرک فیتا red tape *n*
سراہنا admire *v*	سرکانا displace *v*
سرائے inn *n*	سرکٹ circuit *n*

س

سرکردہ leading *adj*	سڑک road *n*
سرکس circus *n*	سڑک پر لگی بتی streetlight *n*
سرکش rebel *n*	سڑکنا sniff *v*
سرکشی mutiny *n*	سڑنا گلنا decompose *v*
سرکشی کرنا rebel *v*	سزا punishment *n*
سرکنا budge *v*	سزا دینا punish *v*
سرکنڈا reed *n*	سزا سنانا sentence *n*
سرکہ vinegar *n*	سزا کا التوا reprieve *n*
سرگرم zealous *adj*	سست languish *v*
سرگرمی zeal *n*	سست بنانا slacken *v*
سرگزشت chronicle *n*	سست حرکتی slow motion *n*
سرگوشی whisper *n*	سستا cheap *adj*
سرگوشی کرنا whisper *v*	سستانا repose *v*
سرما winter *n*	سستی laziness *n*
سرمایا funds *n*	سسر father-in-law *n*
سرمایا داری capitalism *n*	سسرال والے in-laws *n*
سرمایا مہیا کرنا fund *v*	سسکارنا hiss *v*
سرمایاکار investor *n*	سسکی sob *n*
سرمایاکاری investment *n*	سسکی بھرنا sob *v*
سرمایاکاری کرنا invest *v*	سطح surface *n*
سرمساری contrition *n*	سطح پیما level *n*
سرمی قلم pencil *n*	سَعی attempt *n*
سرمئی gray *adj*	سعی کرنا endeavor *v*
سرنگ tunnel *n*	سفارت diplomacy *n*
سرنگ بنانا undermine *v*	سفارت خانہ embassy *n*
سرنگ علاقہ minefield *n*	سفارتی diplomatic *adj*
سریع quick *adj*	سفارش کرنا recommend *v*
سریناد serenade *n*	سفاک یا ظالِم atrocious *adj*
سڑاند stench *n*	سفر journey *n*

سفر پر روانہ ہونا v set out	سلاد n salad
سفر کرنا v sail, travel	سلائی n sewing
سفرکا راستہ n itinerary	سلجھانا v unravel
سفوف n powder	سلسلہ n continuation
سَفیر ۔ ایلچی n ambassador	سلطان n monarch
سفید adj white	سلطنت n kingdom
سفید کرنا v whiten	سلگانا v kindle
سفیر n diplomat	سلگن n combustion
سکارف n scarf	سلنڈر n cylinder
سکالر n scholar	سلوٹ n cuff
سکائٹ n scout	سلوک کرنا v treat
سکتہ n comma	سلے ہوءے کپڑے n clothes
سکرٹ n skirt	سلی n sleigh
سکری n dandruff	سلیپر n slipper
سکڑائو n contraction	سلیٹ n slate
سکڑنا v shrink	سم n hoof
سکنا v can	سماعت n hearing
سکہ n coin	سَماعت گاہ n auditorium
سکوٹر n scooter	سماعتی adj acoustic
سکور کرنا v score	سماوی adj celestial
سکول n school	سمت n direction
سکون n calm	سمتی وسعت n dimension
سکونت رکھنا v inhabit	سمجھ n understanding
سکین کرنا v scan	سمجھ دار adj judicious
سگا ۔ رشتہ دار adj akin	سمجھدار adj sensible
سگار n cigar	سمجھنا v understand
سگریٹ n cigarette	سمجھوتہ n compromise
سِل n slab	سمجھوتہ کرنا v compromise
سلاخ n bar	سمسٹر n semester

س

symphony *n* سمفونی	junction *n* سنگم
smuggler *n* سمگلر	cosmetic *n* سنگھار
ocean, sea *n* سمندر	fossil *n* سنگوارہ
overseas *adv* سمندر پار	aggravation *n* سنگینی
seasick *adj* سمندر زدہ	hear, listen *v* سننا
pirate *n* سمندری چور	golden *adj* سنہری
fur *n* سمور	beautify *v* سَنوارنا
furry *adj* سموری	cinema *n* سنیما
numb *adj* سن	senior *adj* سنئیر
sentry *n* سنتری	quarterly *adj* سہ ماہی
seriousness *n* سنجیدگی	resource *n* سہارا
earnestly *adv* سنجیدگی سے	support *v* سہارا دینا
serious *adj* سنجیدہ	sustain *v* سہارنا
certificate *n* سند	convenience *n* سہولت
patent *n* سند حق ایجاد	facilitate *v* سہولت پہنچانا
graduate *v* سند دینا	hundred *adj* سو
anvil *n* سِندان	embark *v* سوار ہونا
caterpillar *n* سنڈی	quiz *v* سوال
sensation *n* سنسنی	debrief *v* سوال کرنا
cynicism *n* سنکمزاجی	questionnaire *n* سوال نامہ
arsenic *n* سَنکھیا	hundredth *adj* سواں
cynic *adj* سنکی	cent *n* سواں حصہ
relentless *adj* سنگ دل	biography *n* سوانح حیات
atrocity *n* سنگ دلی	farce *n* سوانگ
marble *n* سنگِ مرمر	masquerade *v* سوانگ میلہ
gravestone *n* سنگ مزار	except *pre* سوائے
embellish *v* سنگارنا	stepfather *n* سوتیلا باپ
chorus *n* سنگت	stepbrother *n* سوتیلا بھائی
orange *n* سنگترہ	stepson *n* سوتیلا بیٹا

س

سوتیلی بہن stepsister n	سونڈ trunk
سوتیلی بیٹی stepdaughter n	سونگھنا smell v
سوتیلی ماں stepmother n	سویا ہوا asleep adj
سوٹزرلینڈ Switzerland n	سویٹر sweater n
سوٹزرلینڈ کا Swiss adj	سویڈن Sweden n
سوج جانا swell v	سویڈنی Sweedish adj
سوجا ہوا swollen adj	سوئچ switch n
سوجن swelling n	سوئی needle n
سوچ thought n	سیاہ توت blackberry n
سوچنا think, deem v	سیاہ معاہدہ blackmail n
سوختی لکڑی firewood n	سیاہی blackness n
سودا deal n	سیب apple n
سودا بازی bargaining n	سینکنا bask v
سوداگر dealer n	سیاحت tourism n
سوڈا soda n	سیّارچہ asteroid n
سور pig, boar n	سیارہ planet n
سور کا گوشت pork, ham n	سیاستدان politician n
سور کی چربی lard n	سیاق context n
سوراخ puncture n	سیال watery adj
سوراخ کرنا perforate v	سیال مادہ serum n
سورج sun n	سیاہ black adj
سوری کرنا ride v	سیاہی ink n
سوزش inflammation n	سیٹ set n
سوزشِ زائدہ appendicitis n	سیٹلائٹ satellite n
سوزشِ قلب heartburn n	سیٹی whistle n
سوکھی گھاس hay n	سیٹی بجانا whistle v
سولہ sixteen adj	سیخ grill n
سولی gallows n	سیخ پر بھوننا grill v
سونا gold n	سیدھا straight adj

س

unassuming *adj* سیدھا سادھ	senator *n* سینیٹر
erect *adj* سیدھا کھڑا	
stand up *v* سیدھا کھڑے ہونا	
walk *n* سیر	
outing *n* سیر سپاٹا	**ش**
saturate *v* سیراب کرنا	
tourist *n* سیرو سیاحت	
series *n* سیریز	shot *n* شاٹ
ladder *n* سیڑھی	branch *n* شاخ
step *n* سیڑھی کا ڈنڈا	tentacle *n* شاخک
stairs *n* سیڑھیاں	lush *adj* شاداب
lead *n* سیسا	exult *v* شادمان ہونا
leaded *adj* سیسا ملا ہوا	marriage *n* شادی
secretary *n* سیکریٹری	married *adj* شادی شدہ
second *n* سیکنڈ	marry *v* شادی کرنا
learn *v* سیکھنا	infrequent *adj* شاذ
seal *n* سیل	shark *n* شارک مچھلی
damp *adj* سیلا	poet *n* شاعر
flood *v* سیلاب	poetry *n* شاعری
flooding *n* سیلابی	disgruntled *adj* شاکی
saloon *n* سیلون	pupil *n* شاگرد
cement *n* سیمنٹ	evening, eve *n* شام
breed *v* سینا	supper *n* شام کا کھانا
centimeter *n* سینٹی میٹر	include *v* شامل کرنا
sandal *n* سینڈل	annex *n* ۔ ملانا ۔ شامل کرنا
sandwich *n* سینڈوچ	exclude *v* شامل نہ کرنا
toast *v* سینکنانا	ally, join *v* شامل ہونا
horn *n* سینگ	superb *adj* شان دا
senate *n* سینیٹ	pomposity *n* شان و شکوہ

excellent *adj* شاندار	شر *n* evil
oak *n* شاه بلوط	شر مچاکر *adv* noisily
cherry *n* شاه دانہ	شراب *n* liquo, winer
regal *adj* شاہانہ	شَراب خوری *n* alcoholism
voucher *n* شاہد	شرابِ سیب *n* cider
boulevard *n* شاہراہ	شرابور *adj* soggy
masterpiece *n* شاہکار	شراڈ کھیل *n* charade
royal *adj* شاہی	شرارت *n* mischief
perhaps *adv* شاید	شرارتی *adj* naughty
decency *n* شائستگی	شرارے چھوڑنا *v* sparkle
decent *adj* شائستہ	شراکت *n* fellowship
publish *v* شائع کرنا	شرائط *n* terms
nocturnal *adj* شبانہ	شربت *n* syrup
dew *n* شبنم	شرپنل *n* shrapnel
suspicion *n* شبہ	شرح اموات *n* mortality
mistrust *v* شبہ کرنا	شرح نویسی *n* annotation
doubt *v* شبہ ہونا	شَرط *n* bet
ostrich *n* شتر مرغ	شرط لگانا *v* bet
shuttle *v* شٹل	شِرکَت *n* association
person *n* شخص	شرم *n* blush
personality *n* شخصیت	شرمائٹ *n* shyness
intensity *n* شدت	شرمناک *adj* shameful
extenuating *adj* شدت کو کم کرنا	شرمندہ *adj* ashamed
severe *adj* شدی	شرمندہ کرنا *v* shame
drastic *adj* شدید	شَرمیلا *adj* bashful
intensify *v* شدید تر بنا دینا	شرمیلا *adj* shy
yearn *v* شدید خواہش ہونا	شروع کرنا *v* resume
mayhem *n* شدید ضرب	شروعات کرنا *n* outset
intensive *adj* شدید کا حامل	شَریک کَرنا *v* associate

ش

gentleman n شریف آدمی	fracture n شکستگی
partner n شریک	shape, looks n شکل
suspense n شش و پنج	shape v شکل اختیار کرنا
astonish v ششدر کرنا	abdomen n شکم
chess n شطرنج	gastric adj شکمی
ray n شعاع	crease n شکن
radiation n شعاع ریزی	wrinkle v شکن پڑنا
juggler n شعبدہ باز	crease v شکن ڈالنا
department n شعبہ	pleated adj شکن زدہ
verse n شعر	clamp n شکنجہ
flame n شعلہ	grievance n شکوہ
fiery adj شعلہ فشاں	crack, gap n شگاف
pastime n شغل	bud n شگوفہ
cure n شفا	omen n شگون
healer n شفابخش	calculation n شمار
transparent adj شفاف	calculate v شمار کرنا
kind adj شفیق	calculator n شمار کندہ
doubt n شک	statistic n شماریات کا جزو
skeptic adj شک پرست	north n شمال
victim, prey n شکار	northeast n شمال مشرق
hunt v شکار کرنا	northern adj شمالی
hunter n شکاری	solar adj شمسی
hound n شکاری کتا	crematorium n شمشان
complaint n شکایت	candle n شمع
complain v شکایت کرنا	candlestick n شمع دان
thanks n شکریہ	bell pepper n شملہ مرچ
thank v شکریہ ادا کرنا	annexation n شمول ۔ ضبطی
defeat n شکست	identity n شناخت
overthrow v شکست دینا	identify v شناخت کرنا

ش

acquaintance *n* شناسائی	cub *n* شیر کا بچہ
best man *n* شَہ بالا	toddler *n* شیرخوار
mastermind *n* شہ عقل	lioness *n* شیرنی
meteor *n* شہابیہ	sherry *n* شیری
evidence *n* شہادت	glass *n* شیشہ
beam *n* شہتیر	devil *n* شیطان
honey *n* شہد	diabolical *adj* شیطانی
beehive *n* شہد کا چھتّا	
bee *n* شہد کی مَکّھی	
city, town *n* شہر	
citizen *n* شہری	
citizenship *n* شہریت	# ص
prince *n* شہزادہ	
princess *n* شہزادی	
emperor *n* شہنشاہ	
aphrodisiac *adj* شہوَت انگیز	passive *adj* صابر
martyr *n* شہید	user *n* صارف
gorgeous *adj* شوخ	clean *adj* صاف
noise *n* شور	articulate *v* صاف تلفظ کرنا
noisy *adj* شور مچانے والا	neat *adj* صاف ستھرا
broth, soup *n* شوربہ	outright *adj* صاف صاف
racket *n* شوروغل	manifest *v* صاف ظاہر
frenetic *adj* شوریدہ سر	clean, wipe *v* صاف کرنا
chauffeur *n* شوفر	outspoken *adj* صاف گو
fondness *n* شوق	candor *n* صاف گوئی
boast *v* شیخی بھگارنا	cloudless *adj* صاف مطلع
enthrall *v* شیدا کرنا	virtuous *adj* صالح
lion, tiger *n* شیر	morning *n* صبح
baby *n* شیر خوار	patience *n* صبر
	journalist *n* صحافی
	health *n* صحت

ش
ص

wholesome _adj_ صحت بخش	صَف بَندی _n_ array
healthy _adj_ صحت مند	صفائی _n_ purification
recover _v_ صحت یاب ہونا	صفائی کا آلہ _n_ cleanser
robust _adj_ صحتمند	صفائی کرنے والا _n_ cleaner
desert _n_ صحرا	صفائی کی حالت _n_ cleanliness
courtyard _n_ صحن	صفر _n_ zero
correct _adj_ صحیح	صَفرا _n_ bile
justify _v_ صحیح ثابت کرنا	صلاحیت _n_ capability
preside _v_ صدارت کرنا	صلاحیت آزما _adj_ challenging
authenticity _n_ صَداقَت	صلہ دینا _v_ remunerate
chairman _n_ صدر	صلہ دینے والا _adj_ rewarding
archbishop _n_ صَدَر اُسقُف	صلیب _n_ crucifix
abbot _n_ صدر راہب	صلیبی جنگ _n_ crusade
headquarters _n_ صدردفتر	صمام _n_ valve
vest _n_ صدری	صندوق _n_ chest, bin
centenary _n_ صدسالہ جشن	صنف _n_ gender
shock _n_ صدمہ	صنوبر _n_ cypress
shocking _adj_ صدمہ انگیز	صوابدید _n_ discretion
shock _v_ صدمہ لگنا	صوبہ _n_ province
century _n_ صدی	صوت بندی _n_ recording
clearness _n_ صراحت	صوتیاتی _adj_ phoney
expressly _adv_ صراحتاً	صورت _n_ phase
only _adv_ صرف	صورت بگاڑنا _v_ deform
neglect _n_ صرفِ نظر	صورتحال _n_ situation
positive _adj_ صریح	صوفا _n_ sofa
hardship _n_ صعوبت	صوفہ _n_ couch
parade _n_ صف آرائی	صومعہ _n_ synagogue
deployment _n_ صف آرائی	ضامن _n_ pledge
deploy _v_ صف آرائی کرنا	ضائع کرنا _v_ waste

ص

ضبط repression n	ط
ضبط کر لینا confiscate v	
ضبطی confiscation n	
ضخیم enormous adj	طاق shelf n
ضَدِ نامِیَہ antibiotic n	طاق (جمع) shelves n
ضدی stubborn adj	طاقت strength n
ضرب multiplication n	طاقت سے forcibly adv
ضرب المثل proverb n	طاقت ور mighty adj
ضرب لگانا hit v	طاقتور powerful adj
ضرر رساں detrimental adj	طاقتور بنانا strengthen v
ضرورت necessity n	طالب علم student n
ضرورت مند needy adj	طایفہ choir n
ضرورت ہونا need v	طبّاخ baker n
ضروری necessary adj	طبع مکرر reprint n
ضروری شے prerequisite n	طبقہ امرا nobility n
ضعف collapse n	طبیب physician n
ضعیف feeble adj	طربیہ ناٹک comedy n
ضم کرنا merge v	طرز pose n
ضمانت bail n	طرف side n
ضمانت پر چھوڑنا bail out v	طرفدار partisan n
ضمانت دینا underwrite v	طرفداری predilection n
ضمنی پیداوار by-product n	طریق طرز procedure n
ضمنی عنوان subtitle n	طریقہ manner n
ضَمِیمَہ appendix n	طریقہ کار method n
ضمیر pronoun n	طشت tray n
ضمیر کی چبھن qualm n	طشتری saucer n
ضوابط بندی کرنا codify v	طعام گاہ dining room n
ضَیافت banquet n	طغیانی deluge n
ضیافت feast n	طفل دماغ moron adj
	طفلانا puerile adj

طفولیت	infancy n
طلاق	divorce n
طلاق دینا	divorce v
طلب کر لینا	call out v
طلب کرنا	invoke v
طلب کرنارنا	seek v
طلسم سے آزاد	disenchanted adj
طلوع آفتاب	sunrise n
طُلُوع ہونا	arise v
طمانیت	serenity n
طنجوی نارنگی	tangerine n
طنز	sarcasm n
طنزیہ	sarcastic adj
طہارت خانہ	lavatory n
طوطا	parrot n
طوفان	storm n
طوفانِ برق و باد	thunderstorm n
طوفانی	stormy adj
طول بلد	longitude n
طویل شدہ	protracted adj
طویل مدتی	long-term adj
طویل نیند یا سکتہ	coma n
طَیَارَہ	aircraft n
طے کرنا	determine v
طیارہ اغوا کرنا	hijack v
طیارے کا اغوا	hijack n
طیران پذیر	volatile adj
طیش	fury n

ظ

ظاہر کرنا	reveal v
ظاہر ہونا	emerge v
ظاہری	apparent adj
ظاہری حلیہ	look n
ظاہری وضع	guise n
ظرف	vessel n
ظلم	cruelty n
ظہرانہ	lunch n
ظُہُور	apparition n

ع

عاجزی	meekness n
عاجزی سے	humbly adv
عادت	habit n
عادت ڈالنا	accustom v
عادی	addicted adj
عادی شَرابی	alcoholic adj
عارضہ یاد وطن	nostalgia n
عارضی	temporary adj
عارضی صُلَح	armistice n
عارفانہ	mystic adj
عاشق	lover n
عافیت	impunity n

ط
ظ
ع

عاق کرنا v disinherit	عدم امکان n impossibility
عاقبت اندیشی n premeditation	عدم ابلیت n inability
عاقل sane adj	عدم برداشت n intolerance
عالم learned adj	عدم تحفظ n insecurity
عالمگیر worldwide adj	عدم توازن n imbalance
عام common adj	عدم فائدہ n disadvantage
عام آدمی n layman	عدم فیصلہ n indecision
عام پسند کرنا v popularize	عدم کمال n imperfection
عام طور پر normally adv	عدم یقین n disbelief
عامل exorcist n	عرَبی Arabic adj
عامیانہ vulgar adj	عرض n width
عاید کرنا v inflict, impose	عرض بلد n latitude
عبادت worship n	عرض کرنا v entreat
عبور transition n	عرضی n petition
عبور پٹی n crosswalk	عرف n nickname
عجائب گھر n museum	عرق n sap, juice
عجب prodigy n	عروج n climax
عجلت v hurry, haste	عروسی bridal adj
عجلت میں hastily adv	عریانیت nudity n
عجلتی hasty adj	عریانیت پسند n nudist
عجیب strange, queer adj	عزت n honor, respect
عجیب واقعہ n phenomenon	عزت بخشنا v dignify
عدالت n court	عزت کرنا v respect
عداوت n antipathy	عزت مآب Highness n
عدد n digit	عزتِ نفس n self-respect
عدم اتحاد n disunity	عزم n determination
عدم اتفاق n discord	عزم و استقلال n resolution
عدم استعمال n disuse	عزیزرکھنا v cherish
عدم استقامت incontinence n	عشائیہ n dinner

ع

staff *n* عصا	عکسی مشین *n* copier
nerve *n* عصب	علاج *n* medication
nervous *adj* عصبی	علاج کرنا *v* remedy
organism *n* عضو	علاقائی *adj* regional
award, bestow *v* عطا کَرنا	علاقہ *n* territory
confer *v* عطاکرنا	علاقہ رکھنا *v* pertain
scent *n* عطر	علالت *n* ailment
donation *n* عطیہ	علامت *n* emblem, badge
grant *v* عطیہ دینا	علامت ہونا *v* stand for
donate *v* عطیہ کرنا	علامتی *adj* symbolic
glory *n* عظمت	علامتی ترقیم *n* notation
glorious *adj* عظمت والا	علاوہ *adv* aside from
great *adj* عظیم	علم *n* knowledge
magnificent *adj* عظیم الشان	علم النفس *n* psychology
monster *n* عفریت	علمِ آثار قدیمہ *n* archaeology
pardon *n* عفو	علمِ حساب *n* arithmetic
disinfectant *n* عفونت ربا	علم حفظانِ صحت *n* hygiene
hawk, eagle *n* عقاب	علمِ حَیات *n* biology
creed *n* عقائد	علم سیاست *n* politics
rear *adj* عقبی	علم مادیات *n* physics
backdoor *n* عقبی دَروازَہ	علمِ نُجوم *n* astrology
remarry *v* عقد ثانی کرنا	علیحدگی *n* separation
wise *adj* عقلمند	علیحدہ *v* break up
adoration *n* عقیدَت	علیحدہ کرنا *v* detach
homage *n* عقیدت	علیحدہ ہونا *v* secede
belief *n* عقیدہ	علیل *adj* ailing
image, photo *n* عکس	علیل کرنا *v* sicken
photographer *n* عکس بنانے والا	عمارت *n* building
photograph *v* عکسی تصویر	عمدگی *n* precision

ع

عمدگی سے	nicely _adv_
عمده	fine, nice _adj_
عمده اور جامع بنانا	terse _adj_
عمر	age _n_
عمررسیده کنواری	spinster _n_
عمل	act, deed _v_
عمل تکثیف	condensation _n_
عمل تنفس	breathing _n_
عمل کرنا	process _v_
عملداری	dominion _n_
عملہ	crew _n_
عملی	practical _adj_
عمودی	upright _adj_
عنایت	favor _n_
عنصر	element _n_
عنوان	prelude _n_
عہد	epoch _n_
عہد کرنا	vow _v_
عہدِ ماضی میں	formerly _adv_
عہدہ	rank _n_
عہدوپیمان	covenant _n_
عوام	public _adj_
عورت (جمع)	women _n_
عورت (واحد)	woman _n_
عیار	wily, foxy _adj_
عیب	defect _n_
عیسائی	christian _adj_
عیسائیت	Christianity _n_
عیش پسندی	luxury _n_

عینک	glasses _n_
عینک ساز	optician _n_
عینی شاہد	eyewitness _n_

غ

غار	abyss _n_
غارت کرنا	vandalize _v_
غارت گر	bandit _n_
غارت گری	vandalism _n_
غافل	delinquent _adj_
غالب ہونا	predominate _v_
غائب ہو جانا	disappear _v_
غائب ہونا	vanish _v_
غُبارَہ	balloon _n_
غبن کرنا	embezzle _v_
غدار	traitor _n_
غداری	betrayal _n_
غداری کرنا	defect _v_
غدہ	gland _n_
غذا	food, diet _n_
غذاءی نالی	esophagus _n_
غرارے کرنا	gargle _v_
غرانا	growl _v_
غرضمند	interested _adj_

submerge v غرقآب کرنا	thresh v غلے کو گاہنا
sunset n غروبِ آفتاب	nasty adj غلیظ
pride n غرور	pellet n غلیلہ
poor n غریب	sorrow n غم
antelope n غزال	painful adj غم آلودہ
bath n غُسَل	wail v غم میں چلّان
bathroom n غُسَل خانہ	woes n غم و الم
bathe v غُسَل کرنا	gloomy adj غمگین
anger v غصہ آنا	sorrowful adj غمناک
furiously adv غصے سے	lewd adj غنڈہ
furious adj غصیلا	consider v غور کرنا
tantrum n غضب	ponder v غورو حوض کرنا
delinquency n غفلت	meditate v غوروخوض کرنا
slave, servant n غلام	plunge n غوطہ
slavery n غلامی	diver n غوطہ خور
domination n غلبہ	diving n غوطہ خوری
take over v غلبہ پا لینا	dive v غوطہ لگانا
erroneous adj غلط	amoral adj غیر اِخلاقی
misjudge v غلط اندازہ لگانا	amateur adj غیر پیشہ وَر
misconstrue v غلط تعبیر کرنا	anger n غیظ ۔ طیش
misprint n غلط چھپائی کرنا	oracle n غیبی آواز
miscalculate v غلط حساب لگانا	immoral adj غیر اخلاقی
falsify v غلط ردوبدل کرنا	lowly adj غیر اعلیٰ
misunderstand v غلط سمجھنا	impractical adj غیر افادی
mistake n غلطی	inhuman adj غیر انسانی
detect v غلطی پکڑنا	insignificant adj غیر اہم
infallible adj غلطی سے مبرا	unoccupied adj غیر آباد
err, miss v غلطی کرنا	impartial adj غیر جانبدار
lapse v غلطی ہونا	absent adj غیر حاضر

غ

absence _n_ غیر حاضری	improper _adj_ غیر مناسب
unreal _adj_ غیر حقیقی	unattached _adj_ غیر منسلک
informal _adj_ غیر رسمی	unjust _adj_ غیر منصفانہ
informality _n_ غیر رسمی پن	realty _n_ غیر منقولہ جائیداد
unmarried _adj_ غیر شادی شدہ	ineffective _adj_ غیر موٴثر
unhealthy _adj_ غیر صحتمند	unprofitable _adj_ غیر نفع بخش
needless _adj_ غیر ضروری	obscure _adj_ غیر واضح
undecided _adj_ غیر طے شدہ	disloyal _adj_ غیر وفادار
discontent _adj_ غیر قانع	uncertain _adj_ غیر یقینی
unlawful _adj_ غیر قانونی	unfurnished _adj_ غیرآراستہ
unfamiliar _adj_ غیر مانوس	fair _adj_ غیرجانبدار
unequivocal _adj_ غیر مبہم	neutralize _v_ غیرجانبدار بنانا
immobile _adj_ غیر متحرک	insensitive _adj_ غیرحساس
irrelevant _adj_ غیر متعلق	impure _adj_ غیرخالص
unrelated _adj_ غیر متعلقہ	immortal _adj_ غیرفانی
unforeseen _adj_ غیر متوقع	illegal _adj_ غیرقانونی
unsafe _adj_ غیر محفوظ	manslaughter _n_ غیرقانونی قتل
insincere _adj_ غیر مخلص	inequality _n_ غیرمساوات
invisible _adj_ غیر مرئی	inconsistent _adj_ غیرمستقیم
unequal _adj_ غیر مساوی	genius _n_ غیرمعمولی ذہین
unarmed _adj_ غیر مسلح	indefinite _adj_ غیرمعین
disarm _v_ غیر مسلح کرنا	foreign _adj_ غیرملکی
dissimilar _adj_ غیر مشابہ	foreigner _n_ غیرملکی شخص
absolute _adj_ غیر مشروط	illogical _adj_ غیرمنطقی
sedate _v_ غیر مضطرب	insulation _n_ غیرموصل کاری
dissatisfied _adj_ غیر مطمئن	disloyalty _n_ غیروفاداری
remarkable _adj_ غیر معمولی	furor _n_ غیظ
abnormality _n_ غیر معمولی پن	
unpopular _adj_ غیر مقبول	

غ

ف

cease-fire n	فاعر بندی
victorious adj	فاتح
victor n	فاتح شخص
dove n	فاخته
noxious adj	فاسد
vicious adj	فاسق
blunder n	فاش غلطی
distance n	فاصلہ
afar adv	فاصلے پَر
profound adj	فاضل
surplus n	فاضل رقم یا چیز
starvation n	فاقہ
starve v	فاقے کرنا
superfluous adj	فالتو
spare adj	فالتو رکھا ہوا
paralyze v	فالج کرنا
mortal adj	فانی
advantage n	فائدہ
utilize v	فائدہ اٹھانا
pay off v	فائدہ پہنچانا
benefit v	فائدہ ہونا
file n	فائل
conquest n	فتح
conquer v	فتح کرنا
triumphant adj	فتحیاب
insurrection n	فتنہ
football n	فٹ بال

obscenity n	فحاشی
obscene adj	فحش
flourish v	فخر سے لہرانا
proudly adv	فخریہ
ample adj	فراخ
escapade n	فرار
escape v	فرار ہونا
deserter n	فراری
crest n	فراز
get away v	فراز ہو جانا
France n	فرانس
French adj	فرانسیسی
provision n	فراہمی
luxurious adj	فراواں
corpulent adj	فربہ
fatten v	فربہ کرنا
genial adj	فرحت افزا
exhilarating adj	فرحت بخشنا
banality n	فُرسُودگی
floor n	فرش
angel n	فرشتہ
artichoke n	فَرشوف
leisure n	فرصت
duty n	فرض
presume v	فرض کرنا
sect n	فرقہ
firm n	فرم
precept n	فرمان
furniture n	فرنیچر

ف

فرہنگ glossary n	فقرہ paragraph n
فرو کرنا lay v	فکرمند ہونا concern v
فروتنی کرنا deign v	فلسفہ philosophy n
فروخت sale n	فلسفہ دان philosopher n
فروخت کنندہ seller n	فَلَک شَناسی astronomy n
فروری February n	فَلَکیاتی astronomic adj
فروزاں ablaze adj	فلم film n
فروغ پانا thrive v	فلو influenza n
فریب swindle n	فلیٹ flat n
فریب دینا swindle v	فن fin n
فریب نظر illusion n	فنِ تدبیرات tactics n
فریٹ freight n	فنِ تعلیم pedagogy n
فریفتہ کرنیوالا enthralling adj	فنِ تعمیر architecture n
فریگیٹ frigate n	فنِ تنقید critique n
فساد پیدا کرنا embroil v	فن لینڈ Finland n
فصاحت eloquence n	فن لینڈ کا Finnish adj
فصیل bulwark n	فنی کام artwork n
فضائی atmospheric adj	فہرست catalog n
فضل blessing n	فہرست بنانا list v
فضول rubbish n	فہرست سامان inventory n
فضول خرچ extravagant adj	فہرست نِگاری bibliography n
فضول خرچ کرنا squander v	فوٹو کاپی photocopy n
فضول خرچی extravagance n	فَوج army n
فضیلت excellence n	فوجی ٹوپی beret n
فطانت talent n	فوجی دَستہ battalion n
فطرت nature n	فوجی گشت patrol n
فعل action, verb n	فوراً instantly adv
فقدان lack n	فوری instant n
فقدانِ مرمت disrepair n	فوقیت دینا prefer v

ف

prevail v فوقیت رکهنا	debatable adj قابلِ بحث
steel n فولاد	bearable adj قابلِ بَرداشت
foam n فوم	enable v قابل بنانا
benevolence n فیض رَسائی	dependable adj قابل بھروسہ
per pre فی	binding adj قابل پابندی
currently adv فی الحال	praiseworthy adj قابل تحسین
virtually adv فی الواقع	adjustable adj قابلِ ترتیب
percent adv فی صدی	admirable adj قابلِ تَعریف
apiece adv فی کَس	divisible adj قابل تقسیم
cordon, ribbon n فیتہ	attainable adj قابِل حَصُول
fee n فیس	edible adj قابل خوردنی
fashion n فیشن	approachable adj قابلِ رسائی
decision n فیصلہ	habitable adj قابل سکونت
decide v فیصلہ کرنا	audible adj قابل سَماعت
decisive adj فیصلہ کن	dishonorable adj قابلِ شرم
defuse v فیوز نکالنا	curable adj قابل علاج
	detachable adj قابلِ علیحدگی
	workable adj قابل عمل
	considerable adj قابلِ غور

ق

establish v قاعم کرنا	acceptable adj قابل قبول
dish n قاب	valuable adj قابل قدر
occupant n قابض	avoidable adj قابل گَریز
able adj قابل	lovable adj قابلِ محبت
applicable adj قابلِ اطلاق	agreeable adj قابلِ مُطابقَت
questionable adj قابلِ اعتراض	forgivable adj قابل معافی
regrettable adj قابلِ افسوس	reversible adj قابل منسوخی
	deductible adj قابل منہائی
	comparable adj قابلِ موازنہ
	despicable adj قابل نفرت

قابلِ نفرت بدبو stink n	قبر grave n
قابلِ نكاسى disposable adj	قبرستان cemetery n
قابلِ ہونا merit v	قبض constipation n
قابل يقين believable adj	قبض كشا laxative adj
قابليت ability n	قبضہ possession n
قابو پانا overcome v	قبضہ كرنا occupy v
قابو سے باہر rampant adj	قبل از تاريخ prehistoric adj
قابو كرنا capture v	قبل از وقت precocious adj
قابو ميں ركھنا monopolize v	قبول كرنا accept, admit v
قاتل killer n	قبول نہ كرنا disown v
قادرِ مطلق almighty adj	قَبُوليَت approbation n
قارى reader n	قبيلہ tribe n
قاشيں بنانا slice v	قتل murder n
قاعده regulation n	قتلِ عام massacre n
قافيہ rhyme n	قتل كرنا decimate v
قالب framework n	قتلا chip n
قالين carpet n	قحط famine n
قانون law n	قد size n
قانون ساز lawmaker n	قدر value n
قانون سازى legislation n	قدرتى natural adj
قانون سازى كرنا legislate v	قدرتى طور پر naturally adv
قانون شكنى infraction n	قدردان considerate adj
قانونى lawful adj	قدردانى كرنا appreciate v
قانونى بنانا legalize v	قدرے rather adv
قانونيت legality n	قدم step n
قائد boss n	قَديم archaic adj
قائل كرنا convince v	قديم primitive adj
قائم كرنا institute v	قديم - موروثى ancient adj
قائم مقامى كرنا officiate v	قراءت recital n

altar n	قُربان گاہ	fable n	قصہ
sacrifice n	قربانی	anecdote n	قِصّہ ۔ حَکایَت
scapegoat n	قربانی کا بکرا	fault n	قصور
intimacy n	قربت	faulty adj	قصور وار
disk n	قرص	queue n	قطار
creditor n	قرض خواہ	pole n	قطب
debtor n	قرض دار	diameter n	قطر
loan v	قرض دینا	diagonal adj	قطر سے متعلق
draw n	قرعہ	drop n	قطرہ
lot adv	قرعہ اندازی	drip v	قطرہ قطرہ گرنا
cornet n	قرنا	severance n	قطع تعلقی
adj	قرونِ وسطی کا	amputate v	قَطَع کَر دینا
close, near adj	قریب	intersect v	قطع کرنا
border on v	قریب آنا	irrespective adj	قطع نظر
close to pre	قریب قریب	sector n	قطعہ
nearsighted adj	قریب نظر	patch n	قطعہ زمین
close v	قریب ہونا	definitive adj	قطعی
approach v	قریب ہونا ۔ پاس آنا	terrain n	قطعۂ زمین
nearly adv	قریباً	padlock n	قفل
pound n	قریباً آدھا کلو	locksmith n	قفل ساز
episode n	قسط	acrobat n	قلاباز
sort n	قسم	staple n	قلابہ
assortment n	قِسم بَندی	cardiac arrest n	قلب گرفتی
swear v	قسم کھانا	cardiac adj	قلبی
fortune n	قسمت	cardiology n	قلبیات
crust n	قشر	castle n	قلعہ
butcher n	قصاب	pen n	قلم
butchery n	قصاب خانہ	record v	قلمند کرنا
borough n	قصبہ	clone v	قلمیہ

قمیض *n* shirt
قندی *n* candy
قنوطیت *n* pessimism
قہبہ خانہ *n* brothel
قہر *n* wrath
قہقہہ آور *adj* laughable
قہوہ خانہ *n* cafeteria
قوت *n* energy
قوتِ محرکہ *n* impulse
قوس *n* bow
قوسِ قزع *n* rainbow
قوسین *n* bracket
قول *n* proposition
قولنج *n* colic
قوم *n* nation
قومی *adj* national
قَومی تَرانَہ *n* anthem
قومیانہ *v* nationalize
قومیت *n* nationality
قونصل *n* consul
قونصلیٹ *n* consulate
قے آنا *v* throw up
قیادت *n* leadership
قیاس *n* presumption
قیاس آرائی *n* speculation
قیاس آرائی کرنا *v* speculate
قیاس کرنا *v* guess
قیاسی *adj* abstract
قیام *n* stay
قیام پذیری *n* stability
قیام نا پذیری *n* instability
قید *n* confinement
قید میں ڈالنا *v* imprison
قیدی *n* prisoner
قیر ماہی *n* squid
قیراط *n* carat
قیمت *n* price, cost
قیمت کم کردینا *v* mark down
قیمت ہونا *v* cost
قیمتی *adj* costly
قیمہ *n* mincemeat
قیمہ کرنا *v* mince
قینچی *n* scissors

ک

کا *pre* of
کالج *n* college
کا ہونا۔ *v* belong
کاءیں کاءیں کرنا *v* crow
کاپی رائٹ *n* copyright
کاتنا *v* spin
کاٹ ڈالنا *v* chop
کاٹ کر نکالنا *v* cut out
کاٹنا *v* cut, slash, carve

کاٹنے کا آلہ cutter n	کاشتکاری کرنا till v
کاٹنے کا عمل clipping n	کاغذ paper n
کاٹنے والا stinging adj	کافر godless adj
کاٹھ کباڑ junk n	کافی enough adv
کاج buttonhole n	کاکردگی efficiency n
کار car n	کالا ہرن buck n
کار نمایاں achievement n	کالر collar n
کارآمد worthwhile adj	کالعدم void adj
کارپوریشن corporation n	کالعدم کرنا undo v
کارتوس cartridge n	کالک grime n
کارٹون cartoon n	کالم column n
کارخانہ factory n	کام job, task n
کارخانہ صاف گری refinery n	کام بگاڑ لینا goof v
کارڈ card n	کام شروع کرنا get down to v
کارک cork n	کام کرنا conduct v
کارکن worker n	کام کی ترتیب بنانا schedule n
کارگر ضرب coup n	کام میں لانا employ v
کارندہ agent n	کام میں لگ جانا settle down v
کاروباری آدمی businessman n	کامل total adj
کاروان caravan n	کامیاب successful adj
کاروابی process n	کامیاب ہونا succeed v
کاروبار business n	کامیابی prosperity n
کاروبار کا خاتمہ liquidation n	کان quarry n
کاروباری مہم enterprise n	کان پھاڑنے والا deafening adj
کاریگر artisan n	کان درد earache n
کاسہ scalp n	کان کا پردہ eardrum n
کاشت cultivation n	کان کا میل earwax n
کاشت کرنا cultivate v	کان کن miner n
کاشتکاری agriculture n	کانپ اٹھنا shudder v

ک

كانپنا	tremble, shiver *v*
كانٹا	hook, fork *n*
كانٹے دار	thorny *adj*
كانسی	bronze *n*
كانفرنس	conference *n*
كانگرس	congress *n*
كانوائے	convoy *n*
كانونٹ سكول	convent *n*
كانی	mineral *n*
كابل	sluggish *adj*
كابو	lettuce *n*
كائنات	universe *n*
كائناتی	cosmic *adj*
كائو بوائے	cowboy *n*
كائونٹس	countess *n*
كائونٹی	county *n*
كائی	moss *n*
كب	hunch *n*
كب والا	hunched *adj*
كبڑا	hunchback *n*
كبھی كبھار	seldom *adv*
كبھی نہیں	never *adv*
كبوتر	pigeon *n*
كبود	livid *adj*
كپاس	cotton *n*
كپتان	captain *n*
كپڑا	cloth *n*
كپڑوں كی الماری	wardrobe *n*
كپڑوں كی دراز	dresser *n*

كپڑوں والا صندوق	suitcase *n*
كپڑے كا كنارہ	hem *n*
كپكپاہٹ	shiver *n*
كپكی	shudder *n*
كتا	dog *n*
كتاب	book *n*
كتاب دان	bookcase *n*
كتاب یاداشت	notebook *n*
كتابچہ	booklet *n*
كتب خانہ	bookstore *n*
كتب فروش	bookseller *n*
كتبہ	inscription *n*
كترانا	dodge *v*
كترن	strip *n*
كترنا	gnaw, nibble *v*
كٹھائی	harvest *n*
كٹھائی كرنا	harvest *v*
كٹر	fanatic *adj*
كٹَر پَن	bigotry *n*
كٹّر	bigot *adj*
كٹھَن ۔ دُشوار	arduous *adj*
كٹھور	implacable *adj*
كٹوتی	deduction *n*
كٹّے شہتیر	lumber *n*
كٹیا	cottage, hut *n*
كثافت	density *n*
كثرت	opulence *n*
كثرتِ تعداد	multitude *n*
كثیرالعناصر	multiple *adj*

discourtesy n	کج خلقی	harshly adv	کرختگی سے
crank n	کج دھرا	character n	کردار
raw adj	کچا	Christmas n	کرسمس
floss n	کچا ریشم	chair n	کرسی
override v	کچل ڈالنا	charisma n	کرشمہ
squash v	کچلنا	charismatic adj	کرشمہ ساز
some adj	کچھ	curfew n	کرفیو
anything pro	کُچھ بھی	cricket n	کرکٹ
submit v	کچھ پیش کرنا	crispy adj	کرکرا
nothing n	کچھ نہیں	canvas n	کرمچ
shortly adv	کچھ ہی دیر میں	do v	کرنا
den n	کچھار	have to v	کرنا پڑنا
turtle n	کچھوا	currency n	کرنسی
pie n	کچوری	colonel n	کرنل
slum n	کچی آبادی	sphere, dial n	کرّہ
can v	کر سکنا	atmosphere n	کرہ ہوا ۔ فضا
karate n	کراٹے	crowbar n	کروبار
moan, groan n	کراہ	groceries n	کریانہ
aversion n	کراہَت	merciful adj	کریم
whine, moan v	کراہنا	detestable adj	کریہہ
rent n	کرایہ	saucepan n	کڑاہی
rent v	کرایہ پر دینا	rumble n	کڑک
tenant n	کرایہ دار	bitter adj	کڑوا
hire v	کرائے پر لینا	bitterness n	کڑواہَٹ
distress n	کرب	cousin n	کزن
feat n	کرتب	tighten v	کس دینا
blouse n	کُرتی	oyster n	کستورا مچھلی
harsh, stiff adj	کرخت	custard n	کسٹرڈ
harshness n	کرختگی	fraction n	کسر

کسنا clench v	کفایت شعار thrifty adj
کسوٹی criterion n	کفایت شعاری frugality n
کسے whom pro	کفایتی economical adj
کسی دن someday adv	کفن shroud n
کسی طرح somehow adv	کل tomorrow adv
کسی طور someway adv	کل پرزہ gadget n
کسی قدر somewhat adv	کل مقدار sum n
کسی وقت sometimes adv	کلال bartender n
کسینو casino n	کلاہ hood n
کشادہ spacious adj	کلائی wrist n
کشادہ دل open-minded adj	کلب club n
کشادہ ذہن broadminded adj	کلچر culture n
کشتی boat, ferry n	کلرک clerk n
کشتی چلانا row v	کلسائو carburetor n
کشتی کرنا wrestle v	کلف دار starchy adj
کشش traction n	کلماتِ برکات benediction n
کشش ثقل gravity n	کُلہاڑی ax, hatchet n
کَشَفَ ۔ الھام apocalypse n	کلو میٹر kilometer n
کشمش raisin n	کلوگرام kilogram n
کشمکش conflict n	کلوواٹ kilowatt n
کَشید beverage n	کلی طور پر grossly adv
کشید کرنا distill v	کلیت totality n
کشیدہ estranged adj	کلیسا ministry n
کشیدہ کاری embroidery n	کم slim, short adj
کشیدہ کاری کرنا embroider v	کم از کم minimum n
کف cuff n	کم ازکم least adj
کفِ صابون lather n	کم تر lower, less adj
کفارہ penance n	کم تعداد couple n
کفارہ گاہ purgatory n	کم تعداد کا fewer adj

fluctuate v کم زیادہ ہونا	mass n کمیت
recoup v کم کر لینا	committee n کمیٹی
diminish, lessen v کم کرنا	meanness n کمینگی
alleviate v کم کرنا ۔ گھٹانا	mean adj کمینہ
shortlived adj کم معیا	pettiness n کمینہ پن
go down v کم ہونا	mumps n کن پیڑے
earnings n کماءی	border n کنارا
perfection n کمال	verge, edge n کنارہ
commander n کمان دار	marginal adj کنارے کا
earn v کمانا	innuendo n کنایہ
blanket n کَمبَل	household n کنبہ
company n کمپنی	thyroid n کنٹھ
inferior adj کمتر	miser n کنجوس
waist n کمر	blunt adj کند
belt n کَمَر بَند	boring adj کند ذہن
room n کمرہ	carve v کندہ کرنا
classroom n کمرہ جماعت	shoulder n کندھا
rest room n کمرہء آرام	shrug v کندھے اچکانا
weak, frail adj کمزور	bolt n کنڈی
weaken v کمزور بنانا	bolt v کنڈی لگانا
weakness n کمزوری	canister n کنستر
juvenile adj کمسن	indigent adj کنگال
reinforce v کمک دینا	bracelet n کنگن
noose n کمند	hairbrush n کنگھا
shortage n کمی	comb n کنگھی
furnish v کمی پوری کرنا	comb v کنگھی کرنا
lack v کمی ہونا	engraving n کنندہ کاری
scarce adj کمیاب	engrave v کنندہ کرنا
scarcity n کمیابی	celibate adj کنوارہ

کنواره پن virginity n	کھٹکھٹانا knock v
کنواری maiden n	کھٹولا crib n
کنواری لڑکی miss n	کھجلانا itch v
کنواں well n	کھجور date n
کہاں where adv	کھجور کا درخت palm n
کہاں سے wherever c	کھدائی کرنا excavate v
کہانی story, tale n	کھڈا ditch n
کہاوت saying n	کھڈی loom n
کہر frost, haze n	کھرا،ظاہر plain adj
کہر آلود misty, frosty adj	کھرچنا scrape v
کہر زدگی frostbite n	کھردرہ rough adj
کہر زدہ frostbitten adj	کھرل mortar n
کہرآلود foggy adj	کھرلی manger n
کہکشاں galaxy n	کھریدنا scratch v
کہنا say v	کھڑا کرنا erect v
کہنی elbow n	کھڑکھڑانا rattle v
کہیں اور elsewhere adv	کھڑکی window n
کہیں نہیں nowhere adv	کھڑے ہونا stand v
کھاد ڈالنا manure n	کھڑی چٹان cliff n
کھال ادھیڑنا skin v	کھل کر ہنسنا chuckle v
کھانا eat v	کھلا respective adj
کھانا پکانا cooking n	کھلا خرچ کرنا lavish v
کھانا کھانا dine v	کھلا راستہ freeway n
کھانسی cough n	کھلا کھلا broadly adv
کھانسی کرنا cough v	کھلاپن openness n
کھانے کا چمچ tablespoon n	کھلاڑی sportman n
کھائی trench, chasm n	کھلبلی turmoil n
کھپر tile n	کھلنا bloom v
کھٹا sour adj	کھلونا toy n

barn _n_ کھلیان	crow _n_ کوا
denounce _v_ کھلی ملامت کرنا	coupon _n_ کوپن
mushroom _n_ کھمبی	shortsighted _adj_ کوتاہ نظر
strained _adj_ کھنچا ہوا	coat _n_ کوٹ
blunt _adj_ کھنڈا	lane _n_ کوچہ
bluntness _n_ کھنڈا پن	jumpy _adj_ کودنے والا
rinse _v_ کھنگالنا	code _n_ کوڈ
misplace _v_ کھو دینا	cod _n_ کوڈ مچھلی
coconut _n_ کھوپرا	blank _adj_ کورا
skull _n_ کھوپڑی	courier _n_ کورئیر
explore _v_ کھوج لگانا	lash, whip _n_ کوڑا
explorer _n_ کھوجی	dirt, litter _n_ کوڑا کرکٹ
unearth, dig _v_ کھودنا	garbage _n_ کوڑاکرکٹ
hollow _adj_ کھوکھلا	leprosy _n_ کوڑھ
cavity _n_ کھوکھلی جگہ	mindless _adj_ کوڑھ مغز
open, unfold _v_ کھولنا	leper _n_ کوڑھی
wedge _n_ کھونٹا	flog, lash _v_ کوڑے مارنا
stake _n_ کھونٹی	cuss _v_ کوسنا
cavern _n_ کھوہ	effort _n_ کوشش
cargo _n_ کھیپ	attempt _v_ کوشش کرنا
farm _n_ کھیت	anguish _n_ کوفت
farming _n_ کھیتی باڑی	tack _n_ کوکا
cucumber _n_ کھیرا	flank _n_ کوکھ
fun _n_ کھیل تماشا	cocoa _n_ کوکو
playground _n_ کھیل کا میدان	cocaine _n_ کوکین
play _v_ کھیلنا	cholesterol _n_ کولسٹرول
tow truck _n_ کھینچ گاڑی	cologne _n_ کولون
tow _v_ کھینچن	who _pro_ کون
draw, pull _v_ کھینچنا	which _adj_ کون سا

ک
گ

bud n کونپل	کیڑوں کا لشکر swarm n
crane n کونج	کیڑے مار دوائی pesticide n
hump n کوہان	کیسہ بندی capsule n
coal n کوئلہ	کیسے how adv
char v کوئلہ بنانا	کیفیتِ مزاج mood n
any adj کوئی ۔ کسی	کیکڑا crab n
anyone pro کوئی اکیلا	کیل pin n
else adv کوئی اور	کیمسٹ chemist n
someone pro کوئی ایک	کیمیا chemistry n
anybody pro کوئی بھی	کیمیکل chemical adj
no one pro کوئی بھی نہیں	کینٹین canteen n
something pro کوئی چیز	کینچوا worm n
somebody pro کوئی شخص	کینگرو kangaroo n
either adv کوئی نہ کوئی	کینہ malice n
nobody pro کوئی نہیں	کینہ پرور vindictive adj
banana n کیلا	کیوں why adv
because c کیُونکہ	کئ several adj
over pre کے اوپر	
despite c کے با وجود	
beyond adv کے پار	
during pre کے دوران	
instead adv کی بجائے	گ
keyboard n کی بورڈ	
towards pre کی طرف	
what adj کیا	گءیر gear n
kettle n کیتلی	گاجر carrot n
catholic adj کیتھولک	گاجر کی قسم parsnip n
Catholicism n کیتھولک مذہب	گارنٹی guarantee n
bug, insect n کیڑا	گارنٹی دینا guarantee v
	گارنٹی دینے والا guarantor n

گ

گاڑھا بنانا condense v	گدلا muddy adj
گاڑھا سیال dope n	گدلا کرنا muddle n
گاڑھا منجمد مادہ clot n	گدھ vulture n
گاڑھا ہونا coagulate v	گدھا donkey n
گاڑی vehicle n	گدی cushion n
گاڑی چلانا drive n	گدی رکھنا cushion v
گاڑی کھڑی کرنا park v	گدیاں وغیرہ upholstery n
گالی دینا abuse v	گڈریا shepherd n
گالی گلوچ abuse n	گڈمڈ mixed-up adj
گانا sing v	گذشتہ previously adv
گانٹھ bale n	گرامر grammar n
گاہک customer n	گراں قیمت sumptuous adj
گائوں village n	گرانا demolish v
گائے cow n	گراوٹ decadence n
گائے کا گوشت beef n	گرپڑنا tumble v
گبند دار عمارت pavilion n	گرجا church n
گپ شپ gossip n	گرجنا boom, rumble v
گپ لگانا gossip v	گرد dust n
گتہ cardboard n	گردان کرنا conjugate v
گتھم گتھا ہونا scuffle n	گردآلود dusty adj
گٹار guitar n	گردباد hurricane n
گٹر gutter n	گردبار twister n
گٹھا bundle n	گردش rotation n
گٹھا بنانا bundle v	گردش کرانا circulate v
گٹھڑی pack v	گردن neck n
گچھا bunch n	گردَن اُڑانا behead v
گدا mattress n	گردہ kidney n
گدگدانا tickle v	گردونواح surroundings n
گدگدی tickle n	گرفت grip n

گرفت میں لینا seize v	گَز yard n
گِرَفتار کَرنا arrest v	گَزر transit n
گِرَفتاری arrest n	گزرنا elapse v
گِرگٹ lizard n	گَزشتہ شب last night adv
گرم hot, warm adj	گَزشتہ کل yesterday adv
گرم چشمہ geyser n	گَزند detriment n
گرم مسالہ seasoning n	گُستاخ insolent, rude adj
گرم ہونا warm up v	گُستاخی rudeness n
گرم ہونا/کرنا heat v	گُستاخی کَرنا affront v
گرما دینا enthuse v	گفتگو conversation n
گرمالہ heater n	گفتگو کرنا chat v
گرمائی گھر kiosk n	گل دائودی daisy n
گرمی کی لہر heatwave n	گلِ لالہ tulip n
گرنا drop, fall v	گلاب rose n
گرنے کا عمل drop n	گلاب کی سیج rosary n
گرہ knot n	گلابی rosy adj
گروہ group n	گلابی رنگ pink adj
گرویدہ کر لینا captivate v	گلاگھونٹنا suffocate v
گرے ہائونڈ greyhound n	گلدان flowerpot n
گری core n	گلڈ guild n
گریپ فروٹ grapefruit n	گلنا rot v
گریز کرنا avoid v	گلنا سرنا decay v
گریز کرنیوالا evasive adj	گلناری پھول carnation n
گریس grease n	گلہ throat n
گرین لینڈ Greenland n	گلہری squirrel n
گرینائٹ granite n	گلوبچہ globule n
گڑھا pit n	گلوبند necklace n
گڑھا کھودنا pierce v	گلوٹین guillotine n
گڑیا doll n	گلوکوز glucose n

گ

hoarse _adj_ گلوگرفہ	phosphorus _n_ گندھک
street, alley _n_ گلی	reckon _v_ گننا
gladiator _n_ گلیڈی ایٹر	sinner _n_ گنہگار
glacier _n_ گلیشنیر	deep _adj_ گہرا
disappearance _n_ گم شدگی	deepen _v_ گہرا کرنا
presupposition _n_ گمان	navy blue _adj_ گہرا نیلا رنگ
misguided _adj_ گمراہ	depth _n_ گہرائی
mislead _v_ گمراہ کرنا	eclipse _n_ گہن
misleading _adj_ گمراہ کن	nursery _n_ گہوارہ
seduction _n_ گمراہی	dock, wharf _n_ گھاٹ
missing _adj_ گمشدہ	ravine, gorge _n_ گھاٹی
anonymous _adj_ گمنام	grass _n_ گھاس
cane _n_ گنا	weed _n_ گھاس پھونس
sin _n_ گناہ	haystack _n_ گھاس کا انبار
sin _v_ گناہ کرنا	sod _n_ گھاس کا تختہ
sinful _adj_ گناہ گار	prairie _n_ گھاس کا میدان
dome _n_ گنبد	gash, wound _n_ گھاؤ
gout _n_ گنٹھیا	blackout _n_ گھُپ اندھیرا
bald _adj_ گنجا	dwindle, wane _v_ گھٹنا
dense _adj_ گنجان	shoddy _adj_ گھٹیا
capacity _n_ گنجائش	home, house _n_ گھر
gage _v_ گنجائش ناپنا	get in _v_ گھر آنا
rot _n_ گند	homemade _adj_ گھر کا بنا ہوا
sewer _n_ گند کا نکاس	homework _n_ گھر کا کام
mess _n_ گندگی	homely _adj_ گھریلو
wheat _n_ گندم	domesticate _v_ گھریلو بنانا
dirty _adj_ گندہ	housewife _n_ گھریلو خاتون
pollute _v_ گندہ کرنا	concoct _v_ گھڑنا
dough _n_ گندھا ہوا آٹا	watch _n_ گھڑی

گھڑی ساز	watchmaker n
گھڑی کو چابی دینا	wind up v
گھڑی ہوئی	trumped-up adj
گھڑیال	clock n
گھس بیٹھیا	intruder n
گھس جانا	wear out v
گھسنا	corrode v
گھسنا ہوا	shabby adj
گھسنانا	turn in v
گھسیٹنا	haul, drag v
گھمانا	wind, screw v
گھمبیر	grim adj
گھمنڈ سے	vainly adv
گھمنڈی	arrogant adj
گھن	loathing n
گھن گرج	thunder n
گھنا	dense adj
گھنٹا	hour n
گھنٹہ گھر	belfry n
گھنٹھیا	rheumatism n
گھنٹی	bell, ring n
گھوٹنا	strangle v
گھورنا	stare v
گھوڑا	horse n
گھوڑی	mare n
گھوم جانا	whirl v
گھومنا	rotate v
گھومنے والا	revolver v
گھونسلا	nest n

گھونگھا	snail n
گھونگھریالا	curly adj
گھیر لینا	beset v
گھیرا ڈالنا	seal off v
گھیرا ڈالنا	surround v
گھیراٴو	blockage n
گھیرنا	circle v
گواہ	witness n
گواہی دینا	testify v
گوبر	dung n
گوبھی	cauliflower n
گود	lap n
گود لینا	adopt v
گودا	marrow, pulp n
گودام	warehouse n
گورنر	governor n
گوری اور بھورے	blond adj
گوریلا	gorilla n
گوشت	meat n
گوشت کا قتلا	steak n
گوشت/ماس	flesh n
گول	goal n
گول پتھر	cobblestone n
گول کنکر	pebble n
گول مٹول	chubby adj
گولا	log n
گولہ بارود	ammunition n
گولی	pill, tablet n
گولی چلا دینا	fire v

گ
ل

shoot v	گولی مارنا
boulder n	گوم مثل بٹّا
lump n	گومڑ
quandery n	گومگو کا عالم
boom, echo n	گونج
resounding adj	گونج دار
glue n	گوند
paste n	گوندھا ہوا آٹا
weave v	گوندھنا
speechless adj	گونگا
articulation n	گویائی
singer n	گویّہ
ball n	گیند
eleven adj	گیارہ
eleventh adj	گیارواں
song n	گیت
jackal n	گیدڑ
garage n	گیراج
gas n	گیس
gasoline n	گیسولین
wet adj	گیلا
demoralize v	گیلا کرنا
gallon n	گیلن
rhinoceros n	گینڈا

ل

agnostic n	لا ادری
innumerable adj	لا تعداد
unlimited adj	لا محدود
negligent adj	لاپرواہ
ceaselessly adv	لاپروابی سے
indifferent adj	لاتعلق
indifference n	لاتعلقی
lottery n	لاٹری
cart v	لاد کر لیجانا
burden v	لادنا
caress n	لاڈ پیار
mandatory adj	لازم
compulsory adj	لازمی
wireless adj	لاسلکی
corpse n	لاش
impersonal adj	لاشخصی
incurable adj	لاعلاج
emaciated adj	لاغر
atrophy v	لاغری
everlasting adj	لافانی
millionaire n	لاکھ پتی
expense n	لاگت
cockroach n	لال بیگ
lantern n	لالٹین
greed n	لالچ
covet v	لالچ کرنا
greedy adj	لالچی

endless *adj* لامحدود	لحاف *n* quilt
lawn *n* لان	لدا ہوا *adj* loaded
bring *v* لانا	لذیذ *adj* delicious
derelict *adj* لاوارث	لرزش *n* tremor
immortality *n* لایموت	لڑائی *n* quarrel, fight
inseparable *adj* لاینفک	لڑائی کرنا *v* quarrel
librarian *n* لائبریرین	لڑکا *n* boy, lad
noticeable *adj* لائقِ توجہ	لڑکپن *n* boyhood
punishable *adj* لائقِ سزا	لڑکھڑاتا ہوا *adj* staggering
speaker *n* لائوڈ سپیکر	لڑکھڑانا *v* vacillate
lighter *n* لائیٹر	لڑکی *n* girl, gal
outfit, dress *n* لباس	لڑنا *v* fight
undress *v* لباس اتارنا	لڑنے لگنا *v* open up
dress *v* لباس پہننا	لطف *n* enjoyment
replete *adj* لبالب	لطف اندوز ہونا *v* enjoy
trigger *n* لبلبی	لطیفہ *n* joke
charm *v* لبھانا	لعاب *n* saliva
tempting *adj* لبھانے والا	لعل *n* ruby
gobble *v* لپ لپ کھانا	لعنتِ ابدی *n* damnation
envelop *v* لپیٹ کر ڈھانپنا	لغزش *n* lapse, slip
wrap *v* لپیٹنا	لفافہ *n* envelope
lingering *adj* لٹکا ہوا	لفظ *n* word
hang *v* لٹکانا	لفظ بہ لفظ *adv* verbatim
hanger *n* لٹکن	لفظی *adj* literal
linger *v* لٹکنا	لفظی طور پر *adv* literally
scoundrel *n* لچا	لفظی معما *n* crossword
flexible *adj* لچک دار	لکڑی۔ *n* wood
pliable *adj* لچکدار	لکنت *n* impediment
elastic *adj* لچکیلا	لکھ لینا *v* annotate

لکھا ہوا written *adj*	لو heatstroke *n*
لکھنا write, note *v*	لوازمات furnishings *n*
لکیر row *n*	لوبان incense *n*
لگام bridle, rein *n*	لوبیا سیم bean *n*
لگام سے قابو کرنا rein *v*	لوبیہ kidney bean *n*
لگانا set up *v*	لوٹ کمال booty *n*
لگانا ۔ مطابق بنانا adjust *v*	لوٹ مار pillage *v*
لگڑ بگڑ hyena *n*	لوٹ مار کرنا sack *v*
لگن basin *n*	لوٹنا rob *v*
لگنا seem *v*	لوحِ مزار tombstone *n*
لگے رہنا stick to *v*	لوشن lotion *n*
للکارنا challenge *v*	لوگ folks *n*
لمبا length *n*	لومڑ fox *n*
لمبا قدم strife *n*	لوند کا سال leap year *n*
لمبا کرنا lengthen *v*	لوہا iron *n*
لمبائی کے رک کاٹنا slit *v*	لوہار blacksmith *n*
لمبوترا oblong *adj*	لوہے کا میل cinder *n*
لمبی قلمیں whiskers *n*	لیاقت progress *n*
لمحہ moment *n*	لیبارٹری lab *n*
لمحہ بھر کو momentarily *adv*	لیپنا dope *v*
لمس touch *n*	لیٹر liter *n*
لَنگر anchor *n*	لیٹنا lie *v*
لنگرانداز کرنا moor *v*	لیٹی لگانا glue, paste *v*
لنگڑا limp *n*	لید ore *n*
لنگڑا کر چلنا limp *v*	لیرنکس larynx *n*
لنگوٹیا یار crony *n*	لیزر laser *n*
لہجہ accent *n*	لیس کرنا equip *v*
لہردار wavy *adj*	لیفٹیننٹ lieutenant *n*
لہسن garlic *n*	لیکن but *c*

ل
م

مار گرانا v	shoot down
مارچ n	March
مارچوب n	asparagus
مارشل n	marshal
مارفین n	morphine
ماركر n	marker
ماركسی adj	marxist
ماركہ n	trademark
مارملیڈ n	marmalade
مارنا v	beat
ماسكہ n	focus
ماش كرنا v	massage
ماضی adj	past
ماقَبل n	antecedent
مال n	material
مال خانہ n	depot
مالِ غنیمت n	loot
مال مویشی n	livestock
مال و اسباب n	belongings
مالش n	massage
مالك n	owner
مالك ہونا v	owe
مالكن n	mistress
مالی n	gardener
مالیاتی adj	financial
مالیخولیا adj	paranoid
مالیكیول n	molecule
ماموں n	uncle
ماں n	mother

لیكھ n	furrow
لیگ n	league
لیمپ n	lamp
لیموں n	lemon
لین n	input
لین دین n	dealings
لین دین كرنا v	commute
لینا v	take
لینز n	lense
لینن n	linen
لیور n	lever

م

ماتم n	lament, wail
ماتم كرنا v	mourn
ماتم ہونا v	lament
ماحصل n	output
ماحصل نكالنا v	sum up
ماحول n	environment
مادام n	madam
مادرانہ adj	maternal
مادہ n	female
مادیت n	materialism
مادینی adj	feminine
مار دینا v	assassinate

مانجهنا scour v	مبازر contestant n
ماننا believe v	مبازرت challenge n
ماننا ۔ ہاں کہنا assent v	مبالغہ کرنا dramatize v
مانوس unknown adj	مُبتَدی beginner n
ماہِ عروسی honeymoon n	مُبتَدی ۔ شاگِرد apprentice n
ماہر skillful adj	مبترک blessed adj
ماہر آلات برق electrician n	مبتلا ہونا suffer v
ماہِر تَعمیرات architect n	مبرا exempt adj
ماہِر دندان dentist n	مبلغ missionary n
ماہِر فَلکیات astronomer n	مبہم vague, fuzzy adj
ماہرانہ انتظام maneuver n	مبہم ۔ ذو معنی ambiguous adj
ماہوار monthly adv	مبینہ طور پر allegedly adv
ماہی گیر fisherman n	متاٴمل hesitant adj
ماہر proficient adj	متاثر کن touching adj
مایوس کرنا frustrate v	متاثرکن impressive adj
مایوس کن disappointing adj	متاخر subsequent adj
مایوس ہونا disappoint v	متامل reluctant adj
مایوسی frustration n	متبادل alternative n
مائع liquid n	متبادل چیز substitute n
مائع جذب ہونا soak up v	متجاوز excessive adj
مائل کرنا kneel v	متجسس curious adj
مائیکروسکوپ microscope n	متحد کرنا unite v
مائیکروفون microphone n	متحرک dynamic adj
مآخذ source n	متحرک بنانا mobilize v
مباحثہ dispute n	متحرک فلم movie n
مباحثہ کرنا dispute v	متحرک کاری activation n
مُبارَک auspicious adj	متحرک کرنا activate v
مبارک باد congratulations n	متحمل placid adj
مبارک باد کہنا congratulate v	متحیر کرنا/ہونا amaze v

م

متداخل incoming *adj*	متوجہ ہونا look *v*
مترادف synonym *n*	متوفی deceased *adj*
مترجم translator *n*	متوقع imminent *adj*
متروک obsolete *adj*	متین sober *adj*
متروک شدہ outmoded *adj*	مٹا دینا erase *v*
متروک ہو جانا go out *v*	مٹر pea *n*
متزلزل unsteady *adj*	مٹر گشت کرنا stroll *v*
متضاد incompatible *adj*	مٹکا jar *n*
متعارف کرانا introduce *v*	مٹھاس sweetness *n*
متعدد diverse, various *adj*	مٹھائیاں sweets *n*
متعدی contagious *adj*	مٹھی بھر handful *n*
متعفن fetid *adj*	مٹی clay, mud *n*
متعلق فعل adverb *n*	مٹی سے آلودہ soiled *adj*
متعلق ہونا concern *v*	مٹی کا تیل petroleum *n*
متعلقہ relevant *adj*	مٹی کے ظروف crockery *n*
متعلم learner *n*	مثال illustration *n*
متغیرہ variable *adj*	مثال پیش کرنا exemplify *v*
متفق نہ ہونا disagree *v*	مثالی exemplary *adj*
مُتَفَکِّر anxious *adj*	مثانہ bladder *n*
متلون fickle *adj*	مثل type *n*
متلی nausea *n*	مثل مقدمہ apostle *n*
متماثل identical *adj*	مثلث triangle *n*
متمنی would-be *adj*	مثلہ کرنا maim *v*
متن text *n*	مثنی سازی duplication *n*
متنوع بنانا diversify *v*	مَجاز ٹھہرانا authorize *v*
متواتر consecutive *adj*	مجبور کرنا compel, force *v*
متوازن/برابر کرنا offset *v*	مجبور کن stringent *adj*
متوازی parallel *n*	مجبوری compulsion *n*
متوجہ mindful *adj*	مجتمع ہونا congregate *v*

criminal *adj*	مجرم	defender *n*	محافظ
convict *v*	مجرم ٹھرانا	lifeguard *n*	محافظِ زندگی
culpability *n*	مجرميت	idiom *n*	محاوره
hurt *adj*	مجروح	affection *n*	محبت
offend *v*	مجروح کرنا	loving *adj*	محبت آميز
magistrate *n*	مجسٹريٹ	beloved *adj*	محبُوب
embody *v*	مجسم کرنا	sweetheart *n*	محبوبہ
icon *n*	مجسمہ	pent-up *adj*	محبوس ہونا
sculptor *n*	مجسمہ ساز	penniless *adj*	محتاج
statue *n*	مجسہ	careful *adj*	محتاط
council *n*	مجلس	restrict *v*	محدود کردينا
gregarious *adj*	مجلس پسند	arch *n*	محراب
throng *n*	مجمع	motive *n*	محرک
crowd *v*	مجمع لگانا	deprived *adj*	محروم
collection *n*	مجموعہ	deprive *v*	محروم کرنا
code *n*	مجموعہ ضوابط	deprivation *n*	محرومی
gross *adj*	مجموعی	benefactor *n*	مُحسِن
overall *adv*	مجموعی طور پر	tangible *adj*	محسوس باللمس
demented *adj*	مجنون	feel, sense *v*	محسوس کرنا
suggestive *adj*	مجوز	levy *v*	محصول
scaffolding *n*	مچان	postage *n*	محصول ڈاک
mosquito *n*	مچھر	stark *adj*	محض
fish *n*	مچھلی	concert *n*	محفل موسيقى
front *n*	محاذ	secure, safe *adj*	محفوظ
audit *v*	محاسبہ کرنا	secure *v*	محفوظ بنانا
besiege *v*	مُحاصراه کرنا	record *v*	محفوظ کر لينا
siege *n*	محاصره	preserve *v*	محفوظ کرنا
blockade *v*	محاصره کرنا	protect *v*	محفوظرکھنا
customs *n*	محاصل	palace *n*	محل شاہی

محلل solvent *adj*	مخلص sincere *adj*
محلول solution *n*	مخلوط promiscuous *adj*
محنت industry *n*	مخلوق creature *n*
محوَر axis *n*	مخمل velvet *n*
محوس کیاگیا heartfelt *adj*	مخمور drunk *adj*
محویت preoccupation *n*	مَدّاح admirer *n*
محیط ہو جانا engulf *v*	مداخلت interference *n*
مخالف opponent *n*	مداخلت کرنا interfere *v*
مخالفت hostility *n*	مدار orbit, hub *n*
مخالفت کرنا oppose *v*	مدافعت immunity *n*
مخبر informer *n*	مدت term *n*
مختار attorney *n*	مدت العمر lifetime *adj*
مختصر brief *adj*	مدخول intake *n*
مختصر جامہ shorts *n*	مدد help *n*
مختصر دستخط initials *n*	مدد دینا assist *v*
مختصر دورہ کرنا stop by *v*	مَدَد کَرنا aid, help *v*
مختصر راستہ shortcut *n*	مدد کرنے والا benevolent *adj*
مختصر کرنا curtail *v*	مددگار helper *n*
مختصر نویسی shorthand *n*	مدرسہ seminary *n*
مختصراً briefly *adv*	مدعا علیہ defendant *n*
مختلف different *adj*	مدعو کرنا invite *v*
مختلف الرائے dissident *adj*	مدعی plaintiff *n*
مختلف ہونا differ *v*	مدقوتعلق hectic *adj*
مخروط prism *n*	مَدنی سَہُولتیں amenities *n*
مخروطہ cone *n*	مدھم dim *adj*
مخروطی pyramid *n*	مدھم کرنا dim *v*
مخصوص specific *adj*	مدوجزری موج tidal wave *n*
مخفی کرنا mystify *v*	مڈبھیڑ encounter *n*
مخل nuisance *n*	مذاق کرنا joke *v*

م

negotiation *n* مذاكرات	rooster *n* مرغ
shambles *n* مذبح	cock *n* مرغا
religion *n* مذهب	gull *n* مرغابی
religious *adj* مذهبی	scroll *n* مرغولا
letter, epistle *n* مراسله	chicken, hen *n* مرغی
appeal *n* مرافعہ كرنا	compound *n* مركب
contemplate *v* مراقبہ كرنا	center *n* مركز
square *n* مربع	centralize *v* مركز گير بنانا
conserve *n* مربہ	central *adj* مركزی
dying *adj* مرتا ہوا	epilepsy *n* مرگی
gangrene *n* مرتا ہوا بافت	reparation *n* مرمت
edit *v* مرتب كرنا	repair, mend *v* مرمت كرنا
vibrant *adj* مرتعش	crunchy *adj* مرمری
perpetrate *v* مرتكب ہونا	die *v* مرنا
concentrate *v* مرتكز كرنا	dressing *n* مربم پٹی
center *v* مرتكز ہونا يا كرنا	bandage *v* مرہم پٹی كرنا
wither *v* مرجهانا	prevalent *adj* مروج
pepper *n* مرچ	current *adj* مروجہ
stage *n* مرحلہ	twist *v* مروڑنا
ointment *n* مرحم	Mars *n* مريخ
manliness *n* مردانگی	disciple *n* مريد
manly *adj* مردانہ	infirmary *n* مريض خانہ
virility *n* مردانہ پن	visible *adj* مرئی
census *n* مردم شماری	twisted *adj* مڑا ہوا
homicide *n* مردم كشی	turn *v* مڑنا
dead *adj* مردہ	flavor *n* مزا
mortuary *n* مردہ خانہ	humor *n* مزاح
inlaid *adj* مرصع	resistance *n* مزاحمت
will *n* مرضی	shrine *n* مزار

prank n مزاق		مستعد prompt adj
hindrance n مزحمت		مستعل transient adj
dissuade v مزحمت کرنا		مستغیث prosecutor n
laborer n مزدور		مُستَفید beneficiary n
labor n مزدوری		مستقبل future n
censure v مزمت کرنا		مستقل رہنا persevere v
furthermore adv مزید		مستقل مزاج patient adj
besides pre مزید برآں		مستول mast n
tasty adj مزیدار		مسٹر mister n
wart n مسّا		مسجد mosque n
competitive adj مسابقتی		مسحور کرنا fascinate v
masseur n مساج کرنیوالا		مسحور کن glamorous adj
odometer n مسافت پیما		مسِحیّت baptism n
traveler n مسافر		مسخ کرنا deface v
spicy adj مسالے دار		مسخرہ clown n
pore n مسام		مسرت delight n
porous adj مسام دار		مسرت بخش delightful adj
equation n مساوات		مسرف lavish adj
equivalent adj مساوی		مسرور revel v
tantamount to adj مساوی القدر ہونا		مسرور کرنا delight v
amount to v مساوی ہے		مسکرانا smile v
competitor n مسبق		مسکراہٹ smile n
deserving adj مستحق		مسکن lodging n
deserve v مستحق ہونا		مسکین meek adj
stable adj مستحکم		مسل dossier, file n
reject v مسترد کرنا		مسلح armed adj
mechanic n مستری		مسلک cult n
rectangle n مستطیل		مسلم indisputable adj
rectangular adj مستطیلی		مسلمان Muslim adj

maxim n مسلمہ اصول	drink n مشروب
standard n مسلمہ عمدگی	drink v مشروب پینا
problem n مسلہ	conditional adj مشروط
demolition n مسماری	entail v مشروط بیمہ کرنا
draft n مسودہ	torch n مشعل
draft v مسودہ تیار کرنا	hobby n مشغلہ
invoice n مسودہ قانون	engaged adj مشغول
lentil n مسور	drill n مشق
gum n مسوڑا	exercise v مشق کرنا
Messiah n مسیح	toil v مشقت کرنا
corresponding adj مشابہ	workbook n مشقی کتاب
correspond v مشابہ ہونا	difficulty n مشکل
likeness n مشابہت	barely adv مشکل سے
hairdresser n مشاطہ	precarious adj مشکوک
practising adj مشاق	renowned adj مشہور
resemble v مشابہہ ہونا	advice n مشورہ
observation n مشاہدہ	advise v مشورہ دینا
consultation n مشاورت	consult v مشورہ کرنا
confer v مشاورت کرنا	adviser n مشیر
eager, avid adj مشتاق	counselor n مشیر قانونی
dubious adj مشتبہ	machine n مشین
suspect n مشتبہ شخص	machine gun n مشین گن
apartment n مشترکہ جائیداد	handshake n مصافہ
enrage v مشتعل کردینا	conciliatory adj مصالحتی
irritate v مشتعل کرنا	notary n مصدق الاسناد
comprise v مشتمل ہونا	authentic adj مصدقہ
cocktail n مشربات کا آمیزہ	busy adj مصروف
east n مشرق	engagement n مصروفیت
oriental adj مشرقی	busily adv مصروفیت سے

مصغر miniature *n*	مطیع compliant *adj*
مصف detergent *n*	مطیع ہو جانا capitulate *v*
مصفا بنانا cleanse *v*	مظاہرہ display *n*
مصلحت expediency *n*	مظاہرہ کرنا demonstrate *v*
مصلوب کرنا crucify *v*	معاءنہ کرنا inspect *v*
مُصَنِف author, writer *n*	معاش sustenance *n*
مصور painter *n*	معاشرہ society *n*
مُصَوَر ۔ آرٹِسٹ artist *n*	معاشقہ courtship *n*
مصیبت suffering *n*	معاف کرنا forgive *v*
مصیبت زدہ miserable *adj*	معافی forgiveness *n*
مضافات suburb *n*	معافی چاہنا excuse *v*
مضبوط strong *adj*	معالجہ therapy *n*
مضبوطی firmness *n*	معاملہ affair, case *n*
مضحکہ خیز ridiculous *adj*	معاملہ کرنا deal *v*
مضر pernicious *adj*	معانت سے متعلق subsidiary *adj*
مضطرب tumultuous *adj*	معاندانہ hostile *adj*
مضمر implication *n*	معاہدہ treaty *n*
مضمون essay *n*	معاہدہ ۔ میثاق alliance *n*
مطابق کرنا adapt *v*	معاوضہ pay *v*
مطابقت conformity *n*	معائنہ review *n*
مطابقت پذیر adaptable *adj*	معائنہ کار inspector *n*
مطالبہ کرنا require *v*	معائنہ کرنا examine *v*
مطالعہ study *v*	مُعائنہ لاش autopsy *n*
مطالعہ ماحول ecology *n*	معتبر reliable *adj*
مطب clinic *n*	معتمد confidant *n*
مطلب ہونا signify, mean *v*	معتمدِ خاص henchman *n*
مطلع کرنا notify *v*	معجزاتی miraculous *adj*
مطمئن content *adj*	معجزہ miracle *n*
مطمئن کرنا satisfy *v*	مَعدنی تارکول asphalt *n*

معدنی چشمہ	spa *n*	معوقع	likely *adv*
معدہ	stomach *n*	معیاد	period *n*
معدوم	extinct *adj*	معیار	standard *n*
معدوم ہو جانا	die out *v*	معیار سے کم	substandard *adj*
معذرت	apology *n*	معیار گھٹانا	impair *v*
معذرت خواہی	excuse *n*	معیاری بنانا	standardize *v*
معذرت کرنا	apologize *v*	معیشیت	economy *n*
معذور	disabled *adj*	معین	definite *adj*
معذور کرنا	incapacitate *v*	مغالطہ	fallacy *n*
معذوری	disability *n*	مغرب	west *n*
معرکہ مارنا	champion *v*	مغربی	western *adj*
معروف	well-known *adj*	مغرور	proud *adj*
معزز	noble *adj*	مغرور بانکا	cocky *adj*
معزز شخص	dignitary *n*	مغلوب	subdued *adj*
معصوم	innocent *adj*	مغلوب کرلینا	overpower *v*
معصومیت	innocence *n*	مغلوب کرنا	oppress *v*
معطل کر دینا	suspend *v*	مغلوب ہو جانا	succumb *v*
معقول	reasonable *adj*	مفت	free *adj*
معکوس طور پر	conversely *adv*	مفرور	fugitive *n*
معکوسی	reciprocal *adj*	مفروضہ	supposition *n*
معلم	instructor *n*	مفعت	gain *n*
معلومات	data *n*	مفلر	muffler *n*
معمار	mason *n*	مفلس	destitute *adj*
معمول	routine *n*	مفلس کرنا	impoverished *adj*
معمول کا	usual *adj*	مفلسی	poverty *n*
معمولی ذکر کرنا	touch on *v*	مفلسی سے	poorly *adv*
مَعمُولی مَرض	benign *adj*	مفلوج	cripple *adj*
معنی	meaning *n*	مفلوج کرنا	cripple *v*
معنی نکالنا	implicate *v*	مفہوم ہونا	imply *v*

مفید	useful _adj_	مقعد	rectum _n_
مفید ۔ کار آمد	beneficial _adj_	مقلد	conformist _adj_
مقابلہ	competition _n_	مقناطیس	magnet _n_
مقابلہ کرنا	contend _v_	مقناطیسی	magnetic _adj_
مقابلہ کرنیوالا	contender _n_	مقناطیسیت	magnetism _n_
مقاسیہ	module _n_	مقننہ	parliament _n_
مقاطعہ	boycott _v_	مقولہ	motto _n_
مقالہ	thesis _n_	مقوی	tonic _n_
مقام	standing _n_	مقیقت بینی	realism _n_
مقام بندی	location _n_	مقیم ہونا	settle _v_
مقامی	local _adj_	مکءی کا بھٹّہ	cob _n_
مقامی لہجہ	dialect _n_	مکا مارنا	punch _v_
مقبرہ	tomb _n_	مکار	cunning _adj_
مقبولیت	fame _n_	مکافات	retaliation _n_
مقتدرِ اعلیٰ	sovereign _adj_	مکالمہ	dialogue _n_
مقدار	quantity _n_	مکان مالک	landlord _n_
مقدار خوراک	dosage _n_	مکان مالکن	landlady _n_
مقدس	holy _adj_	مکتوب الیہ	addressee _n_
مقدس قرار دینا	consecrate _v_	مکرر قبضہ کرنا	recapture _v_
مقدم ہونا	precede _v_	مکروہ	hideous _adj_
مقدمہ	lawsuit _n_	مکڑا	spider _n_
مقدمہ بازی	litigation _n_	مکڑے کا جالا	spiderweb _n_
مقدمہ بازی کرنا	litigate _v_	مکڑی کا جالا	cobweb _n_
مقدمہ چلانا	prosecute _v_	مکعب	cube _n_
مقرر	speaker _n_	مکعب جیسا	cubic _adj_
مقرر کردہ	assign _v_	مکل کرنا	make up _v_
مُقَرَر کَرنا	allocate _v_	مکمل	complete _adj_
مقسوم	dividend _n_	مکمل تباہی	holocaust _n_
مقصد	purpose _n_	مکمل تلاشی لینا	ransack _v_

م

entirely *adv* مکمل طور پر	adulterate *v* ملاوٹ کرنا
complete *v* مکمل کرنا	tenderness *n* ملائمت
feasible *adj* مکن	creamy *adj* ملائی دار
fist *n* مکہ	debris *n* ملبہ
butter *n* مکھن	adjourn *v* ملتوی کرنا
fly *n* مکھی	atheist *n* مُلحِد
boxer *n* مکے باز	adjacent *adj* ملحق
boxing *n* مکے بازی	adjoining *adj* ملحقہ
strike *v* مکے مارنا	extradite *v* ملزم سپرد کرنا
popcorn *n* مکی بھوننا	indict *v* ملزم قرار دینا
corn *n* مکئی	compost *n* ملغوبہ
alligator *n* مگر مچھ	convoluted *adj* ملفف
crocodile *n* مگرمچھ	enclose *v* ملفوف کرنا
reconcile *v* مل جانا	country *n* ملک
capture *n* ملاپ	deport *v* ملک بدر کرنا
sailor *n* ملاح	deportation *n* ملک بدری
consideration *n* ملاحظہ	queen *n* ملکہ
employee *n* ملازم	ownership *n* ملکیت
use *v* ملازم رکھنا	possess *v* ملکیت رکھنا
employment *n* ملازمت	meet *v* ملنا
waitress *n* ملازمہ	sociable *adj* ملنسار
meeting *n* ملاقات	monarchy *n* ملوکیت
call on *v* ملاقات کرنا	milligram *n* ملی گرام
visitor *n* ملاقاتی	millimeter *n* ملی میٹر
enrich *v* ملامال کرنا	malaria *n* ملیریا
condemnation *n* ملامت	million *n* ملین
condemn *v* ملامت کرنا	similar *adj* مماثل
mingle, mix *v* ملانا	semblance *n* مماثلت
blender *n* مِلانے والا	tangent *n* مماسی

forbid v ممانت کرنا	deft adj منجھا ہوا
prohibition n ممانعت	pervert adj منحرف
prohibit v ممانعت کرنا	dependent adj منحصر
motherhood n ممتا	depend v منحصر ہونا
probable adj ممکن	sinister adj منحوس
contraband n ممنوعہ شے	temple n مندر
thankful adj ممنون	contents n مندرجات
mummy n ممی	heal v مندمل ہونا
hereafter adv من بعد	delegate n مندوب
from pre من جانب	downturn n مندے کا رحجان
concoction n من گھڑت کہانی	hover v منڈلانہ
appropriate adj مناسب	market n منڈی
rapport n مناسبت	goal n منزل
sightseeing v مناظر بینی	cross out v منسوخ کردینا
profit n منافع	revoke, annul v منسوخ کرنا
hypocrite adj منافق	repeal n منسوخی
hypocrisy n منافقت	charter n منشور
celebrate v منانا	bookkeeper n منشی
consequent adj منتج	judge n منصف
choose v منتخب کرنا	justly adv منصفانہ طور پر
confound v منتشر	design n منصوبہ
disperse v منتشر کرنا	compact adj منضبط
look forward v منتظر ہونا	logic n منطق
manager n منتظم	logical adj منطقی
housekeeper n منتظم خانہ	spectacle n منظر
transmit v منتقل کرنا	consent v منظر کرنا
minute n منٹ	scenario n منظرنامہ
frozen adj منجمد	organize v منظم ہونا یا کرنا
freeze v منجمد کرنا	approve v مَنظور کَرنا

م

مَنظوری approval n	مہربان gracious adj
مَنع کرنا ban, bar v	مہربانی kindness n
منعکس کرنا reflect v	مہربانی سے kindly adv
منفی negative adj	مہرہ vertebra n
منکسر modest adj	مہلک lethal, fatal adj
منکشف exposed adj	مہلک بیماری pest n
منگل Tuesday n	مُہِم adventure n
منگنی engagement n	مہم جو pushy adj
منگنی کرنا engage v	مہم چلانا campaign v
منگیتر fiancé n	مہمان guest n
منہ بند کرنا shut up v	مہمان نوازی hospitality n
منہ تک بھے جانا brim n	مہمل nonsense n
منہ چڑانا mugging n	مہنگا expensive adj
منہ کے بل prone adj	مہیا کرنا provide v
منہا کرنا deduct v	مہیا کرنے والا supplier n
منہدم کرنا dismantle v	مہیج stimulus n
منہمک ہونا engrossed adj	مہیمیز سے ہانکنا goad v
منوا لینا vindicate v	مہینہ month n
منور کرنا illuminate v	موءثر influential adj
منی آرڈر money order n	موءقف viewpoint n
منی سکرٹ miniskirt n	مواد stuff n
منیمی bookkeeping n	موازنہ comparison n
مہاجر emigrant n	موازنہ کرنا compare v
مہارت skill n	موافق compatible adj
مہاسا pimple n	موبائل ٹیلی فون cellphone n
مہذب civil, polite adj	موت death n
مہذب بنانا civilize v	موتی pearl n
مہر stamp, seal n	موتیا cataract n
مہر لگانا seal v	موٹا thick, fat adj

م

موٹا بنانا v	thicken
موٹائی n	thickness
موٹر n	motor
موٹر سائیکل n	motorcycle
موٹل n	motel
موج n	wave
موجود ہونا v	subsist
موجودگی n	presence
موچ آنا v	sprain
موچنا n	tweezers
مور n	peacock
مورت n	sculpture
مورچہ n	barricade
مورچہ بند adj	entrenched
مورخ n	historian
موروثی adj	hereditary
موڑ n	diversion
موڑ دینا v	avert
موڑنا v	distract, divert
موزہ n	stocking
موزوں adj	suitable
موزوں بننا v	compete
موزونیت n	competence
موسم n	season
موسمِ گرما n	summer
موسمی adj	seasonal
موسیقار n	musician
موسیقی n	music
موصل n	conductor

موضوع n	subject, topic
موقع n	opportunity
موکل n	client
مول تول n	bargain
مول تول کرنا v	negotiate
مولی n	radish
موم n	wax
موم پھلی n	peanut
مونچھ n	mustache
مونڈنا v	shear
مونہہ n	mouth
مویشی n	cattle
مویشی خانہ n	ranch
میزان n	balance
مے کدہ n	tavern
میٹر n	meter
میٹرک کرنا v	matriculate
میٹھا adj	sweet
میٹھا آلو n	yam
میٹھا کرنا v	sweeten
میجر n	major
میخ محور n	linchpin
میدان n	arena, field
میرا adj	my
میراث n	heritage
میز n	table
میزان n	scale
میزائل n	missile
میزبان n	host

tablecloth n میزپوش	ن
makeup n میک اپ	
mechanize v میکانی بنانا	
mechanism n میکانیہ	unheard-of adj نا شنیدہ
magazine n میگزین	unspeakable adj نا گفتہ بہ
combination n میل	misdemeanor n نا مناسب رویہ
socialize v میل جول پیدا کرنا	unfair adj نا واجب
sewage n میل کچیل	despair n ناامیدی
accord n میل ملاپ	injustice n ناانصافی
get together v میل ملاقات کرنا	unjustified adj ناانصافی پر مبنی
defile v میلا کرنا	incompetent adj ناابل
tendency n میلان	disqualify v ناابل قرار دینا
penchant n میلان طبع	incompetence n ناابلیت
incline v میلان ہونا	knob n ناب
fair n میلہ	annihilate v نابُود کر دینا
mammoth n میمتھ	profane adj ناپاک
mammal n میمل	unstable adj ناپائندار
kid n میمنہ	immaturity n ناپختگی
I pro میں	immature adj ناپختہ
myself pro میں خود	dislike v ناپسند کرنا
look through v میں سے دیکھنا	dislike n ناپسندیدگی
turret n مینار	undesirable adj ناپسندیدہ
lighthouse n مینارء نور	gauge v ناپنا
frog, toad n مینڈک	inexperienced adj ناتجربہ کار
ram n مینڈھا	celibacy n ناتخدائی
braid n مینڈھی	exhaustion n ناتوانی
mayor n مینر	illegitimate adj ناجائز
May n مئی	malpractice v ناجائز فعل
	undeserved adj ناحق
	nail n ناخن

نافرمان defiant adj	ناخوانده illiterate adj
ناقابل unable adj	ناخوش unhappy adj
ناقابلِ ادراک indiscreet adj	ناخوشگوار unpleasant adj
ناقابلِ اصلاح incorrigible adj	نادان fool, silly adj
ناقابلِ برداشت unbearable adj	نادانی indiscretion n
ناقابلِ بھروسہ unreliable adj	نادر peculiar adj
ناقابلِ پیش گوئی unpredictable adj	نادرست inaccurate adj
ناقابلِ تردید undeniable adj	نادم penitent n
ناقابلِ تسخیر invincible adj	ناراض angry adj
ناقابلِ تشریح inexplicable adj	ناراضی displeasure n
ناقابلِ تصور unthinkable adj	ناراضی کا سبب displeasing adj
ناقابلِ تقسیم indivisible adj	نارضامندی سے unwillingly adv
ناقابلِ تلافی irreparable adj	نارمل بنانا normalize v
ناقابلِ رسائی inaccessible adj	ناروا unreasonable adj
ناقابلِ شکست adamant adj	ناروے Norway n
ناقابلِ عذر inexcusable adj	نازک tender adj
ناقابلِ فراموش unforgettable adj	نازل ہونا come down v
ناقابلِ قبول inadmissible adj	ناسور ulcer n
ناقابلِ مزاحمت irresistible adj	ناشائستگی indecency n
ناقابلِ واپسی irrevocable adj	ناشائستہ impolite adj
ناقابلِ یقین unbelievable adj	ناشپاتی pear n
ناقص defective adj	ناشتہ breakfast n
ناقص غذا malnutrition n	ناشر publisher n
ناک nose n	ناشکرگزار ungrateful adj
ناک ڈبکی nosedive v	ناشکری ingratitude n
ناکافی inadequate adj	ناظر bystander n
ناکام ہونا fail, flunk v	ناف belly button n
ناکامی failure n	نافِ چرخ nave n
ناکامیاب unsuccessful adj	نافذ کرنا enforce v

viper n ناگ	novelist n ناول نگار
inevitable adj ناگزیر	rare adj نایاب
panic n ناگہانی خوف	aide n نائب
distasteful adj ناگوار	regent n نائب السلطنت
distaste n ناگواری	knight n نائٹ
gutter n نالہ	nitrogen n نائٹروجن
duct, hose n نالی	botany n نباتیات
name n نام	pulse n نبض
surname n نام کا ثانوی جزو	pulsate v نبض کا چلنا
so-called adj نام نہاد	nostril n نتھنا
incoherent adj نامربوط	affix v نَتھی کَرنا
impotent adj نامرد	outcome n نتیجہ
nominate v نامزد کرنا	deduce, infer v نتیجہ نکالنا
unfavorable adj نامساعد	prose n نثر
absurd adj نامعقول	salvation n نجات
incomplete adj نامکمل	savior n نجات دہندہ
impossible adj ناممکن	filth n نجاست
unsuitable adj نامناسب	filthy adj نجس
repudiate v نامنظور کرنا	astrologer n نَجُومی
rejection n نامنظوری	downstairs adv نچلی منزل
correspondent n نامہ نگار	squeeze v نچوڑنا
famous adj نامور	oasis n نخلستان
celebrity n نامور شخصیت	arrogance n نَخوت
reputedly adv ناموری سے	remorse n ندامت
misfit adj ناموزوں	novelty n ندرت
prominent adj نامی گرامی	stream, creek n ندی
hopeless adj نامید	intrepid adj نڈر
granny n نانی دادی	tribute n نذر
uneven, bumpy adj ناہموار	male n نر

masculine *adj* نَر کا	starch *n* نشاسته
sperm *n* نرتولیدی ماده	mark, sign *n* نشان
rate, tariff *n* نرخ	freckled *adj* نشان زده
nurse *n* نرس	earmark *v* نشانِ شناخت
nursery *n* نرسری	mark *v* نشانَ لگانا
mild, soft *adj* نرم	shot *n* نشانه
soften *v* نرم بنانا	marksman *n* نشانه باز
lenient *adj* نرم دل	token *n* نشانی
clemency *n* نرم دلی	low *adj* نشبی
plush *adj* نرم رواندار کا کپڑا	broadcast *v* نشر کرن
softness *n* نرمی	broadcast *n* نشریه
relaxing *adj* نرمی برتنے والا	addictive *adj* نشہ آور
softly *adv* نرمی سے	course *n* نصاب
delicacy *n* نزاکت	textbook *n* نصابی کتاب
beside *pre* نَزدیک	midnight *n* نصف شب
by *pre* نزدیک	radius *n* نصف قطر
proximity *n* نزدیکی	hemisphere *n* نصف کرہ
flu *n* نزلہ	admonition *n* نصیحت
artery *n* نَسّ	scenery, view *n* نظارہ
denominator *n* نسب نما	system *n* نظام
ratio *n* نسبت	systematic *adj* نظام کا حامل
formula *n* نسخہ	hierarchy *n* نظام مراتب
generation *n* نسل	neglect *v* نظر انداز کرنا
racist *adj* نسل پرست	revision *n* نظر ثانی
racism *n* نسل پرستی	revise *v* نظر ثانی کرنا
genocide *n* نسل کشی	leave out *v* نظرانداز کردینا
oblivion *n* نسیان	ignore *v* نظرانداز کرنا
oblivious *adj* نسیانی	ideology *n* نظریہ
breeze *n* نسیم	poem *n* نظم

discipline *n* نظم و ضبط	footprint *n* نقش پا
slogan *n* نعره	replica *n* نقشِ ثانی
pantry *n* نعمت خانہ	replicate *v* نقشِ ثانی تیار کرنا
melodic *adj* نغمگین	impress *v* نقش کرنا
composer *n* نغمہ ساز	map *n* نقشہ
imposition *n* نفاذ	drawing *n* نقشہ کشی
ordination *n* نفاذ فرمان	draftsman *n* نقشہ نویس
disgust, hatred *n* نفرت	drawback *n* نقص
hateful *adj* نفرت انگیز	harm *n* نقصان
hate, detest *v* نفرت کرنا	injure, harm *v* نقصان پہنچانا
spirit *n* نفس	damaging *adj* نقصان دہ
prurient *adj* نفس پرست	point *n* نقطہ
mortification *n* نفس کشی	dot *n* نقطہ
carnal *adj* نفسانی	standpoint *n* نقطہٴ نظر
psychic *adj* نفسیاتی	copy, imitation *n* نقل
psychopath *n* نفسیاتی مریض	mime *v* نقل اتارنا
profit *v* نفع اٹھانا	duplicate *v* نقل کرنا
lucrative *adj* نفع آور	relocation *n* نقل مکانی
gain *v* نفع حاصل کرنا	relocate *v* نقل مکانی کرنا
benefit *n* نفع منفعت	herald *v* نقیب
permeate *v* نفوذ کرنا	trumpet *n* نقیری
pretty *adj* نفیس	outlet, vent *n* نکاس
mask *n* نقاب	drainage *n* نکاسی
unmask *v* نقاب اتارنا	drain *v* نکاسی آب کرنا
burglar *n* نقب زن	oust, expel *v* نکال باہر کرنا
burglary *n* نقب زنی	eject *v* نکال پھینکنا
heist *n* نقب زنی کرنا	turn out *v* نکال دینا
burglarize *v* نقب لگانا	withdraw *v* نکالنا
print *n* نقش	tie *n* نکٹائی

نکڑ	corner n	نمدار بنانا	moisten v
نکل	nickel n	نمک	salt n
نکما	frivolous adj	نمک حرام	felon n
نکوٹین	nicotine n	نمکین	salty adj
نگاہ	glance n	نمو	growth n
نگاہ ڈالنا	glance v	نمو پانا	germinate v
نگاہ میں آنا	show up v	نمونہ	model, pattern n
نگران	caretaker n	نمونیا	pneumonia n
نگرانی	supervision n	نمی	humidity n
نگرانی کرنا	supervise v	نن	nun n
نگل لینا	devour v	ننگا	bare, nude adj
نگلنا	swallow v	ننگا کرنا	uncover v
نگلنے کاعمل	gulp n	ننگاہ	naked adj
نگہبان	custodian n	ننگے پاؤں	barefoot adj
نگہداشت	upkeep n	نہ ختم ہونے والا	unending adj
نل بند کرنا	turn off v	نہ ہی	nor c
نل کاری	plumbing n	نہ یہ نہ وہ	neither adv
نلیا،ساکن پانی	pool n	نہانے کا ٹب	bathtub n
نماز	prayer n	نہایت عمدہ	exquisite adj
نمائش	presentation n	نہایت کجوس	stingy adj
نماۂشی	plausible adj	نہتا	defenseless adj
نمایاں	outstanding adj	نہر	canal n
نمایاں کرنا	highlight n	نہیں	not adv
نمائش	exhibition n	نو	nine adj
نمائش کرنا	exhibit v	نو جوان	youthful adj
نمائشی	ostentatious adj	نو مذہب	convert n
نمائندگی	agency n	نوالہ	morsel n
نمائندگی کرنا	represent v	نواں	ninth adj
نمٹنا	tackle, cope v	نوآبادی	colony n

ن

نوآبادی بنانا colonize v

نوآبادیاتی colonial adj

نوآموز novice n

نوبیاہتا newlywed adj

نوٹس notice n

نوجوان youngster n

نوجوانی adolescence n

نوچنا claw v

نوخیز teenager n

نوع species n

نوعِ انسانی mankind n

نوعمر شخص juvenile n

نوک tip n

نوکدار pointed adj

نوکرانی maid n

نوکری کرنا serve v

نومبر November n

نومولود newborn n

نووارد newcomer n

نوے ninety adj

نیچے اُتَرنا alight adv

نیستی ۔ فَنا annihilation n

نیم وا ۔ آدھ کھُلا ajar adj

نیا new adj

نیا بھرتی شدہ recruit n

نیا جنم rebirth n

نیت intention n

نیچے down, below adv

نیچے کی طرف downhill adv

نیدرلینڈز Netherlands n

نیزہ spear n

نیزے کی انّی spearhead v

نیست و نابود ہونا perish v

نیکی charity n

نیلا blue adj

نیلام کرنا auction v

نیلامی auction n

نیم خوابیدہ drowsy adj

نیم گرم lukewarm adj

نیند sleep n

نیوکلیائی nuclear adj

ہ

ہاتھ hand n

ہاتھ پائوں extremities n

ہاتھ پائوں پر چلنا scramble v

ہاتھ ریڑھی wheelbarrow n

ہاتھی elephant n

ہاتھی دانت ivory n

ہار garland n

ہارمون hormone n

ہارنا lose v

ہارنے والا loser n

ہاضم digestive adj

بال	hall, lobby *n*
بالہ	corollary *n*
بالینڈ	Holland *n*
باں	yes *adv*
بانپنا	gasp *v*
بانکنا	drive *n*
بائیڈروجن	hydrogen *n*
ہپناٹاعز کرنا	hypnotize *v*
ہتھ کڑی لگانا	handcuff *v*
ہتھکڑی	handcuffs *n*
ہتھوڑا	hammer *n*
ہتھیار	weapon *n*
ہتھیانا	loot *v*
ہٹ دھرمی	tenacity *n*
ہٹا کرجگہ لینا	supersede *v*
ہٹانا	remove *v*
ہجا	syllable *n*
ہجرت کرنا	emigrate *v*
ہجوم	crowd *n*
ہجوم کرنا	mob *v*
ہجے	spelling *n*
ہجے کرنا	spell *v*
ہچکچاتے ہوئے	reluctantly *adv*
ہچکچانا	hesitate *v*
ہچکچاہٹ	hesitation *n*
ہچکولے	jolt *n*
ہچکولے دینا	jolt *v*
ہچکی	hiccup *n*
ہدایت دینا	instruct *v*

ہدایت کار	director *n*
ہدایت کرنا	admonish *v*
ہدف	target *n*
ہَدَف لینا	aim *v*
ہدیہ کرنا	give away *v*
ہڈی	bone *n*
ہڈی کا گودا	bone marrow *n*
ہر ایک	each, every *adj*
ہر روز	everyday *adj*
ہر شخص	everybody *pro*
ہر شے	everything *pro*
ہر کوئی	everyone *pro*
ہرا بھرا	prosperous *adj*
براول دستہ	vanguard *n*
ہرجانہ	penalty *n*
ہردلعزیز	popular *adj*
ہرروز	daily *adv*
ہرگھنٹے بعد	hourly *adv*
ہرن	deer *n*
ہرن کا گوشت	venison *n*
ہڑپ کر جانا	gulp *v*
ہڑتال کرنا	walkout *n*
ہزار	thousand *adj*
ہزاریہ	millennium *n*
ہسپانوی	Spaniard *n*
ہسپتال	hospital *n*
ہسٹیریا	hysteria *n*
ہسٹیریائی	hysterical *adj*
ہشاش بشاش	cheerful *adj*

digest v هضم کرنا	counterpart n ہم منصب
Saturday n ہفتہ	compatriot n ہم وطن
weekly adv ہفتہ وار	synchronize v ہم وقت ہونا
astound v ہَکا بَکا کر دینا	our adj ہمارا
daze v بکابکا کر دینا	guts n ہمت
stutter v ہکلانا	dismay v ہمت توڑنا
plow v ہل چلانا	gruelling adj ہمت شکن
onslaught n ہلا	dismay n ہمت شکنی
shaken adj ہلا ہوا	sympathy n ہمدردی
fuss n ہلچل	sympathize v ہمدردی کرنا
hooligan n ہلڑ باز	accompany v ہمراہ ہونا
portable adj ہلکا	neighbor n ہمسایہ
shower n ہلکا چھینٹا	neighborhood n ہمسائیگی
unload v ہلکا کرنا	totalitarian adj ہمہ گیر
quake, shake v ہلنا	smooth adj ہموار
assail v بَلَہ بولنا	smooth v ہموار بنانا
we pro ہم	plot n ہموار قطع زمین
simultaneous adj ہم آہنگ	smoothness n ہمواری
concur v ہم آہنگ ہونا	always adv ہمیشہ
harmony n ہم آہنگی	forever adv ہمیشہ کے لیے
adjustment n ہم آہنگی ۔ تطابق	us pro ہمیں
classmate n ہم جماعت	casserole n ہنڈیا
ourselves pro ہم خود	practice n ہنر
coordinate v ہم ربط بنانا	goose n ہنس
coordination n ہم ربطگی	jovial adj ہنس مکھ
contemporary adj ہم عصر	laugh v ہنسنا
abreast adv ہم قدم	laughter n ہنسی
peer n ہم مرتبہ	uproar n ہنگامہ
concentric adj ہم مرکز	emergency n ہنگامی حالت

hitherto *adv*	ہنوز
may *v*	ہو سکتا ہے
air, wind *n*	ہَوا
aviator *n*	ہَوا باز
aviation *n*	ہوا بازی
airtight *adj*	ہَوا بَند
inflate *v*	ہوا بھرنا
air *v*	ہَوا دینا
lift off *v*	ہوا میں اٹھنا
flip *v*	ہوا میں اچھالنا
soar *v*	ہوا میں بلند ہونا
deflate *v*	ہوا نکالنا
ventilation *n*	ہواداری
airfield *n*	ہَوائی اڈّا
airplane *n*	ہَوائی جَہاز
airmail *n*	ہَوائی ڈاک
airline *n*	ہَوائی کَمپَنی
hotel *n*	ہوٹل
lust *n*	ہوس
lust *v*	ہوس ہونا
conciousness *n*	ہوش
watch out *v*	ہوشیار
look out *v*	ہوشیار ہونا
appalling *adj*	ہولناک
honk *v*	ہوں ہوں کرنا
be *v*	ہونا
become *v*	ہونا آنا
lip *n*	ہونٹ
smack *v*	ہونٹ چٹخارنا

grisly *adj*	ہیبت ناک
turbulence *n*	ہیجان
diamond *n*	ہیرا
hero *n*	ہیرو
heroism *n*	ہیروکی خصوصیات
heroin *n*	ہیروئین
cholera *n*	ہیضہ
helmet *n*	ہیلمٹ
hello *e*	ہیلو
helicopter *n*	ہیلی کاپٹر
handout *n*	ہینڈآئوٹ
perspective *n*	ہیت
transform *v*	ہیئت بدلنا
format *n*	ہیئیت

ہ
و

و

attachment *n*	وابَستَگی
attached *adj*	وابَستَہ
involve *v*	وابستہ ہونا
back *adv*	واپس
reimburse *v*	واپس ادا کرنا
repayment *n*	واپس ادائیگی
back up *v*	واپس آنا
go back *v*	واپس جانا
refund *n*	واپس شدہ رقم

give back v واپس کرنا	fatherhood n والديت
back v واپس کرنا/لینا	parents n والدین
bring back v واپس لانا	walrus n والرس
move back v واپس لے لینا	volleyball n والی بال
withdrawal n واپس لینے کا عمل	virus n وائرس
come back v واپس ہونا	violin n وائلن
return n واپسی	violinist n وائلن نواز
watt n واٹ	plague n وبا
due adj واجب	outbreak n وبا کی پھوٹ
payable adj واجب الادا	vitamin n وٹامن
dues n واجب الادا رقم	ecstasy n وجد
monologue n واحد کلامی	intuition n وجدان
valley n وادی	ecstatic adj وجدآور
heir n وارث	reason n وجہ
heiress n وارثہ	existence n وجود
warrant n وارنٹ	exist v وجود رکھنا
varnish n وارنش	personify v وجود قرار دینا
varnish v وارنش لگا	originate v وجود میں لانا
avowed adj واشگاف	unification n وحدت
clear, obvious adj واضح	brutal adj وحشی
clear v واضح بنانا	barbaric adj وحشیانہ
clearly adv واضح طور پر	brutality n وحشیانہ پن
explicit adj واضع	inherit v ورثہ پانا
preacher n واعظ	entice v ورغلانا
abound v وافر ہونا	meningitis n ورم
located adj واقع	ministry n وزارت
happen v واقع ہونا	load, weight n وزن
event n واقعہ	load v وزن اٹھانا
father n والد	weigh v وزن کرنا

و

minister n وزیر	colon n وقف توضیحی
intercession n وساطت	devote v وقف کرنا
middle n وسط	interval n وقفہ
midsummer n وسطِ گرما	respite n وقفہ برائے آرام
immensity n وسعت	stop over v وقفہ کرنا
escalate v وسعت دینا	ocurrence n وقوع
misgiving n وسوسہ	come about v وقوع پذیر ہونا
comprehensive adj وسیع	advocate v وکالت کرنا
intermediary n وسیلہ	lawyer n وکیل
receive v وصول کرنا	wig n وگ
payee n وصول کنندہ	delivery n ولادت
clarity n وضاحت	penny n ولایت کا پیسہ
explain v وضاحت کرنا	villain n ولن
homeland n وطن	Dutch adj ولندیزی
patriot n وطن پرست	saint n ولی
repatriate v وطن واپس آنا/لانا	canonize v ولی گراننا
litany n وظیفہ	windshield n ونڈ شیلڈ
sermon n وعظ	that adj وہ
preach v وعظ کرنا	those adj وہ (جمع)
allegiance n وَفا داری ۔ اطاعت	she pro وہ (عورت)
faithful adj وفادار	he pro وہ (مرد)
loyalty n وفاداری	themselves pro وہ آپ (جمع)
federal adj وفاقی	they pro وہ لوگ
delegation n وفد	there adv وہاں
majesty n وقار	whim n وہم
time n وقت	obsession n وہم کا تسلط
punctual adj وقت کا پابند	same adj وہی
faint n وقتی بے ہوشی	wheelchair n وہیل چینر
fad n وقتی فیشن	whale n وہیل مچھلی

ووٹ n	vote
ووٹ ڈالنا v	vote
وولٹیج n	voltage
ویب سائٹ n	web site
ویٹو v	veto
ویران adj	deserted
ویرانی n	desolation
ویکسین n	vaccine
ویگن n	wagon
ویلڈ کرنے والا n	welder

و
یا

یا

یا c	or
یاد n	recollection
یاد تازہ کرنا v	commemorate
یاد دلانا v	remind
یاد دہانی n	reminder
یاد رکھنا v	remember
یاد کرنا v	recall
یاداشت n	memoirs
یادگار adj	memorable
یادگاری adj	monumental
یادگاری نشانی n	memento
یاسمین n	jasmine
یاسیت پسند adj	pessimistic

یاقوت n	saphire
یتیم n	orphan
یتیمی n	orphanage
یچیدگی n	complexity
یرغمال n	hostage
یعنی adv	namely
یقین n	certainty
یقین دلانا v	assure
یقین کامل n	conviction
یقینی adj	certain
یقینی بنانا v	ensure
یقینی طور پر adv	surely
یک اسلوبی n	monotony
یک بیک adj	plump
یک رخا adj	singleminded
یک زوجی n	monogamy
یک طرفہ adj	unilateral
یکتا adj	unique
یکجان کرنا v	blend
یکجہتی n	solidarity
یکساں ۔ ایک سا adj	alike
یکسانیت n	uniformity
یہ (جمع) adj	these
یہ (واحد) adj	this
یہاں adv	here
یہودی adj	Jewish
یہودی فقیہہ n	rabbi
یہودیت n	Judaism
یورپ n	Europe

یونانی Greek *adj*

یونیورسٹی university *n*

یورپی European *adj*

یوم پیدائش birthday *n*

یونان Greece *n*

یا

Word to Word® Bilingual Dictionary Series

Language - Item Code - Pages ISBN #

Albanian - 500X - 306 pgs
ISBN - 978-0-933146-49-5

Amharic - 820X - 362 pgs
ISBN - 978-0-933146-59-4

Arabic - 650X - 378 pgs
ISBN - 978-0-933146-41-9

Bengali - 700X - 372 pgs
ISBN - 978-0-933146-30-3

Burmese - 705X - 310 pgs
ISBN - 978-0-933146-50-1

Cambodian - 710X - 348 pgs
ISBN - 978-0-933146-40-2

Chinese - 715X - 340 pgs
ISBN - 978-0-933146-22-8

Farsi - 660X - 328 pgs
ISBN - 978-0-933146-33-4

French - 530X - 320 pgs
ISBN - 978-0-933146-36-5

German - 535X - 352 pgs
ISBN - 978-0-933146-93-8

Gujarati - 720X - 334 pgs
ISBN - 978-0-933146-98-3

Haitian-Creole - 545X - 322 pgs
ISBN - 978-0-933146-23-5

Hebrew - 665X - 316 pgs
ISBN - 978-0-933146-58-7

Hindi - 725X - 320 pgs
ISBN - 978-0-933146-31-0

Hmong - 728X - 294 pgs
ISBN - 978-0-933146-31-0

Italian - 555X - 362 pgs
ISBN - 978-0-933146-51-8

Japanese - 730X - 372 pgs
ISBN - 978-0-933146-42-6

Korean - 735X - 344 pgs
ISBN - 978-0-933146-97-6

Lao - 740X - 319 pgs
ISBN - 978-0-933146-54-9

Pashto - 760X - 348 pgs
ISBN - 978-0-933146-34-1

Polish - 575X - 358 pgs
ISBN - 978-0-933146-64-8

Portuguese - 580X - 362 pgs
ISBN - 978-0-933146-94-5

Punjabi - 765X - 358 pgs
ISBN - 978-0-933146-32-7

Romanian - 585X - 354 pgs
ISBN - 978-0-933146-91-4

Russian - 590X - 298 pgs
ISBN - 978-0-933146-92-1

Somali - 830X - 320 pgs
ISBN- 978-0-933146-52-5

Spanish - 600X - 346 pgs
ISBN - 978-0-933146-99-0

Swahili - 835X - 274 pgs
ISBN - 978-0-933146-55-6

Tagalog - 770X - 294 pgs
ISBN - 978-0-933146-37-2

Thai - 780X - 354 pgs
ISBN - 978-0-933146-35-8

Turkish - 615X - 348 pgs
ISBN - 978-0-933146-95-2

Ukrainian - 620X - 337 pgs
ISBN - 978-0-933146-25-9

Urdu - 790X - 360 pgs
ISBN - 978-0-933146-39-6

Vietnamese - 795X - 324 pgs
ISBN - 978-0-933146-96-9

All languages are two-way:
h-Language / Language-English.
ages in planning and production.

Order Information

To order our Word to Word® Bilingual Dictionaries or any other products from Bilingual Dictionaries, Inc., please contact us at (951) 296-2445 or visit us at **www.BilingualDictionaries.com**. Visit our website to download our current Catalog/Order Form, view our products, and find information regarding Bilingual Dictionaries, Inc.

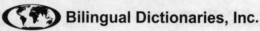 **Bilingual Dictionaries, Inc.**

PO Box 1154 • Murrieta, CA 92562 • Tel: (951) 296-2445 • Fax: (951) 461-3092
www.BilingualDictionaries.com

Special Dedication & Thanks

Bilingual Dicitonaries, Inc. would like to thank all the teachers from various districts accross the country for their useful input and great suggestions in creating a Word to Word® standard. We encourage all students and teachers using our bilingual learning materials to give us feedback. Please send your questions o̶ ments via email to support@bilingualdictionaries